WELL DONE

ADVANCE PRAISE FOR
WELL DONE

"It's a winner! Every business that practices the principles that Ken explores in this book will find solutions to their biggest problems and the success that comes from doing business with vision, integrity, and thoughtfulness. My partners and I used these principles with the various NBA teams that we operated, and they will work if they are implemented and embraced. I highly recommend this insightful book for business and life."

Pat Williams
Co-founder of the Orlando Magic
Author of *How To Be Like Walt: Capturing the Disney Magic Every Day of Your Life*

"This warm, wonderful, deeply insightful book shows you the timeless principles and universal wisdom behind all success."

Brian Tracy
New York Times Best-Selling Author, Speaker, Consultant

"In his book, *Well Done*, Ken does a masterful job of bringing the timeless success principles in the bible to the business world."

Gino Wickman
Author of *Traction* and Creator of EOS

"What does it take to build a God-honoring, successful business that enjoys favor from the Lord? Ken Gosnell lays a foundation of biblical principles that every Christian business leader should follow along the path toward true success in God's eyes."

Tom Harper
CEO of BiblicalLeadership.com
Author of *Servant Leader Strong: Uniting Biblical Wisdom and High-Performance Leadership*

"If ever a book was well-named, *Well Done* is it! As long as I've known Ken Gosnell, I've been consistently impressed with his innovative spirit, his deep business acumen, and his ability to clearly convey powerful business principles. This extensively researched book reflects every bit of Ken's capabilities. As a CEO and as a coach, too many CEOs, I'm confident in recommending *Well Done* as a resource for any business leader committed to pursuing excellence."

Michael Sipe
Chairman, 10x Catalyst Groups
Author of *The AVADA Principle: How an Ancient Word Holds the Key to Your Highest and Best Life*

"I love this book! Ken has written a helpful and comprehensive list of practical suggestions to help leaders live out their faith at the same time they advance their organization. Though written with the CEO in mind, this book will be helpful for leaders at any level."

Ron Edmondson
CEO, Leadership Network
Author of *The Mythical Leader*

"Ken's book will inspire you to become a more principle-centered leader. It provides a lot of great advice and concepts that will make you and your organization better. Well done!"

Jon Gordon
Best-selling author of *The Carpenter* and *Power of Positive Leadership*

"Ken Gosnell's book is impactful and powerful, a 'well done' teaching that combines Scriptural truths with practical, real-world illustrations. I think many of the marketplace ministry leaders I have worked with over the years would agree it contains many useful insights. I recommend it to any businessperson who is looking to make a difference for eternity."

Rich Marshall
Author, *God@Work* (Vol. 1-2) and *God@Rest*,
Host of "God@Work" program on GodTV

"Ken Gosnell has produced a great new resource for business leaders who desire success not only in business but also with their family and God. Drawing from a wide range of personal experience, renowned experts, and biblical wisdom, this book will inspire you to put what you read immediately into practice."

Richard Blackaby
Author of *Spiritual Leadership* and *God in the Marketplace*

"Ken's book *Well Done* can be a tremendous resource for any leader who is looking to enhance their business skills and personal performance. His insightful way of examining proven and timeless principles is both refreshing and inspiring. Busy leaders will be able to grab insights and apply the principles immediately to implement effective change in their business. You will enjoy this book and find it an essential tool to help you grow your business."

Chris Widener
Author of the *Art of Influence* and *Leadership Rules*
ChrisWidener.com

"I am proud to offer my endorsement for my friend and my brother in Jesus Christ, Mr. Ken Gosnell's book *Well Done*. He is a Chief Servant Leader at CEO Experience and successful, a wonderful Businessman and Husband, father. I do 100% recommend his book to Christian CEOs and Leaders and especially to young Christian entrepreneurs."

Anil Anwar
President/CEO Christian Times Magazine & CTM News Channel

"*Well Done* is one of the best (faith based) business leadership books that I have ever read. Ken's compilation of real life stories, perspectives, and biblical truths, paints a clear picture of how to integrate one's faith, proven experience, and God's word in business and life."

Francis X. Kelly III, CLU, RHU, REBC
Chief Executive Officer, KELLY

"*Well Done* by Ken Gosnell is very well done. The principles and lessons in this book are timeless, no matter what religion you practice. We are living in a time that tests our character and reputation. Reading the right material, often will refocus you on the right way to lead your life and lead others. *Well Done*, I believe, will do just that. Remember, the only thing you can take with you and leave behind is your legacy."

Lee Cockerell
Executive Vice President (Retired and Inspired), Walt Disney World® Resort
Author of *Creating Magic: 10 Common Sense Leadership Strategies from a Life at Disney, The Customer Rules, The 39 Essential Rules for Delivering Sensational Service, Time Management Magic,* and *Career Magic*

"I have always believed that God's law and the best business practices are in harmony. Ken has done an exceptional job of melding both into a useful framework. This book provides a valuable roadmap for any Christian business operator."

Joel Trammell
CEO Khorus
Author of *CEO on a Tightrope*

"Ken doesn't just teach us about biblical business principles; he lives them. By exploring the proclamations, parables, and practices of Jesus, *Well Done* offers sound counsel for business leaders and, more broadly, for people who want to steward their lives with eternity in mind. I'm eager to incorporate these principles into my life and work!"

Peter Greer

President & CEO, HOPE International

Author of *Mission Drift*

"In the beginning God wove principles into the very fabric of his creation. These principles are like gravity, and they work if you believe in God or not. Ken Gosnell, in his new book *Well Done*, highlights 12 of these principles drawn from scripture, which have to power to transform both our work and our organizations. This is a must read for anyone in business from the first-year clerk to the CEO."

Hugh C. Whelchel

Executive Director of the Institute for Faith, Work & Economics

Author of *How Then Should We Work*

"*Well Done* by Ken Gosnell captures perfectly what my desire is as a leader: to come to the end of my time knowing that I have given my very best to the people I was called to serve. The wisdom Ken shares will not only help you grow your team, but it will grow your understanding of what it means to lead well."

Mark Cole

CEO John Maxwell Enterprise

"As a student of the good words the Bible has for business, I have a few good words for Ken Gosnell's book *Well Done*: Practical, wise, thorough, doable, real-world, inspiring, encouraging, insightful, and well done. Important insights for business leaders, of course, but also for the church, NPOs and government leaders as well."

Bill Peel

Executive Director, Center for Faith & Work at LeTourneau University

Author of *Workplace Grace*

"Ken does a fantastic job of delivering practical business advice alongside interesting and engaging lessons from biblical scripture. This book makes you stop and think. Providing an incredible resource for modern-day leadership and team problem solving with some of the most famous stories ever told. A wonderful read from a brilliant author."

Chris Lamontagne
CEO Teespring

"Drawing equally from Biblical Wisdom, Personal Experience, and Noteworthy Executive Stories, Ken Gosnell provides a practical guide for business leaders to run their companies with the ultimate end in mind: the commendation of Jesus, "Well done." This is essential reading for all who are serious about God honoring faith and practice in their work life. I highly recommend it."

Dr. Chip Roper
President and lead consultant at the VOCA Center in New York City

"Hearing God say 'well done' is the end to which all of us strive. Ken has rightly described the intersection of faith and work in Scripture. The principles in God's Word are similarly the foundation for all Christian ministry. Proverbs 27:17 says, 'As iron sharpens iron, so one person sharpens another.' Leaders in both business and ministry would do well to listen to, and heed, Ken's incisive reflections on God's truths."

Dr. Bruce A. Smith
President - Wycliffe Associates
Author of <i>Living Translation: Peace Children—The Sawi Story</i>

"The Bible has a lot to say about how to run a business and be an effective leader. In his new book, <i>Well Done</i>, Ken Gosnell unpacks these truths and provides us with practical applications that, if applied, can help us be the business leaders that God has called us to be."

Todd Hopkins
Founder and CEO, Office Pride Commercial Cleaning Services
Author of <i>The Stress Less Business Owner</i>

"In a world of lost souls, failing businesses and spiritual bondage, many people try to operate a business with no spiritual foundation, where there is no knowledge the people perish! Ken Gosnell shares insights into the knowledge of kingdom principals that every person should read and understand. A MUST READ! Truly a blueprint for living a life of abundance."

Velma Trayham
CEO & President of Millionaire Mastermind Academy, Inc.
Author of *When God Says Go: Turn Your Storms into an Unshakable Relationship with God, Leaving It All Behind*

"Current, useful, actionable, and true. It's gold! Leadership is a language that's best learned via a guided journey. Read this book to master true biblical inspired leadership principles in the land of information overload and disinformation. This is a roadmap to visionary pursuits and stewardship worth reading."

Erica Nicole
Founder and CEO, YFS Magazine/MSNBC Contributor

"Ken Gosnell's book *Well Done* is indeed well done! It is filled with executable Biblical principles that will guarantee the success of any venture! And here is my favorite part of Ken's book: Ken includes in each chapter questions that you can use to Lead Your Team With Questions to execute that principle in your context!"

Bob Tiede
Blogger @ LeadingWithQuetions.com
Author of *Great Leaders ASK Questions, 339 Questions Jesus Asked* and *Now That's a Great Question*

"'Well done' is the highest compliment any servant leader can receive. Ken Gosnell provides leaders the guidebook and road map for leaders who want to eternally impact both their customers and employees in his book, *Well Done*. Read it and find the tools you need to grow your servant leadership."

Dee Ann Turner
Best-selling author, *Bet on Talent: How to Create a Remarkable Culture that Wins the Hearts of Customers*, Vice President, (Retired) Chick-fil-A, Inc.

"Warning - *Well Done* is NOT for the marginal or occasional believer but exclusively for those marketplace warriors who passionately desire to impact their spheres of influence for the Kingdom. This power-packed, how-to executive guide challenges every Christian in business to a higher level of focus, commitment consecration, and activation of the power of God into their business and communities. I exhort you to join the *Well Done* executive leadership tribe to transform the business mountain for the glory of God."

Dr. Jim Harris
Founder and Managing Partner of Dynatos Global Inc.
Author of 14 award-winning books, including
Our Unfair Advantage: Unleash the Power of Holy Spirit in Your Business

"A book I couldn't put down. Grounding, reminding me of true leadership principles from the greatest leader of all. Inspires me to keep my compass pointed in the right direction, head down, and working hard for what truly matters to hear from Our Lord at the end of the race, 'Well done.'"

Steve Newton
Founder and CEO of Mission BBQ

"This book has the potential to impact generation! The principles are doable and transferrable."

Tim Goad
Founder and CEO of Goad International,
founder and pastor of G5 Church,
and author of *Vocabulary of a Leader*

WELL

12 BIBLICAL BUSINESS PRINCIPLES
for Leaders to Grow Their Business
with Kingdom Impact

DONE

Ken Gosnell

NEW YORK

LONDON • NASHVILLE • MELBOURNE • VANCOUVER

WELL DONE

12 Biblical Business Principles for Leaders to Grow Their Business with Kingdom Impact

Published in New York, New York, by Morgan James Publishing. Morgan James is a trademark of Morgan James, LLC. www.MorganJamesPublishing.com

ISBN 9781631950964 paperback
ISBN 9781631950971 eBook
Library of Congress Control Number: 2020934385

Cover Design by:
Chris Treccani
www.3dogcreative.net

Interior Design by:
Christopher Kirk
www.GFSstudio.com

Morgan James is a proud partner of Habitat for Humanity Peninsula and Greater Williamsburg. Partners in building since 2006.

Get involved today! Visit
MorganJamesPublishing.com/giving-back

DEDICATION

This book is dedicated to my father and mother, Brian and Mary Gosnell.
My parents modeled for me faith, authenticity, and hard work.
The lessons that they taught and modeled for me have prepared me
for life and for eternity for which I will always be grateful.

TABLE OF CONTENTS

FOREWORD

Work is central to our lives. For many, it serves to shape and define who we are. So, it is vitally important that we see work clearly for what it is – an opportunity to steward some of the greatest gifts that God has given. For some, work is simply a means whereby that person makes a living. However, there is a big difference between making a living and making a life. When someone is simply making a living, they are primarily consumed by a career, making choices that enhance their professional pursuits. On the other hand, making a life is about making a positive difference in the lives of others and having an eternal perspective, while choosing to prioritize those elements that bring richness of relationships to life.

Believers who possess such a relational and eternal perspective tend to thrive, no matter what the professional context. They embrace the notion that work is a form of worship. And, how they work shows what they worship.

In the grand scheme of life, it makes little difference what one does in terms of vocational pursuits. Titles, trinkets, and accolades will have no eternal significance. However, why and how one works will determine the lasting significance of their pursuits. If work is merely for self-promotion and self-fulfillment, then one may attain power and status and yet be relationally poor in the process. On the other hand, if work is to honor God and serve to extend his love into the workplace, then movements of good can be created that will ripple into eternity.

Within these pages, Ken Gosnell unpacks principles that will challenge any leader to reconsider the very nature of work. He reminds the reader that leadership must be about something more than self-interest, more impactful than self-service and more noble than self-fulfillment. He moves the reader to go beyond simply having a mission to actually being on mission.

When someone embraces and embodies these principles, then they will truly be working "as unto the Lord." They are more likely to lead well and love the least among us in such a way as to have a profoundly positive impact. And, at the end of the day, they are likely to be affirmed by the Master with the words, "Well done!"

Dr. Randy Ross
CEO of Remarkable!
Author of *Remarkable!* and *Relationomics*

INTRODUCTION

"Well done, good and faithful servant." The moment I first read those words, my spirit leaped, and I knew that those words would become my life's mission. I wanted to live and work in such a way that when I finished my race and stood before my maker, that I could hear those words from my creator's lips.

As I launched into business, the words "Well Done" became my mission in everything that I did. I wanted to hear the words Well Done from every customer, vendor, and employee. I wanted to be recognized as a leader in my field, and I wanted to know that when I completed my work, I could lay my head on the pillow at night, knowing that I did everything that day to the best of my ability. Every day I wanted to work too Well Done.

When I would meet other faith-driven leaders, I found that they, too, were motivated by words Well Done. Although we might be in different businesses doing different work, we had the same purpose and mission. I discovered that almost every leader who is shaped by their faith wants to hear these words but often wrestle with how to embrace more of the Well Done principles in their life and work.

Those two words led me on several years of study to understand how to lead a business and live a life in a way that would please God. I read the Bible from cover to cover and studied every passage that could be related to business. I wanted to find clues for how to measure my actions, decisions, and results against the standard that God might use when He decides to dispense those two powerful words.

What I unearthed as the studied the Bible was both exciting and intriguing. This search encouraged me to understand how business leaders in different generations interpreted and applied these words to their life and business. I read books from a variety of Christian CEOs as well as leaders in their fields. I studied their companies and listened to the voices of those that knew these leaders. What I found amazed me.

Through my study, I found that in the teachings of Jesus as related by the business owner Matthew, there were twelve thought-out biblical business principles that every faith-driven leader should master on their way to hearing the words Well Done. The apostle Matthew was a first-century business owner in the form of a tax collector. To be a tax collector was one of the most important businesses in the time of Jesus. Of all the books in the Bible, Matthew has the ability to speak to business owners and leaders since he was one. Matthew's Gospel is a personal account of how Matthew viewed Jesus and his teachings as they would apply to him personally and all that would read his writings. Every business owner and CEO should embrace the Gospel of Matthew for a view of the teachings of Jesus.

As I reviewed business leaders and CEOs from the past, I found that Christian CEOs over a considerable span of time practiced these principles and went on to find success both in this world and in the world to come. These biblical business principles are enduring and have been proven over and over again. In this book, I reference examples from many companies. Among them are JCPenney, Forever 21, and Tom's Shoes. Each company mentioned within these pages has achieved a high level of success, but some of them are currently in decline. I would suggest that the biblical business principles that these companies practiced are what helped them to achieve good results, but neglecting these principles has been at least partially responsible for the decline of these companies and organizations.

In this book, I have attempted to show you leaders from over 100 years ago that were leaders in their field using these same Well Done principles. In this book, you will discover such Well Done leaders from the past, such as J.C. Penney, P.T. Barnum, and Booker T. Washington. These Well Done leaders from past generations have something to teach current CEOs and leaders. These leaders from the past lived out their faith in the marketplace and found that they could impact both their business and the Kingdom of God through their work. Further, these leaders teach modern-day leaders that you can grow your business and influence with Kingdom impact.

I also reference modern-day faith-driven leaders such as David Novak (former President of YUM Brands), Truett Cathy (Founder of Chick-fil-A), John Maxwell (author of close to 100 leadership books,) and Todd Hopkins (CEO of Office Pride). These fortune 500 companies and successful CEOs show that these principles work today as well as they did 150 years or two thousand years ago when Jesus first taught these principles to His disciples.

I also point you to small, privately-held businesses whom I personally work with each month as they seek to hear the words Well Done. Although their names might not be familiar, their stories will motivate and encourage any leader who picks up this book. They will teach CEOs and leaders that they can have a significant Kingdom impact even when leading a smaller organization, as they make a difference in the lives of others. In fact, I believe that some of the smallest businesses that are led by Well Done leaders have the biggest opportunity to make an impact for the Kingdom of God. Catch that. Any leader can make a difference using these principles, and one leader did in my life many years ago.

I experienced the difference a biblical business principle can make first hand as I grew up watching the impact of a Well Done CEO who made the difference in my family. This book is dedicated to my father, who was the wisest man I ever knew even though he never went to college or even finished high school. My father was the oldest brother of five siblings. When he was fifteen years old, a drunk driver killed his father. My dad quit school and went to work to help his mother provide for their family. My dad always had hard labor jobs. He wore a hard hat his entire life. His hard work taught me the value of working your best at any position. My father taught me first hand that no task is too tough to accomplish, and if you work hard enough at anything, you can create an impact.

Finally, in my youth, a company named Christy Minerals that was led by a Well Done CEO, Frank O'Brien hired my father. Frank placed a higher premium on a person's character than on their education. My dad went on to work for that company for more than 25 years, and his work became a defining moment for my father and our family. That company helped my father to grow in his new faith and helped to challenge him to share his faith with his family and friends.

When I related to Frank O'Brien, the CEO of Christy Minerals, the company where my father worked, that I was writing a book about the Well Done principles that were founded in the Bible, I asked him to read the book and tell me he thoughts. He responded with these kind words:

"I had the pleasure of working with Ken's father, Brian, for over twenty years. Brian was the union president, and I was the company president. We did not always agree. Despite that, Brian always treated me respectfully, and his word was his bond. If he said anything, you knew he believed it. It is clear that Brian passed on his Christianity to Ken successfully. Some say we can't take anything with us when we die. That is not true. It looks like Brian will be welcoming his son home someday."

I was honored and touched by Frank's words. He is correct that my father did share his faith, and Frank's company set the example of the power of a company that seeks to hear the words Well Done. I am passionate about sharing these principles with other Well Done leaders so that they can grow their company with Kingdom impact.

One defining moment with my father came when I was ten years old. I had a conversation with my father about his work and his faith. My dad always took two things to work every day. He would take his hard hat and his Bible. One day I asked dad why he took his Bible to work. He said that the Bible helped him, and he wanted to read it during his breaks. Those two items that he introduced me to have shaped my life and my work.

I value the Bible and continual learning. My father taught me the value of education and self-improvement. I was the first in my family to go to college. I graduated with honors and then went on to receive two master's degrees, one in business and one in divinity. The most valuable lesson one can learn in life is that they have the power to improve, grow, and develop. Therefore, I decided to grow every day of my life. I knew that every day I should be learning something new and, most important, listening to what God might be teaching me that day.

The most significant source of inspiration and instruction is the book that my father introduced to me, the Bible. The Bible has business and life principles that have been proven true for thousands of years. Over the years, I have read the Bible for consolation, education, inspiration, and empowerment.

I have embraced the principles of the Bible. I live these principles, and I use them to guide and build my business and the businesses that work with at CEO Experience. These principles guided Solomon to become the wisest and richest man in the world. These principles guided every single leader of the Bible and helped them to hear the words Well Done. Further, when I began to look at how these principles are applied in culture and in business, I found that every successful business has learned how to apply and adapt these principles to their business, even though most of them never knew that the principle came from the Bible.

In this book, I highlight a few businesses that would be seen as highly successful, but not led by a Well Done leader. I do this because I want to show any reader of this book the wisdom and truth of these principles. Further, if secular businesses can not only embrace but apply these twelve principles to their business, how much more should leaders who are driven by their faith to hear the words Well Done embrace and apply these principles.

To that end, I have included Win Activities and Experience Questions throughout each chapter. Win Activities and Experience Questions are included in each CXP Executive Retreat Guide that is produced at CEO Experience each month for Well Done CEOs to help the leader apply these principles with clarity and application.

I have a fundamental belief that what you (the reader) writes is more important than what I write. Therefore I want you to write as much in this book as I have written. The experience questions are designed to help you consider the different leadership experiences that have shaped you as a leader. It is important to review and strategically consider how those experiences can mold your leadership decisions and choices. The Win Activity is a deeper dive into how a best idea or new piece of information can be applied in your life and business. The more that you can embrace and apply the principles outlined in this book, the bigger the impact you can have for the Kingdom of God.

It is my hope that this book can inspire and challenge every business that is led by a Christian business owner, and business leaders who may desire to learn a biblical business principle or two. I believe that there is a movement that is growing around the world for leaders who are shaped by their faith, to take a stand, and to honor God in and throughout the platform of their business. One way to promote Him and His Kingdom is to embed His values and elevate His principles in everything that is done in and through the business.

The principles I have written about in this book have shaped almost all of my life and business decisions. These principles have brought clarity to me in difficult and trying times. They have shown me what God expects of me as a leader. They challenge me to go further and work harder than I would if I was left to my own nature. They inspire me by seeing what others have done when they have applied these principles. And these principles remind me of what God is pleased with as I seek to build a business and fulfill the calling that He has given to other business owners and me so that we together can hear the words Well Done.

THE 12 PRINCIPLES SUMMARY

PART I: The Proclamations of Jesus

Biblical Business Principle #1: Take the Second Step
"If anyone forces you to go one mile, go with them two miles." Matthew 5:41

Biblical Business Principle #2: The Golden Rule Works If You Work It
"So in everything, do to others what you would have them do to you." Matthew 7:12

Biblical Business Principle #3: Grow Profit with a Purpose
"What good will it be for someone to gain the whole world, yet forfeit their soul? Or what can anyone give in exchange for their soul?" Matthew 16:26

Biblical Business Principle #4: Know Your 'Yeses' and Your "Nos"
"And do not swear by your head, for you cannot make even one hair white or black. All you need to say is simply 'Yes' or 'No'; anything beyond this comes from the evil one." Matthew 5:36-37

PART II: The Parables of Jesus

Biblical Business Principle #5: Make the Move From Owner to Overseer
"Well done, good and faithful servant. You have been faithful over a little; I will set you over much. Enter into the joy of your master." Matthew 25:27

Biblical Business Principle #6: Trust the Law of Sowing and Reaping
"Still other seed fell on good soil, where it produced a crop—a hundred, sixty or thirty times what was sown." Matthew 13:8

Biblical Business Principle #7: Believe and Ask for the Impossible
"Jesus looked at them and said, "With man this is impossible, but with God all things are possible." Matthew 19:26

Biblical Business Principle #8: Build to the 4th Generation
"Therefore everyone who hears these words of mine and puts them into practice is like a wise man who built his house on the rock. The rain came down, the streams rose, and the winds blew and beat against that house; yet it did not fall, because it had its foundation on the rock." Matthew 7:24-25

PART III: The Practices of Jesus

Biblical Business Principle #9: Know the Order of Things and Work the Order
"But seek first his kingdom and his righteousness, and all these things will be given to you as well." Matthew 6:33

Biblical Business Principle #10: Improve Your Team to Improve Your Organization
"'Come, follow me,' Jesus said, 'and I will send you out to fish for people.' At once they left their nets and followed him" Matthew 4:20

Biblical Business Principle #11: Do Things Today that Impact Today and Tomorrow

"Store up for yourselves treasures in heaven, where moths and vermin do not destroy, and where thieves do not break in and steal. For where your treasure is, there your heart will be also" Matthew 6:20-21.

Biblical Business Principle #12: Work to "Well Done"

"Therefore go and make disciples of all nations, baptizing them in the name of the Father and of the Son and of the Holy Spirit, and teaching them to obey everything I have commanded you. And surely I am with you always, to the very end of the age." Matthew 28:19-20

Part I:

The Proclamations of Jesus

Chapter 1

TAKE THE SECOND STEP

Too Many Companies Expect Second Mile Results
While Only Providing First Mile Effort.

"If anyone forces you to go one mile, go with them two miles."
Matthew 5:41

W ell Done are the words that inspire any faith-driven business leader to strive for excellence in building their business and ordering their life. Although Well Done has a noble connotation to it, many business leaders, including myself, have a difficult time describing and defining what Well Done looks like in the life a business that is led by a person of faith. In this book, I will attempt to describe and practically apply the twelve biblical business principles that can help any leader who desires to grow their business with Kingdom impact to know how they can hear the words Well Done at the end of their journey. Life is too short, and business is too challenging to labor and work all

3

one's life and not hear the words Well Done. Now, let's start on the journey by examining the first principle: take the second step.

There is always another step! Have you ever driven by a Chick-fil-A and seen cars lined up out into the street, even when it's well past the lunch hour? Have you seen the crowds at a mall food court spilling out into the hallway? Calling the chicken chain "popular" is like saying California surfers enjoy ocean waves. Only three of the fifty states in the U.S. don't have a Chick-fil-A, which in 2019 was forecast to soon bypass Wendy's, Burger King, and Taco Bell en route to becoming the nation's third-largest fast-food chain.

Back in 2008, then COO (and now CEO and President) Dan Cathy outlined the secret of their business success, one grounded in Matthew 5:41: "If anyone forces you to go one mile, go with them two miles."

In an interview with The Christian Post, the son of founder S. Truett Cathy said, "We make sure the first mile is taken care of, and then we go beyond that to the second mile. We provide hostesses, carry trays if necessary, (and) have table tray liners. We've even gone so far as to change a tire for someone."[1]

Is it any wonder, since that interview, Chick-fil-A has tripled in size to more than 2,200 locations? Or that it fields more than 20,000 franchisee applications annually while accepting less than one-half of 1 percent? That it makes more money per restaurant than any other fast-food chain? Is it any wonder that the restaurant is so popular that even malls requiring stores to be open on Sunday will waive that rule because they want all the customer traffic they know a Chick-fil-A will bring to their food court? This compelling success story is a real-life example of the maxim: "Always take the second step."

Always Take the Second Step

Those five powerful words contain a secret that successful business leaders and companies have been practicing for two thousand years. Companies that wish to differentiate themselves from their competitors always go a little further and find the second step, whether it be with customer service, as in the case of Chick-fil-A, or with treatment of staff, as in the case of The Container Store, which offers first-year employees two hundred hours of training compared to the industry average of eight. Companies might also differentiate themselves by building their products to last, just as Buck Knives does by offering a life-time guarantee that each knife will be free of defects in material and work-manship. They might also pay attention to details to enhance experiences as Disneyland does, which does not allow employees to point with one finger or tell a guest, "I don't know." Regardless of how they apply the maxim, these companies have learned the art of going a little further, or, as I call it, always taking the second step.

Going a little further is not just a good idea; the "Second-Step Mentality" is a biblical business principle and one proven effective in growing successful businesses. Business leaders seeking to embrace God's pattern for their business will help their organization develop this mindset by building a strong team culture and encouraging their people to "always take the second step." As mentioned in the opening story about Chick-fil-A, this principle comes from Matthew 5:41, where Jesus taught the wisdom of taking the second step. The truth underlying it follows: it is wise and beneficial to do more than is expected or anticipated.

> **Experience Question:** Where have you observed a second-mile mentality in a business that you use? How does it feel to receive unexpected actions or service?

S. Truett Cathy built Chick-fil-A with this attitude. In his memoir, *Eat Mor' Chikin*, he wrote about how—while delivering newspapers as a teen—he tried not to lose a single customer by treating each like they were the most important person in the world. He delivered each paper as if it were destined for the governor's mansion. "That's an image that still works to improve customer service," Cathy said. "If you were working in a restaurant and suddenly the President of the United States showed up, your voice and facial expressions would change. . . . If we're willing to do that for the President, why not treat every customer that well?"[2]

He delivered each paper as if it were destined for the governor's mansion.

Biblical Business Principle #1: Take the Second Step
"If anyone forces you to go one mile, go with them two miles."
Matthew 5:41

Practice a Second-Mile Mentality. Do more than anticipated and expected. Find Second Step Solutions. Pay attention to the little things that others don't. Be different by serving. Give Second Step Surprises.

Jesus teaches the "Second Step" principle as a way of life. He wants His disciples to think and act differently from the world. He shows His followers a model designed to help them to separate themselves from the culture, in order to help others see Him and understand His message more clearly. In business, companies also need to separate themselves from their competition. The company that decides to take a second step in all that they do will become a company that creates more value for those for those they serve. An excellent leadership axiom is, "as a person or company creates more value, they become more valuable." Excellent companies work to show themselves as valuable as they create a differential factor through always doing more than expected. As these companies create they become more recognizable in the market and more rememberable to their customers. The second step model is the best model for adding value to your company and for your customers.

As a person or company creates more value, they become more valuable.

How the "Second Step" Separates You from the Crowd
The second step perspective works in life and business. Leaders who wish to one day hear the words Well Done will embrace why Jesus taught this principle. They will think of strategic ways to apply it their business as they teach it to their people.

1. The Second Step Employs a Double Blessing
One reason this behavior is important for Well Done CEOs is because it blesses those who receive it. When Jesus talks about going the second mile, He is challenging His followers to do twice as much as is asked or expected of them. A person cannot follow this advice without blessing the person who receives it. In the Kingdom, God blesses His followers beyond measure. So

doing twice as much as people expect will amaze them.

CEO Experience member Tom Boyer leads a company called IR.Tools™, an infrared technology company that produces patches, targets, and vehicle IDs for the military and police units around the world. Tom added the second step concept to the company's core values, which include "To Be A Blessing" to everyone they serve. One creative way they do this is through shipping and delivery. In each of the company's shipments, they add a box of Girl Scout cookies. This seemingly simple act serves as a double blessing. They bless the purchasers of their materials while blessing local Girl Scout troops by buying cookies to support their cause.

Well Done CEOs can find many ways to take the second step in their business if they look for them. The second step is not only good for business but it is mandatory for leaders looking to make an impact for God's Kingdom.

2. The Second Step Empowers the Giver

When Jesus made His bold and outrageous statement, He was talking to slaves and people who had been forced to go the first mile. Don't miss this point! The listener had no options for the first mile; it was mandated. Jesus understood that by going the second mile voluntarily, He was helping the one who was a slave to become free. The second mile (or second step) lay in the power of the walker. Though not required to do it, they could choose to walk the extra mile—an empowering choice. When Well Done leaders lead their teams to do more than expected, it empowers employees to better understand their power to make decisions. This act of teaching the second step will help employees and every team member to think more like an owner of their area and department. The second step will help employees develop an ownership mentality. The second step is one of the most empowering steps any person can take to better their life and to enhance their work.

> **The second step is one of the most empowering steps any person can take to better their life and to enhance their work.**

3. The Second Step Excels Over Those that Stand Still

Many people and businesses are content to stand still; they believe what they are doing at present is "good enough." But good enough is never enough in business. God does not call His people to a minimum effort. He calls the believer to do things

The second step person and organization will always outshine and beat the person or organization who stands still.

with excellence. Businesses that strive for this kind of excellence will always out-compete the business that just does enough. The employee who does more than asked will always be promoted before the employee who only does what is asked. The leader who goes above and beyond the expected will always attract more followers than one who does the ordinary. The second step person and organization will always outshine and beat the person or organization who stands still.

4. The Second Step Exalts Values over Demands

An integral part of why Jesus gives such a declaration to His followers is He wants those who come into contact with His people to notice the difference. Taking the second step shows the higher calling and deeper values that a Well Done person exhibits. Kingdom impact is more likely to happen when someone is served in such a way that they ask, "Why?" The soldier who encountered a second mile person would feel compelled to ask the one carrying the bag why they would do so. In fact, in Jesus's era, people had the opportunity to walk that extra mile as they discussed the matter. Many businesses today are missing opportunities to take a second step with people. The next step provides the biggest opportunities to make an impact on recipients and for the Kingdom of Heaven and therefore making a Kingdom impact. Kingdom is anything that is done that make a difference for eternity. I believe more businesses should be concerned more about their Kingdom impact than their bottom line.

5. The Second Step Expands Kingdom and Business Opportunities

The second step provides opportunities that would never be discovered otherwise. When people go further than expected, they discover new insights and see new horizons. Taking the extra step or going an extra mile provides extra opportunities to improve business and expand existing offerings. Great companies go to great lengths to find opportunities to grow. The best way to find new opportunities is by expanding current opportunities. This can come in the form of expanding lines with current customers, improving existing products, or investing in current employees. Some of the best opportunities for your business are at your disposal through your current projects and people.

While all companies would be wise to cultivate a second mile mentality, the great companies are those that embrace it. They learn the art of taking the second step, even in the way they design themselves. Too many companies expect second-mile results without giving second-mile effort. The "second step" can often make the difference between success and failure.

Business leaders who lead their companies in developing a second-step mentality will realize real results, as shown by Chick-fil-A's growth and profitability. Other results may come in the form of customer satisfaction, word-of-mouth referrals to other potential customers, or in a compliment about an employee who did more than expected after recognizing a customer issue they could resolve. A second-step mentality provides a good return on investment.

How To Develop a Second-Step Mentality
Develop An Attitude of Always Doing More Than Anticipated and Expected

No one is inspired to go the second mile unless they have been challenged to do so. Leaders must challenge themselves and those that follow them to have an attitude of always doing more than anticipated and expected. Businesses that practice this art provide the best customer experiences—the surprising or unexpected experiences.

Companies that love their customers create new ways to improve service. Author Tommy Newberry notes the wisdom of continually asking yourself how to increase your service and contribution: "Ask, 'How can I triple my value to my boss, to my clients, to the marketplace, to my family?' Write it down. No one can do the minimum and reach the maximum."[3] The business that seeks to provide more value to those that they serve will become more valuable.

The business that seeks to provide more value to those that they serve will become more valuable.

When a company creates more value for their customers, their customers generate more value for the company. As legendary Dallas Cowboys quarterback and Hall of Famer Roger Staubach once quipped, "There are no traffic jams along the extra mile."[4] Indeed, businesses and business leaders that choose to take the second step will find many rewards and benefits. Magic Kingdom legend Walt Disney instilled this idea into the creation of Disneyland. "That's just the point," Disney said. "We should do the parade precisely because no one's expecting it. Our goal at Disneyland is to always give the people more than they expect. As long as we keep surprising them, they'll keep coming back. But if they stop coming, it'll cost us ten times that much to get them to come back."[5]

When leaders and companies commit to doing more than anticipated or expected, they build a business made to last. Second step leaders think longer and see further than those who focus strictly on today because they act today while thinking about tomorrow.

Find and Develop Second-Step Solutions

To go a little further means to develop a second-step mentality, which inspires team members to find solutions that please the customer and serve the business' best interest. Customer service is really customer creativity. The secret of a successful business is freeing employees to resolve the problems customers face. Management experts Chris DeRose and Noel Tichy—co-authors of the book *Judgment on the Front Line: How Smart Companies Win by Trusting Their People*—emphasize the importance of empowering all employees to become problem solvers: "Frontline workers not only see service breakdowns but also opportunities for serving customers in entirely new ways. Teaching frontline leaders the basics of designing simple experiments enables organizations to test many more ideas than could ever be orchestrated centrally."[6]

> **Customer service is really customer creativity.**

A second-step mentality is the best way to serve your customers and create opportunities to create moments of kingdom impact. Those who find creative solutions cause customers to notice the distinct difference in their company compared to other companies that don't seem to care. These innovators solve problems, inspire customer loyalty, and become referral stories customers want to share with others. Noted management consultant and author Peter Drucker once said: "The purpose of business is to create a customer,"[7] while marketing and digital executive Shiv Singh observes: "The purpose of business is to create a customer who creates customers."[8] For Well Done leaders, the purpose of business is to create customers they can serve and impact for the Kingdom of God.

It has often been said that businesses do not exist until they create customers. However, the businesses that succeed will be those that create a solution for customers to share with other customers. The company or organization that becomes a master at problem-solving by finding new solutions will become a leader in its field. It will be recognized as "top-of-class" in every industry.

Second-step solutions are the best tool for finding solutions for customers.[9] A second-step mentality is not satisfied with just giving a customer a good experience. Instead, it requires finding unexpected solutions for customers that leave them amazed and surprised, which drives the organization. In other words, first-rate companies find second-step solutions.

When a customer encounters a problem, a business has an opportunity to create a meaningful customer experience by paying attention to the little details others miss. An essential step in building customer relationships consists of people in the organization listening to customers' real needs. Too many businesses have stopped listening to customers. Those with empathy seek to understand their customers' problems and then walk alongside them to find creative solutions. Solutions begin once companies empower their employees to help customers find them. Many businesses make a critical error in dealing with customers at this juncture. While many companies develop policies and procedures to solve customers' problems, they often don't work in real life. These possible solutions are flawed because most customers are not satisfied with a standard solution; they want a specific, tailor-made answer. Great companies empower their employees to find solutions.

First-rate companies find second-step solutions

Going the second step will produce more customers while developing new products and processes.

> **Experience Question:** Do you have a place to record the customer stories your company has created? Where?

Pay Attention to the Little Things Others Don't
Customer satisfaction begins once companies employ entrepreneurial thinking—out-of-the-box solutions. This process includes helping employees think like

owners, finding creative ways to leave the customer not only satisfied, but amazed the company actually cares. In their book, *Satisfaction: How Every Great Company Listens to the Voice of the Customer*, J.D. Power and Associates, executives Chris Denove and James D. Power IV write: "Every day your customers provide a steady stream of anecdotal feedback; all you need to do is learn to stop and listen. Warranty records, letters of gratitude, and even a screaming tirade to a service rep are all pieces of the puzzle. The better able you are to collect, synthesize, and mine all of these disparate inputs, the better you will understand your customer."[10]

Every day your customers provide a steady stream of anecdotal feedback; all you need to do is learn to stop and listen.

Second step satisfaction should be every Christian business's goal. Meeting customer expectations produces customer satisfaction. Every customer brings expectations, whether for delivery of a product order or a certain level of functionality from the product. Wise companies and organizations consider what expectations will bring someone into their store or website.

> **Experience Question:** Have you genuinely considered the expectations of your customers and the first step in how to exceed those expectations?

A business would be wise to look at four areas that every customer will experience to discern the first step to a second step level of service. Those four areas include first impression or reception of a customer, product reliability, reusability, and response to issues.

Level 1 - Second Step Reception in the Purchasing of Products. Excellent customer service happens beforehand. Good customer service starts at the door or the portal page, not the cash register or order click.

Level 2 - Second Step Reliability of Product or Service Delivery. Customers expect a specific delivery time when purchasing or ordering; when this fails to meet their expectations, problems occur.

Level 3 - Second Step Reusability of Products and Services. Customers expect a product or service to include certain benefits and durability. If experience fails to align with expectations, it also produces problems.

Level 4 - Second Step Response to Customer Issues and Concerns. Customer service starts with listening to the customer to understand the issues the customer is having and what the customer needs to help resolve those issues.

An essential step to creating second-step satisfaction is to understand what your customers expect and then surpass those expectations.

> **Win Activity: Second Step Expectations:** Where in your business could you use a second-mile principle? List one to four areas that could improve your customer experience by developing a second-mile mentality.
>
> 1.
>
> 2.
>
> 3.
>
> 4.

Be Different By Serving

Amid often-impersonal technology advancements, companies must not miss the most critical ingredient to business success: friendliness. In a hyper-paced world, friendliness stands out and helps a company develop the art of the second-mile surprise. In today's technological age, many customers no longer expect the personal touch; often, too many businesses sacrifice friendliness for efficiency—a fundamental error that can sabotage a business. Successful companies learn how to be friendly while still striving for efficiency. They never sacrifice the personal touch and the power of human relationships.

Being different by serving is a mark of a second-step mentality. It takes time and thoughtfulness to serve well. However, both customers and employees recognize an organization and leader that cares for and serves their people well.

One example of a second step company that cares about their people is the online shoe retailer Zappos, whose customer service is legendary. In a story on the website of the help desk software company, Help Scout, executive Gregory Ciotti wrote about a customer shopping for shoes for her elderly mother, whose medical condition caused very sensitive feet; hard-soled shoes often left her in pain. So the customer bought six pairs from Zappos; after trying them, her mother only kept two, which she wears for long periods.

When it was time for her mother to return the other four pairs, she called Zappos. That's when her mother discovered the Zappos employee who related to her plight because the employee's father had suffered from similar foot problems because of diabetes. The employee ended the conversation by saying that she would pray for the woman to feel better, but the story doesn't end there: "My mom called me to relay the news, and I could hear the smile on her face from 600 miles away. She said that the lovely Zappos person had sent her an enormous bouquet of lilies and roses to let her know she was thinking of her. My sister emailed the company to thank Zappos for taking such good care of my mom. Two days later, my mom, sister, and I were contacted and told we are now 'Zappos VIP Members,' which entitles us to free expedited shipping on all our orders. My sister vows to buy every pair of shoes, from now on, from Zappos."[11]

This story illustrates the business model that Zappos CEO Tony Hsieh writes about in *Delivering Happiness: A Path to Profits, Passion, and Purpose*. In the book, he explains how the first core value of Zappos is to deliver WOW through great service: "Wow is such a short, simple word, but it really encompasses a lot of things. To WOW, you must differentiate yourself, which means to be a little unconventional and innovative. You must do something that's above and beyond what's expected."[12]

Experience Question: Why should you try to wow your customers? How could you teach your employees to serve to the wow?

Like Zappos, great businesses wow their both their internal and external customers. They genuinely care about those that they serve and want to solve their problems. These businesses and business leaders understand that customers desire to be heard—and understood. Sometimes, all customers want is to have someone listen to their issues and care about their situation. Second step companies care about their customers and will always have customers to care for.

Digital marketing and social media whiz Gary Vaynerchuk writes about the power of connecting with the customer in his book, *The Thank You Economy*: "What if you were able to build a relationship, make a connection, tilt the person's emotions toward you, and capture 30, 60, or even 100 percent of what he or she

Second step companies care about their customers and will always have customers to care for.

spends? Your small customer would become a lot bigger. That's why you have to take every customer seriously. This is a basic business principle that has been talked about and written about a great deal, and some companies take it seriously. . . . Valuing every single customer is mandatory in the Thank You Economy."[13]

Companies that have a kingdom impact focus will pivot from finding customers to making their customers their friends. Friendship places a high premium on wanting your customers to like your company and employees with whom they interact consistently. Friendship does not mean that you can produce a weak product or have poor customer service. Friendliness in business contributes a significant role in the loyalty and longevity of customer relationships. I will discuss this further in chapter 2 when I discuss the principle of The Golden Rule Works if You Work It. Companies must understand that, knowingly or not, while customers are buying a service, they are also seeking a relationship.

Give Second Step Surprises

Companies that create an impact will give extras to their customers, both internal and external, to help to make a memorable experience. Jesus was a master of giving second step surprises. He told Zacchaeus that he wanted to come to his house. He told Peter to walk on water. He encouraged Thomas to put his fingers into the holes in his hands. Jesus consistently found ways to surprise the people who walked with him and around him.

Focusing on the customer experience can be difficult for any business. Businesses can spend years developing goodwill toward customers, all to have one bad experience wipe it all out. That's why great companies learn how to surprise and delight their customers by practicing the art of the second mile surprise.

In today's evolving economy, the second step principle will make the difference between good customer experiences and memorable ones. Office Pride, the premier office cleaning franchise, was started by Well Done CEO Todd Hopkins.

The idea for them is that customers hire and expect them to give 100%, but they brag and tell their friends when the company and their employees go just 1% above that (or they take a second step).

Using his research and commitment to customer satisfaction, Hopkins started Office Pride Commercial Cleaning Services and earns rave reviews from franchisees, clients, and competitors. From the beginning, he was determined to build a long-term profitable business that glorified God while serving the community. Starting with just $20,000 from his personal savings and a little help from his family and friends, Hopkins worked out of his home, cleaning at night and signing up customers during the day. It wasn't always easy, but he persevered, relying on his faith and business skills. One of their core values is to "Go the Extra Mile." The idea for them is that customers hire and expect them to give 100%, but they brag and tell their friends when the company and their employees go just 1% above that (or they take a second step).

One example of the impact of their second step thinking at Office Pride was when a franchise owner noticed that after a customer had completely remodeled their break room, they put the table back and was still using the same old table cloth that was aged and had a small tear in it. So, the franchise owner delivered to them a new table cloth as a gift to their remodeling effort. The customer loved it and would often share the story as the small made a big difference to the customer. The customer thought this act was even more impressive considering all the extra work the Office Pride employee had to do each night to keep the facility clean during the remodeling. The Office Pride franchise owner not only paid for the extra work, but took the extra step to give a gift to the company that they were working to clean.

> **Experience Question:** If small actions make big impressions, why don't you think more companies focus on small things that make a difference? What small second step could you take in your business to make a difference with your customers?

A Second Step Case Study

I experienced this recently after my father died, and my mother decided to visit me on the East Coast after his funeral. I attribute much of my success to my mother. I believe that the example she modeled enabled me to learn the benefits of hard work and entrepreneurship.[14] I grew up in the Midwest with a diligent and hardworking mother, as the youngest of four sons. Although life was not always easy, I learned many leadership lessons from my mother as she worked, led the path at home, and raised us. I decided that her first flight should be on Southwest because of their friendliness. I thought that it was a fantastic example that, although my mother was seventy-five years old at the time, she had decided to do something she had never done before by taking her first flight. Although I purchased her a ticket on a Southwest Airlines flight to Baltimore, she insisted she would only fly if I came to St. Louis to travel with her back to my home area. As the flight time approached, she grew more and more nervous.

I made sure to get her to the airport early so I could show her around—three hours ahead of time. When I took her up to the check-in counter, the agents behind the counter noticed me explaining everything to her. One asked politely, "Do you work for Southwest?" I replied, "No, this is my mother's first flight, and I was explaining how everything works." At that, the agent went into action. She said, "Wow, your first flight. That is wonderful." She then asked my mother's age and why she was traveling. After the explanation, the agent said, "Wait here. We have a special gift and prize for you." When she returned from the back, she handed my mother a funny-looking hat and said, "This is just for you; you must wear it onto the plane."

Customer Service Can Be Fun

When Mom and others around her saw the blow-up Southwestern balloon hat, everyone burst into laughter; many people remarked: "That's fantastic." Though a simple gesture, it communicated a vital message: We care. They cared about my mother's nervousness, so they tried to introduce a little laughter into a stressful situation.

Customer Service Always Means Going the Second Mile

While my mother felt a lot better after her experience at the counter, Southwest was just getting started. A few hours later when we boarded, the flight attendant at the front of the plane noticed that my mother was carrying the Southwest balloon hat. As my mother boarded, the flight attendant asked my mother where she got such a unique gift. My mother quickly explained what happened.

The flight attendant didn't just express excitement for my mother; she showed it. After Mom took her seat and the plane was fully boarded, the flight attendant found my mother and brought her a special certificate for her first flight, along with a thank-you card, a luggage tag, and a giant bag full of individual packets of peanuts. The last item touched my mother's heart: Dad's favorite snack was peanuts. All together, these items were probably worth less than five dollars, but they created a valuable, memorable moment for my mother and the other passengers.

Don't Forget the Final Touch

My mother had an enjoyable flight, but Southwest wasn't done yet. As the plane taxied to the gate, the flight attendant began speaking over the intercom. After asking for everyone's attention, she said, "We have two special first-time flyers on our plane today. The first is flying for the first time at seventy-five years of age. Mary, can you touch your call button? Because we have a special gift for you." Then the flight attendant walked to her seat with a large bottle of champagne as the other passengers applauded and smiled broadly. Then the attendant added, "And the second first-time flyer is a man who is eighty-seven and celebrating his birthday today. Please give a round of applause to our captain." Again, the plane broke out in applause and laughter.

> **Experience Question:** Have you ever been surprised by how your employees have solved a customer issue or celebrated a customer in a special way? Capture the details and share this story with other team members.

Former Southwest CEO Herb Kelleher (who died in early 2019) wanted to establish an airline that was built on love, or, as Southwest likes to say it: LUV. "We are interested in people who externalize, who focus on other people, who are really motivated to help other people," Kelleher once said. "We are not interested in navel-gazers, regardless of how lint-free their navels are. If you are careful about hiring loving people, it should come as no surprise that acts of love and generosity will naturally spill out of them. It should also come as no surprise that when you get enough people with these attributes in the same company, a corporate character is created that practices love as a way of doing business."[15]

It should also come as no surprise that when you get enough people with these attributes in the same company, a corporate character is created that practices love as a way of doing business.

When you do something unexpected for the customer, it shows love for the customer. Second mile surprises are always appreciated, and they create memorable experiences.

One more second step comment:

Every company has the power to create amazing customer experience moments. Unfortunately, they also can create bad experiences. Customer service is about thoughtfulness toward the customer. Businesses that practice a second-mile mentality will create unexpected experiences that will translate into unexpected customer stories. Companies are wise when they pay attention to the stories that they create, which can happen on any day, with any customer. These kinds of stories occur when a business embraces the first principle of taking the second step. Well Done leaders always take the second step.

Best Ideas: Write down two or three best ideas that you heard or learned from this chapter.

WELL

DONE

Chapter 2

THE GOLDEN RULE WORKS
IF YOU WORK IT

When you think about the customer,
the customer thinks about you.

"So in everything, do to others what you would have them do to you."
Matthew 7:12

I t's never been about you! Amazon has been a game-changer for businesses and business leaders. For years now, retailers have grumbled about the presence of the online giant Amazon. Many Christian retailers would say that Amazon is largely to blame for the announcement in the spring of 2019 that LifeWay Christian Stores would close all its 170 retail outlets by the end of the year. Although LifeWay retains an online operation (indeed, its online sales ranked five times those of its brick-and-mortar locations), it was the last major Christian store chain left after the 2017 demise of 240 Family Christian Stores.

However, amid the retail rubble lies a lesson for all businesses: above all else, pay attention to the customer. This sentiment appeared in a 2016 letter to shareholders from Amazon's president and CEO, Jeff Bezos. In it, Bezos discussed his obsession with customer focus, which drove his company to pay attention to customers' desire to make purchases online instead of having to drive to a retail outlet. There are many ways to center a business, Bezos said: for example, your business can be product-focused, technology-focused, or business model-focused. Moreover, in his view, obsessive customer focus offers the best assurance of vitality.

Thinking about others first is good business. Indeed, as with Amazon, it must always come first. Many companies begin to decline when they become so internally focused they forget to serve—and care for—their customers. Lack of customer care is the number one reason for companies losing customers. Great and successful businesses always put people first. They come before profits and products because without people you cannot have a business or discover success.

The leader and the business that forgets to put people first need a refresher course in the fundamentals of business. Companies that succeed are ones that elevate people. The most successful businesses use a single guidepost that has helped them thrive over many years. It is known as the Golden Rule, first stated in Christ's "Sermon on the Mount" in Matthew (and a similar version in Luke 6:31). The verse from Matthew 7:12 says: "So in everything, do to others what you would have them do to you." Today those words have gained worldwide recognition as the Golden Rule.

Many great businesses have built on the foundation of this one biblical business principle. In fact, department store magnate J.C. Penney relied on it to start and grow his company into a thriving corporation. Even after the retail recession of recent years, in 2019, Penney's still had 850-plus stores and more than 95,000 employees—more than a century after its beginnings. Its founder once commented: "I cannot remem-

I cannot remember a time when the Golden Rule was not my motto and precept, the torch that guided my footsteps.

ber a time when the Golden Rule was not my motto and precept, the torch that guided my footsteps."[16]

> **Experience Question:** Would your team or vendors say that you practice the Golden Rule? What actions do you think that they would point to make their decision?

The concept embedded in the Golden Rule: to consider others first, works in any economy at any age. Well Done CEOs and business organizations will always treat others as they themselves would like to be treated. In his spiritual autobiography, *Fifty Years with the Golden Rule*, J.C. Penney wrote about learning this biblical business principle from his father: "My confidence that business progress and a literal interpretation of the golden rule could be worked out together went straight back to my father's example. From the time I was a young boy I had understood, that though he worked at two separate callings, by his way of working at them he made them interchangeable. He was a farmer, and he was a preacher, and to him, there was no real difference in what these two occupations demanded of a man. He plowed, planted, harvested—and then, when he preached his sermons, applied his industry with the same quality of feeling so that, in effect, he had one over-all ministry: to serve."[17]

Biblical Business Principle #2: The Golden Rule Works If You Work It
"So in everything, do to others what you would have them do to you."
Matthew 7:12

Treat others as you want to be treated. Understand Other People's Viewpoint. Consider Your Customers' Point of View. Make Friends with Your Customers.

Why the Golden Rule Still Works

I believe that the Golden Rule works. I believe that the Golden Rule works today as well as it has at any time in history. I also believe that businesses should apply the Golden Rule to how they treat everyone who enters into contact with the business.

In an article for Forbes magazine, I wrote the following principles as to why every business should embrace the Golden Rule as a standard for their business.

1. **The Golden Rule Challenges People to Put Relationships First**

Principles provide perspective. Key concepts and philosophies lead to better decision-making. When companies or organizations place people first, then decisions can be made within the framework of what is in the best interests of the customer. When a company finds a solution that is in the best interest of the customer and the organization, then the company has found a good option and is able to make good decisions, which will lead to better outcomes. One-sided decisions may work temporarily, but they do not work in the long run. Too many companies make decisions with only a short view.

2. **The Golden Rule Clarifies Core Behaviors, Which Shape Decisions**

Well Done CEOs who practice the Golden Rule become principle-driven leaders. The Golden Rule can become an arbiter of your business decisions. The first measure of any decision in your company should be an evaluation of how the decision impacts others. When a company strives to make decisions based on what is best for others, it can protect against other motives that may not produce the best results. Companies that put others first through their actions often become the leaders in their field or industry.

Your belief in the Golden Rule can lead you to develop other fundamental values and core principles that can guide the decision-making process in your company. When you understand what is important and why it is important, decisions become easier to make. Every leader needs to know their values, and every team member needs to know the values of the leader. When team members understand how the leader would make a decision, decisions in the company become easier to make.

> **When you understand what is important and why it is important, decisions become easier to make.**

3. **The Golden Rule Calls Team Members to Achieve the Highest Standard of Action**

There is no better core value in the business than to treat others as you would want to be treated. J.C. Penney also wrote of how the Golden Rule inspired his organization to set a new standard for the merchandising profession: "Day by day we were infiltrating the organization with evidence that standards of merchandising could be as high as those of any profession. The idea of partnership was dynamic and encompassing. Not only our store managers but also the communities we serve were partners. Our formula comprised a basic liking for human beings, plus integrity, plus industry, plus creative imagination expressing itself in the capacity to see the other fellow's point of view."[18] J.C. Penney wrote those words almost one hundred years ago, and yet the principle behind those words works as well in 2020 as it did in 1920 when J.C. Penny was building his company.

Brenton Hayden, the founder of Renters Warehouse—which since its founding in 2007, became America's leading real estate investment services company—highlighted the importance of the Golden Rule in an article for *Entrepreneur* magazine. In *Why the Golden Rule Must Be Practiced in Business*, Hayden wrote: "In today's ultra-competitive marketplace, where companies start and fail at a drastic rate, having a solid set of ethics could be just what your company needs to stand head and shoulders above the rest."[19]

Ethics and integrity are needed in every age and in every business. Many businesses desire to know how to hire people of high integrity. The answer can be found in the Golden Rule. The Golden Rule question can be asked at any interview or placed on any recruiting assessment. Ask potential employees: Do you believe in the Golden Rule (treat others as you would want to be treated) and why? This one simple question can be a gatekeeper to the integrity of your company.

4. The Golden Rule Creates Consistency Throughout the Organization

When a business consistently practices the Golden Rule, it always leaves the customer feeling heard and validated. The Golden Rule is not only good for every customer; it is suitable for every leader. Real leadership is setting a standard and then influencing others to rise to the level of that standard in all situations and circumstances. The Golden Rule is one such principle since it helps every leader and organization to treat others as they themselves would like to be treated.

As noted earlier, the J.C. Penney chain has been in existence for more than one hundred years. Although they have had many twists and turns and may even be on the decline, the principle of the Golden Rule helped them to achieve lasting success. The Golden Rule is just as valuable today for businesses as it was in 1902, the year that Penney opened his first Golden Rule Store. Let's look at a few ways to apply the Golden Rule in your business.

> **Experience Question:** How many of your team members are familiar with the Golden Rule? What steps could you take to introduce your company to the Golden Rule principle?

What Does It Look Like to Implement the Golden Rule?

Treat Others Like You Want to Be Treated

The Golden Rule is an excellent principle for interacting with others, since treating others like you would want to be treated establishes priorities, particularly putting the customer first. Every kingdom business or Well Done CEO who hopes to make an impact on God's Kingdom will build into the fabric of the organization's structure and the company values the Golden Rule principle. Lee Iacocca, who orchestrated Chrysler's revival in the 1980s, once said: "In the end, all business operations can be reduced to three words: people, product, and profit. People come first."[20]

When a business is only concerned about its own products or services, they cease to be effective. Business has always been about people. Companies provide a service to others, and the best companies offer the product or service while also establishing a relationship with the customer.

Business author Patrick Lencioni writes about the importance of people in his book, *The Advantage*. He states that "every organization must contribute in some way to a better world for some group of people, because if it doesn't, it will, and should, go out of business."[21]

Many businesses could be out of business today because they have forgotten the value of people. News outlets and business publications consistently report in articles and news stories that many companies no longer make decisions in the best interests of people, but only consider the bottom line. Bottom line only thinking is shortsighted and will never provide long-

Bottom line only thinking is shortsighted and will never provide long-term success.

term success. The better way is to put people first in everything. The first question that every business should ask is, "Is this decision good for the customer?" When the decision is good for the customer, it is usually right for the company.

Recently, my wife and I went to a store to buy ten gift cards for the teachers of our two youngest children. We were going to put $25 on each gift card and give them to the teachers as an end-of-the-school-year thank you for investing their time and energy in our children that year.

We walked into the store and up the counter. My wife asked the individual standing behind the counter if they had any gift cards that we could purchase. The person at the register looked at us with a puzzled look as if to say, "The gift cards are at a stand close to the counter, stupid!" We noticed the stand and also noticed that there were no gift cards on it, which we then stated to the person at the register. Then we asked if she could find some gift cards someplace else in the store. She replied, "We have what we have," as if to say that she had done her job by answering the question we asked.

The end of the school year was the next day, and I knew we needed something to get the teachers, and this was a very popular store. I noticed a manager nearby, so I went and asked her if she could possibly find ten gift cards so we could spend $250 in her store. She responded,

"Yes! of course!" ("Yes" is always the right answer to give to the customer. We will look at this in more depth in the chapter entitled "Know Your Yeses and Noes"). She walked back to the same register where we had just spoken to the other store representative and asked the person to step back from the register for a moment. She opened the drawer under the register and pulled out ten gift cards. Actually, she pulled out about 50 gift cards, handed us ten, and then placed the rest on the rack close to the register.

The manager noticed two problems that needed to be solved; the first was to help the current customer, and the second was to help potential future customers that might have the same need. The manager was considering our needs, but she also was thoughtful of the needs of other prospective customers. That was leadership in action.

In the end, the item that we needed was in the drawer at the register where we initially had been standing and well within reach of the first representative.

If the person at the register had really cared about us or even the business, she would have pulled the drawer out and looked. She thought she was doing her job by answering our question, and did not consider the fact that she was going to cost the company $250 and two potential long-term customers. The manager knew she was doing her job by finding us a solution and trying to solve our problem. The manager treated us genuinely like she would have wanted to be treated. When an employee does not practice the Golden Rule, they cost the company customers, who are then lost to a company that does practice the Golden Rule.

Understand the Other Person's Viewpoint

Consideration is innovation. Every successful business starts with a product or service that can do something better, faster, or quicker for the customer. The secret of consideration can lead to new innovation, improved service, and higher quality. When a business strives to understand its customers and spends effort in developing the organization around the thoughts of others, the business will truly find traction.

Consideration is innovation.

Consider the thought processes of the following businesses. Each business began by thinking about what the customer would like, enjoy, or find useful. In other words, first, these companies considered what other people wanted rather than focusing on what the company wanted to produce.

Amazon: They considered their customers' desire to make purchases online and not have to go to a store. To return to my earlier remarks on CEO Jeff Bezos' 2016 shareholder letter, he also wrote that "there are many advantages to a customer-centric approach, but here's the big one: customers are always beautifully, wonderfully dissatisfied, even when they report being happy and business is great. Even when they don't yet know it, customers want something better, and your desire to delight customers will drive you to invent on their behalf. No customer ever asked Amazon to create the Prime membership program, but it sure turns out they wanted it, and I could give you many such examples."[22]

Starbucks: They considered their customers' desire to have a "third place" to gather outside the home and office. While their customers loved coffee, the coffee shop chain's management considered how they could introduce coffee to a group of people who desired to have a place to meet as well as work.[23] Although Starbucks is about coffee, the Starbucks model includes what the customer desired, which had little to do with coffee.

Walt Disney World: They considered their customers' desire to have fun experiences as a family. This attitude started with Walt Disney's own desire and belief that other people would benefit from a place to experience fun together.[24]

Lee Cockerell, the former executive vice president of operations at Walt Disney World, writes about the value of the customer in his outstanding book, *The Customer Rules, The 39 Essential Rules for Delivering Sensational Service*. Rule number 14 is "Treat Customers the Way You'd Treat Your Loved Ones." He writes, "In a way, your customers are like your family; without their loyalty and trust, the road ahead for your business would be rocky indeed. That's why you should treat customers the way you would want your mother and father, spouse and children, and other loved ones to be treated…By the same token, if you're a manager and you want your employees or direct reports to treat your customers the way they would their loved ones, you need to make sure you treat them the way you would your customers. Think of this as the Golden Rule of customer service: Do unto your employees as you would have them do unto your customers. Customers don't want just a good product; they also want to feel valued, they want to be respected as individuals, and they want authentic human connection. Well, that's what your employees want, too. And if you give it to them, they'll pass it along to those they serve."[25]

Chick-fil-A: They consider their customers' desire to be treated with respect in a fast-food environment. That is the motivation for customers being greeted: "How can I assist you?" and thanked with: "It's my pleasure."[26]

Chick-fil-A sells great chicken, but they do it with kindness and friendliness. They sell chicken with the customer in mind and not just the chicken. That is a recipe for success. Chick-fil-A would not be the company that they are today if they had not stressed the value of being friendly and nice to their customers.

Airbnb: CEO Brian Chesky and fellow cofounders Joe Gebbia and Nathan Blecharczyk helped disrupt the $500 billion hotel industry, with Airbnb's valuation challenging such giants as Hilton and Marriott. In March of 2019, a technology news website, Recode, reported that US consumers spent more money on Airbnb in 2018 than they did on Hilton and its subsidiary brands like DoubleTree and Embassy Suites. That's according to data from Second Measure, a company that analyzes billions of debit and credit card purchases.[27] In her engaging book, *The Airbnb Story, Fortune* senior editor-at-large Leigh Gallagher wrote of how the three partners launched their business after considering customers' desire to find cheap, comfortable rooms to stay at while on travel instead of in impersonal hotels: "They thought, why not create a bed-and-breakfast for the conference out of the empty space in their apartment?"[28]

> **Experience Question:** How do you show your customers that you have thought of them?

This list is a small sample of the breakthroughs that have occurred because a business followed the Golden Rule of treating others like they would like to be treated. Your next breakthrough is at your fingertips when you put the other person first in your business' decision-making and product development processes. New innovation already exists for your business in the minds of your customers. Your business can determine what to do next if you listen to your customers and treat them as you would want to be treated. You don't need an innovation team or some new AI technology; you just need to have your team members listen to your customer by asking them what they would like you to offer that you are currently not offering.

> **Win Activity: What Your Customers Really Want:** Think about the desire of your customers. Then answer: what do your customers really want from your business?
>
> 1.
>
> 2.
>
> 3.
>
> 4.

Consider the Customer's Point of View

Well Done leaders and companies that wish to develop repeat purchases and increase customer retention rates should examine the customer experience by asking critical questions from the customer's point of view (CPOV).[29] The customer point of view assessment is a great practice to implement in the business to ensure that you are embracing the Golden Rule.

A quick assessment of helpfulness to the customer will help your company identify gaps in your service. It can also help you identify where to place resources or training to see a better return on your customer interactions. Review the four statements below to determine how helpful your company is in the marketplace.

Give your company a rating on a scale of Poor (0-10), Moderate (11-15), Very Good (16-20), or Outstanding (21-25) for each of the following statements. Then add your four scores together to get an overall rating.

1. The customer enjoys buying products and services from my company.

Your customer experience is a fundamental element to the success of your company. If your customers have a problematic buying experience or are forced to go through hurdles or difficulties in obtaining your service or product, you will lose customers. Smart businesses focus on ensuring an enjoyable buying process to enhance repeat business and referrals.[30] Businesses practice the Golden Rule when they consider what changes they could make to enhance the buying experience and make it easier for the customer to purchase their product.

2. The customer would report that they were treated with kindness and happiness.

An old Chinese proverb applies here: "A man without a smiling face must not open a shop." Friendly companies focus their attention on teaching employees how to be happy and kind to coworkers and customers. Companies that reward employees for being nice will see the result in how employees treat customers in a friendly way. Companies that focus on customer service do not neglect to teach employees the value of friendliness.[31] A focus on friendliness can include metrics in performance reviews and employee training. Some companies even reward employees for their level of kindness to customers. Customers should always be greeted when they enter into your business and should be treated with respect, even when problems occur.

3. The Customer Feels Appreciated for Their Purchases.

One essential component of friendliness is appreciation. People do not stay friends with someone for very long if they don't feel appreciated. The same goes for businesses. Your customers want to be valued. There are ten statements and expressions that are essential for every team member to learn and embrace. Phrases such as "thank you" and "we appreciate you" can go a long way in enhancing customer service and customer experiences. Do you teach team members to practice these statements and questions in your business?

> **Phrases such as "thank you" and "we appreciate you" can go a long way in enhancing customer service and customer experiences.**

- Please come again.
- Have a nice day.
- Did you find everything okay?
- Do you have any questions?
- We are glad that you came in today.
- Is there anything else I can help you with?
- Can we get your email or phone number so we can stay in touch?
- We love our customers.

Experience Question: What is the most important phrase for your team to remember and repeat?

Too many companies are becoming apathetic about customer interactions. It is still good business to make the customer feel appreciated for their business. One of the best ways to do that is through the right questions or statements.

4. Customer would state that you solve their Problems and Listen to Their Concerns.

Listening is an under-appreciated art in the world of business.[32] Effective companies teach their employees how to hear complaints and solve problems.

In today's economy, listening can be more important than actually solving the problem. The reality is that customers have very few places where they can go to have someone listen to their concerns, thoughts, and complaints. Famed business titan John D. Rockefeller once said, "A friendship founded on business is better than a business founded on friendship."[33] His statement points to the truth that businesses who focus on friendship as a business model will have a better chance of success and long-term customer retention.

Noted digital marketing and social media entrepreneur Gary Vaynerchuk writes about the power of connecting with the customer in his book, *The Thank You Economy*. He encourages businesses and business owners with these words: "What if you were able to build a relationship, make a connection, tilt the person's emotions toward you, and capture 30, 60, or even 100 percent of what he or she spends? Your small customer would become a lot bigger. That's why you have to take every customer seriously. This is a basic business principle that has been talked about and written about a great deal, and some companies take it seriously. . . . Valuing every single customer is mandatory in the Thank You Economy."[34]

Experience Question: How can you thank your customers for their business?

Rate your company a rating on the scale of Poor (0-10), Moderate (11-15), Very Good (16- 20), or Outstanding (21-25) for each of the following statements. Then add your four scores together to get an overall rating.

1. The customer enjoys buying products and services from my company. Rating _____
2. The customer would report that they were treated with kindness and happiness. Rating _____
3. The customer feels appreciated for their purchases. Rating _____
4. Customer would state that you solve their problems and listen to their concerns. Rating _____

Overall rating: _____

> **Experience Question:** In which area of the CPOV (Customer Point of View) Assessment were you strongest? The weakest? What can you do to improve your score?

Make Friends With Your Customers

One fundamental error that can sabotage a business is to sacrifice friendliness for efficiency.[35] Successful companies learn how to be efficient and friendly. These companies understand the importance of process improvement by employing new technologies, but they do not sacrifice the personal touch of the power of human relationships. One trend that is doomed to fail in business is using AI to replace all human interaction. People still come first. Customers want to connect to another person. AI can be helpful in enhancing business processes, but it should never replace all human interaction.

CEO Experience mentor Doug Hillmuth—the owner of Hillmuth Auto Care in the Washington, DC area—has a key question that he asks his staff. Though simple, it provides the roadmap for everything in their business: "Have you made any friends today?" Through this question, he communicates to his team that friendship with the customer means more than just achieving a sale. He understands customers are friends of the business, and thus the business should focus on treating them that way. Doug has used this concept to build his business into a successful enterprise that has endured for forty successful years.

I no longer call you servants because a servant does not know his master's business. Instead, I have called you friends, for everything that I learned from my Father I have made known to you.

Jesus taught the biblical business principle when He communicated to His disciples the idea of friendship as a way to consider others. He tells His disciples in John 15:15, "I no longer call you servants because a servant does not know his master's business. Instead, I have called you friends, for everything that I learned from my Father I have made known to you." Jesus did not want his disciples to look at him only as their teacher or leader; He wanted them to call Him a friend.

Friendliness can become a differentiator in the business world. While it cost nothing to install or instill, friendliness and kindness are crucial factors in the customer experience. When customers feel cared for and listened to, they will be more likely to consider a personal relationship with the product or organization.

Earlier, I mentioned J.C. Penney's *Fifty Years with the Golden Rule*, which related the story of the origins and development of the Penney's department store chain and how the Golden Rule shaped each step of the process of the founder's life and business. An especially memorable statement from the book comes when Penney writes, "When people ask me, 'What one factor do you believe has contributed most to the growth and influence of your organization?' I don't have to stop and think about an answer. Unquestionably it has been the emphasis laid from the very beginning upon human relationships—toward the public on the one hand, through careful service, and giving the utmost in values; toward our associates on the other hand."[36]

Those who think the Golden Rule is no longer relevant have forgotten its timeless application. In Brenton Hayden's article in Entrepreneur, he discusses how applying the Golden Rule in business makes a lot of sense from a practical standpoint. He wrote that treating customers right means that they will be happier, more likely to come back, and more inclined to recommend you to friends and family. Likewise, treating your workers fairly means that they will be motivated to provide excellent service. That leads to satisfied and committed customers, which leads to excellence, which leads to increased profits.

"And the numbers don't lie," Hayden said. "In most industries, companies that are the loyalty leaders have a compound annual growth rate that is more than twice that of their competitors. . . . When it comes to the Golden Rule, this simple yet timeless guideline holds more value than first meets the eye. In a world where the question of ethics and moral dilemmas often arise, having a standard that you can refer to in your decision-making process can be invaluable."[37]

One more second step comment:

In one of the most intriguing stories that Jesus told, He highlighted the importance of consistent behavior in how one person treats another. In Matthew 18:23-35, Jesus tells a story about a man who owes the king a debt that he cannot pay. The king forgives the man, and the man then goes out and punishes another servant who owes him money. The story is specifically about forgiveness, but ultimately it is about the Golden Rule. Matthew 18:35 states, "This is how my heavenly Father will treat each of you unless you forgive your brother or sister from your heart." The story is about treating others like you want to be treated so that the measure of your life will be judged on how you judged others. The point is that it is wise to treat others the way you want to be treated. The Golden Rule still works if you work it. The Golden Rule still works if you apply it in life and business.

Whether it's J.C. Penney or Lee Iaccoca from long ago, or contemporaries like Jeff Bezos or Brenton Hayden, it pays to listen to the voices of others, and specifically the voices of your customers. No great business was ever built unless the business listened and treated their customers with a high level of respect, care, and intimacy. Treat others the way you want to be treated, and you will be practicing a Biblical business principle that will guide you and your business to hearing the words Well Done. Well Done leaders work the Golden Rule, because they know the Golden Rule works when they work it.

Best Ideas: Write down two or three best ideas that you heard or learned from this chapter.

WELL
DONE

Chapter 3

FOCUS ON PROFIT
WITH A PURPOSE

Profit is good, but profit used for good is better.

"What good will it be for someone to gain the whole world, yet forfeit their soul? Or what can anyone give in exchange for their soul?"
Matthew 16:26

D on't just build a bigger barn! Blake Mycoskie, the founder of TOMS shoes, states, "If you are doing good, customers have a greater reason to care about your work."[38] TOMS Shoes has a story that is quite familiar to millions of people nearly fifteen years after its founding, especially since founder Blake Mycoskie chronicled his story in the book, *Start Something That Matters*. It's a story that hasn't grown old, as shown in a 2019 interview with the cutting-edge pastor, Levi Lusko, whose multisite church has a dozen campuses spread across three states. In their chat, Mycoskie shared how his faith and entrepreneurial vision helped propel TOMS to international prominence.[39]

Mycoskie is a sterling example of a CEO who set a bigger "why?" than profits as his primary motivation. As a result, over the years—with the help of numerous partners—TOMS Shoes has given away tens of millions of shoes, helped restore eyesight for more than a quarter of a million people, improved access to clean drinking water, provided better birthing conditions for more than 175,000 mothers, and supported anti-bullying initiatives such as training school staff and crisis counselors to help prevent and respond to instances of bullying. In 2015, it launched the TOMS Entrepreneur Fund to help for-profit startups address societal issues.

In his book, Mycoskie communicates how it was the bigger vision that helped TOMS not only to be successful, but that also helped him find significance. "Conscious capitalism is about more than simply making money—although it's about that too," he writes. "It's about creating a successful business that also connects supporters to something that matters to them, and that has a great impact in the world. As consumers, customers will want your product for the typical reasons—because it works better, because it's fashionable, because the price is competitive, because it offers an innovation—but as supporters they also believe in what you're doing; they've bought into your story because it taps into something real, and they want to be a part of it."[40]

An Underlying Bigger 'Why'

Every successful business creates a profit; healthy businesses are designed for that purpose. Not only can their profits be a gauge for determining the health of a company, but a lack of profits can also alert business leaders of the need to inspect the processes, to refine the products, and to engage with the customers. In his legendary book, *Beyond the Crisis*, leading statistician and business consultant Edward Deming says that "Profit in business comes from repeat customers, customers that boast about your product and service, and that bring friends with them."[41]

> **Experience Question:** How do you feel about profit? Do you believe that profit can be a useful resource if used in an impactful way for kingdom purposes?

The Well Done stewards in the "Parable of the Talents" (Matthew 25:14-30) all produced profitability. Yet, while enabling sustainability and growth for Christian business owners, profits alone can be terribly unsatisfying. Steward leaders understand that an excessive focus on the bottom line can be damaging. This is why Well Done leaders

Purposeful profits can be the funnel through which God brings resources into the hands of the business, so they can, in turn, be used for kingdom purposes.

seek to build businesses with an underlying purpose that is bigger than just profits alone. Without a purpose, earning money leaves one feeling powerless. As Jesus asks His followers in Matthew 16:26: "What good will it be for someone to gain the whole world, yet forfeit their soul?"

> **Experience Question:** What do you think it would look like for a person to be profitable and yet lose their soul?

When a company focuses on profits with a purpose, it sets itself ahead of its competition. It also leaves a legacy because of the way the leaders have used their wealth. Purposeful profits can be the funnel through which God brings resources into the hands of the business, so they can, in turn, be used for kingdom purposes.

Biblical Business Principle #3: Grow Profit with A Purpose

"What good will it be for someone to gain the whole world, yet forfeit their soul? Or what can anyone give in exchange for their soul?"
Matthew 16:26

Know your priorities. Lead your business with purpose and vision. Profit is powerful. Profit used well can lead to both success and significance. Find Creative Ways to Build Margin. Be Generous.

Profits are the lifeblood of successful companies, allowing them to make bolder decisions, respond to needs, make wise investments for properly-timed growth, and generously help causes or organizations that are involved in the work of God's kingdom. You know that you have a purposeful profit when you see the following in your leadership and your organization:

> **Experience Question:** In what ways can you apply the biblical business principle of having a bigger "why" to your business?

5 Boundaries You Need to Establish With Your Business

In Mark 8, Jesus gives a definitive statement about priorities and perspective by reminding His followers that what seems right in the moment can actually be damaging for eternity. Jesus is making the point with this statement that it is easy for anyone to become self-sufficient and think they don't need a Savior. If this statement is true for every Christian, it is much more so for faith-driven leaders who aspire to hear, Well Done when they step into eternity. Many Christian leaders have sold their souls to their businesses for a variety of reasons. Those leaders work their entire lives to build something for themselves and their families, only to lose everything in eternal matters.

The Message translation of the Bible records Mark 8:37 this way: "What good would it do to get everything you want and lose you, the real you? What could you ever trade your soul for?" The phrasing of this verse is quite interesting.

Every Well Done leader has an ultimate purpose that they are striving to complete. And, while they use their business profoundly to meet this goal, they never allow the business to become their sole purpose. CEO Experience mentor Harry Plack, CEO of the Plack Group, often states, "a business will ask a leader to give it everything you have and then still demand more."

A business will ask a leader to give it everything you have and then still demand more.

The Well Done leader does not lose himself or herself to the point that the leader and the business are the same. To not allow the business to become the ultimate ruling force in their life, the Well Done leader knows when and how to set healthy boundaries so they do not forfeit their soul. These five essentials include:

1. **You need to set a boundary on your business when God is calling you to something greater.**

Well Done entrepreneurs who lead businesses have God's calling on their life. They have been specially selected to lead and grow businesses in the marketplace that can provide a service for customers, employment for team members, and impact for the kingdom of God. However, the calling of business might be only one calling on their life. Just as some business owners lead multiple companies, God might be calling these leaders to multiple tasks. When a second call on your life becomes brighter and more encouraging, it is a sign you need to establish a boundary around your first call. This might come in the form of time given to the business and perhaps the vision of growth for the future. It could be that God is calling the business to remain stable as a platform so that something new in your life can become a startup.

2. **You need to set a boundary on your business before your Greed becomes too great.**

Greed is real—and dangerous. For any business leader to ignore the possibility of greed is to start down a dangerous path. This warning to Jesus's disciples appears in Luke 12:15: "Then he said to them, 'Watch out! Be on your guard against all kinds of greed; life does not consist in an abundance of possessions.'" I will write more about this verse in the biblical business principle about working on things today that impact today and tomorrow. However, this statement by Jesus can stand alone. Since large sums of money often change hands in a business, it is easy for business owners to focus too much attention on profits and wealth. Before greed becomes the primary reason for the company or for the work of the business owner, it's time to set boundaries. Alan Barnhart of Barnhart Crane and Rigging (who with his brother legally deeded the company to God) did that for himself through creating a financial finish line. They decided how much money they would need and decided to give the rest to Christian organizations.

3. **You need to set a boundary on your business when your Goals are becoming too blurry.**

Vision is critical for the success of any leader and any organization. When a leader forgets—or is not clear on where the business is going and why the company exists—it is time to establish boundaries so that the leader can recapture passion and excitement for the future. Business owners often struggle with burn-out. Burnout happens when leaders forget the purpose of their work. Passionate people never burn out. Passionate people

Clarity leads to energy. burn hot for an issue or a goal they are trying to accomplish. Each month at the CXP CEO Retreat, the chief experience officers guide CEOs to identify a focus wheel where each leader examines areas of their life to determine passion vs. burnout. When the score in an area is robust, it signifies a passionate person. When the score is an area is weak, that means that a person is close to burnout in that area. Leaders should never settle for blurriness. The leader must be clear about the future and where they are called to work. Clarity leads to energy.

4. **You need to set a boundary on your business when your Gatekeepers are becoming disheartened.**

Gatekeeper is a term that most business owners are familiar with. It relates to a person close to the leader who erects necessary obstacles for others to overcome in order to get close to the leader. In business, a Gatekeeper usually comes in the form of an administrative assistant. These Gatekeepers help the leader maintain focus by not becoming distracted by things or people who do not need to interact with the leader. A successful leader has effective Gatekeepers, who should be one of a CEO's most important and first hires.

The Gatekeepers I am referring to relate to those closest to the leader (spouse, children, or other family members). Before the people closest to the leader feel neglected or that they rank second to the business, the leader must establish a boundary. When the business is taking so much out of the leader that there is nothing left for the leader to give in other areas of their life, it is a signal the busi-ness has begun to negatively impact the leader's soul negatively.

God never gave a business to a faith-driven leader to hurt the leader. It should never become the leader's only priority. Family members need to know they are important—in fact, more important—than the business. I teach every CEO that they should treat their spouse like their number one customer. Spouses are often with a business owner for 40 to 50 years; even the best of customers typically fall well short of that. This model comes from the Garden of Eden, where Adam was to become one with his wife, not with the work that God had given him to accomplish. Family is important and should be honored by every Well Done leader.

5. **You need to set a boundary on your business when your Gifts are being ignored.**

Every leader has gifts and talents, but not every business calls on the leader to use their gifts and talents in the best way. CEOs and business leaders have a variety of tasks to start and accomplish in order to successfully lead a business. Many leaders can become disillusioned with the business because they are doing those tasks they have to do, not necessarily the tasks they are gifted to do. When a leader finds himself or herself in a period of time where they are not using the full plethora of their gifts and abilities, it is time to set a boundary on the business and reorganize their tasks so that they fully utilize their giftedness. Gifts and talents are too valuable not to be used effectively. Companies are better, and leaders lead better when they lead according to their gifts, talents, and passions.

> **Many leaders can become disillusioned with the business because they are doing those tasks they have to do, not necessarily the tasks they are gifted to do.**

Establishing boundaries for a business can be difficult and extremely hard for the leader to implement. However, difficult things are often essential. No leaders like to pull back or feel that they are not making significant progress. CEOs and leaders are motivated to push forward. However, at times, the best thing that can be done for a business is to set healthy boundaries for growth to follow your vision, and to make sure that you are doing what is best for both you and the business to succeed. Make it your goal to grow your business without sacrificing your soul.

A better way forward is to grow both profits and purpose. The profit with purpose principle will help the leader be clear-minded and to ensure that he/she does not become distracted with things that may gain the world, but which may cause him/her to lose their soul. This principle calls every Well Done leader to engineer his/her business in a way that he/she never forget why the company was established in the first place. This model proves profitable for both the business and for those that work in and for the business. In fact, it is so profitable that it will help the faith-driven leader hear the words Well Done.

How You Can Grow Both Profits and Purpose: You Know Your Priorities

God has priorities. He knows the most important and essential ingredients for success in life. As the ultimate owner of your business, God is concerned about profitability. In His leadership, Jesus often directed His disciples to principles that were good and efficient. He didn't want them wasting their time on projects or actions that had no purpose. Godly things grow—sometimes exponentially. In the good soil the seeds produced a crop with 40, 60, and even 100% returns. God does not give people businesses as a punishment, but rather as a tool to gain profits with a purpose.

God does not give people businesses as a punishment, but rather as a tool to gain profits with a purpose.

Legendary automaker Henry Ford once made the statement that "business must be run at a profit, else it will die. However, when anyone tries to run a business solely for profit, then also the business must die, for it no longer has a reason for existence."[42] Despite this truism, some steward CEOs flee from profitability; they feel as if making money is evil. However, purposeful profits may be beneficial for making the right investments for future growth.

This goal begins when a leader understands the value of managing the business in a way that can help produce significant outcomes in their community and around the world. Christian companies that focus on profits not only operate their business needs adequately; they also use their business as a platform to accomplish a greater mission. Because the leaders of these companies are working with the end in mind, they know that their final end will come in eternity when they hear, "Well done, good and faithful servant!" (Matthew 25:21).

King David was a great leader who acquired wealth from the countries he defeated in battle, which also expanded his kingdom. God gave King David a vision for the possibilities because of the available resources under his care, including building a beautiful temple for God. Amid his wealth, David recognized that God was the one who owned everything, so he was moved to do something with what God had given him.

Businesses and business owners have the opportunity to keep their leading priorities in front of them every day. Well Done CEOs believe that they have been given the business for a much bigger purpose than themselves. This kind of perspective is

No matter how small you start something, start something that matters.

a priority that matters. Echoing the title of Blake Mycoskie's book, author and business coach Brendon Burchard once wrote that "no matter how small you start something, start something that matters."[43]

Lead Your Business with Purpose and Vision

Profit with a purpose can happen at any time. It would be better if every business launched with a B.A.S.H. - "Big Awesome Spiritual Hunger" to do something for God and His kingdom. For existing businesses, a key place to start is to focus on moving the needle to better profitability, which can also help uncover an eternal purpose.

Well Done leaders focus on utilizing their resources to produce the best results for their company or organization. While not concerned with promoting themselves, they are concerned about propelling the company's performance and aligning that performance with the organization's broader vision and purpose. Steward leaders build organizations that produce healthy margins to enable their companies to perform influential acts of service for their internal team and in the communities where they are located.

Mission is what motivates me. It energized me to start CEO Experience, the business in which I hold the title of Chief Servant Officer. I believe that I have been called to work with CEOs and business owners so they will one day hear the rewarding words, Well done, when they stand before God in heaven. Through the years, God has enhanced my mission and my purpose. For many years, my mission in life was to hear, Well Done when I finished my life. Then, God revealed to me that I could build an organization that could help thousands—even millions—of steward CEOs to hear those same words.

That mission is critical to everything we do at CEO Experience. Our seven core pathways are models the Chief Experience Officers (the network of Christian consultants that have been licensed through CEO Experience) can use to help CEOs achieve this satisfying result. We do that by offering a variety of retreats where leaders can hear the voice of God. One pathway might be by the CEO meditating alone as they go through the CXP Executive Retreat Guide that my company produces each month. The *CXP Executive Retreat Guide* is a unique resource prepared monthly to help leaders embrace and practice the 12 Biblical Business Principles that lead to them hearing the words Well Done. The guide is one part business magazine, one part executive journal, and one part executive coach. Other pathways include one-on-one strategy sessions or monthly CEO Peer or Team Retreats where we bring together a dozen or so Christian CEOs to learn about a biblical business principle and then to share best ideas with one another so that they return to their businesses with increased vigor to inspire those they lead.

The big awesome spiritual hunger to help every Christian CEO led CEO Experience to put the Christian CEO ahead of a particular product or service. By understanding what a CEO needs and how the CEO learns best, I was able to follow the model of how Jesus learned and taught and make it the service model for the CEOs we serve. Most organizations try to shoehorn a CEO into their plan by getting the Christian CEO to buy into the product or service that the organization is offering. Instead, I wanted to start with how CEOs learn and develop a process to help them wherever they sit on the learning continuum. I followed the model that Jesus himself used as he taught his disciples. Jesus spent time alone in prayer as an example. Jesus spent time individually with disciples to discuss critical issues that the disciple was struggling with or to impart essential teaching that the disciple would need. Jesus engaged with his peers to discuss key issues of the day. Jesus also spent time with the entire team as he taught them the deep meaning of parables and gave them insight into the Kingdom of God. Finally, he took them places to add extra meaning and significance to the truth he was trying to impart. At CEO Experience, we use this model to work with CEOs in seven important ways.

1. **Private Retreats:** Every leader needs time alone to review and reflect those "aha" moments of growth and development that require an application to execute. Leaders who purchase the *CXP Executive Retreat Guide* and use it by themselves experience a personal retreat. These CEOs are still a part of the CEO Experience Team, and they have access to other members and resources, but they desire to do much of their strategic learning and planning by themselves.

2. **Partner Retreats:** This retreat option is for those leaders who use the *CXP Executive Retreat Guide* with an executive coach or, as we call them, Chief Experience Officers. Chief Experience Officers see themselves as partners with CEOs in their businesses, just like regular business partnerships, but without costing a CEO half of the profits. In this model, the Chief Experience Officer guides the CEO down a pathway to enhance growth and practice accountability to deliver real results.

3. **Peer Retreats:** CEO Experience has created the most engaging mastermind model for those CEOs who wish to use the *CXP Executive Retreat Guide* with their peers in a monthly, day-long retreat. These day-long retreats are with a group of up to 15 CEOs to hear best ideas, share case stories, celebrate win walls, and strategically plan together in a memorable experience and through lasting accountable relationships with other CEOS.

4. **Personnel Retreats:** Many leaders like to learn with their team. In fact, Jesus spent more time with His team than anywhere else. Leaders who use the *CXP Executive Retreat* Guide on-site with their next level leaders practice the biblical business principle of improving their team to improve their organization. In this model, a Chief Experience Officer will lead a retreat on-site for an organization to help the team to learn together. Even though not everyone on the team is a Christian, they can understand and embrace the Biblical Business Principles that have been outlined in this book and enhance personal and organizational performance.

5. **Planning Retreats:** Clarity for the leader is one of the leader's most valuable assets. This retreat model is for those leaders who use the *CXP Executive Retreat Guide* in addition to the "CXP Masterplans" to drive better clarity for themselves and their organization. CEO Experience has specifically designed five "masterplans" focused on five critical areas for life and business success (Biblical Business Principles, Vision, Operations, Strategy, and Kingdom Impact).

6. **Performance Retreats:** CEOs often know what they need to do, but need help doing it. This retreat model is designed around the CXP Tools

Package, where a leader is held accountable for executing the vision that they have discerned as a steward of the business. The performance retreat model is designed to work more closely with the CEO in weekly or biweekly touchpoints to ensure enhanced performance. The check-ins ensure that CEOs focus on completing the plan that they have created through the use of the CEO Tools.

7. **Perspective Retreats:** CEO Experience is pleased to offer the only business spiritual retreat to CEOs and business owners at no charge. Each perspective or spiritual retreat is a time of prayer and encouragement through the focus on a biblical business concept. These retreats are only an hour in length, but they provide great encouragement, support, and wisdom for people seeking to hear the voice of the true owner of their business - God.

All of CXP CEO Retreats can be offered via a virtual setting, an in-person setting, and/or an excursion setting to enhance the experience.

This mission of helping CEOS hear the words Well Done motivates me and my team. I believe that the words Well Done are the two most powerful words in the English language. CEO Experience is motivated to make a difference, so every faith-driven leader can hear the words Well Done. This purpose is why we give a free CXP CEO executive retreat guide to any leader, and we give a one free CXP CEO Retreat Experience to every CEO who would like to attend a peer retreat that we have running in cities all across America. If you would like to download a guide that will help you grow a business with a kingdom impact, go to www.ceoexperience.com and download your free CXP CEO digital retreat guide.

> **I believe that the words Well Done are the two most powerful words in the English language.**

Every good mission and purpose motivates, which is why every company should strive to make a profit with a purpose.[44]

Understand Profits Are Powerful

Profits are powerful because they allow the company options to use resources in a variety of ways. Without them, the only choice is to use resources in order to keep the business on life support. One technique I encourage companies to use is to set a financial finish line—an idea that came from Alan Barnhart of Barnhart Crane and Rigging in Memphis, Tennessee.

When Alan took over his parents' business, he wanted to ensure that it had a more significant purpose than just making more money. So he set a financial finish line, with anything above that going to missions.[45] He dreamed that throughout the life of the business, it would be able to give away a million dollars to missionaries and related causes. When Alan took that bold stand, God responded in a dramatic way. The company took off like a rocket, moving from a condition of indebtedness to one of profitability. For the next two decades, they saw the annual profits of business increase by 20 percent.

> **Win Activity: Dream Kingdom Dreams:** Make a list of things that you would do that would enhance the kingdom of God if money were of no limit.
>
> 1.
>
> 2.
>
> 3.
>
> 4.

Then Alan and his brother, Eric, took it a step further, a la Stanley Tam. In 2007, they gave the entire company to the National Christian Foundation, in order to keep the allure of wealth from taking over their lives. Although at one time they gave away half of the profits, in a 2017 podcast interview, Alan explained that as far as the IRS was concerned, he and Eric still owned half and if something happened to one of them, the other would face massive estate taxes. So, he said, "We (needed) to try and find a way to make this God's company; let's see if we can find a way to give it away. And so, in 2007/2008 we gave away 99 percent of the company, and then, a few years later, we gave away the last 1 percent. Therefore, we are no longer the owners, although, in our minds, we never were. We were only the stewards of the business."[46] Today,

Barnhart Crane and Rigging gives away more than a million dollars a month to missions.

> **Experience Question:** What kingdom dream could a profit from your business help fulfill?

Profits are powerful, which is why God told His followers that it is not good for a man to gain the whole world and yet lose his soul. Profits will drive you to want more and, ultimately, distract you from what is eternally important for things that are more profitable in an earthly sense. That is why God regularly reminds us that while profits are good, net income used for His purposes are far better. The Well Done steward leader

The Well Done steward leader will make the switch from being driven by profit to driving profits to accomplish a higher purpose.

will make the switch from being driven by profit to driving profits to accomplish a higher purpose.

Understand Profits Can Lead to Significance

History books are filled with stories of men and women who have turned their success in business toward using their wealth to create a lasting legacy. These leaders pivoted at a point in their lives to make the move from acquiring wealth to distributing wealth. Many leaders made it a goal to give away all the wealth that they had accumulated before they died.

For example, there's Andrew Carnegie, who made his wealth in the steel industry. Carnegie was the impetus behind the establishment of a system that would eventually help fund nearly 1,700 public libraries across the nation. Before his death, Carnegie donated funds to build the infrastructure and the foundation of more than 250 libraries. The sixty million dollars he gave to libraries was only a portion of the $350 million he gave away after selling Carnegie Steel to J.P. Morgan in 1901 for almost half a billion dollars.[47]

Fast forward a century and Berkshire Hathaway CEO Warren Buffett and Microsoft billionaires Bill and Melinda Gates have created the Giving Pledge, inviting the world's wealthiest people to pledge more than half their wealth to charitable causes during their lives or in their wills. By the spring of 2019, more than 190 of the world's wealthiest individuals, couples, and families had taken the pledge.[48]

Although the success of men like Andrew Carnegie and Warren Buffet is impressive and the work that they contributed to through their profits have been helpful, it is important to consider if it was eternally significant. When we look at history, we can see a shining example in R.G. LeTourneau, a successful steward leader during World War II. LeTourneau developed two-hundred-ninety-nine patents as he developed earth-moving machines, and his creativity and engineering mind was a major component in helping the United States win the war. However, those contributions were not enough for him. As his business grew, so did his vision and mission. He made a major decision to give away 90 percent of the wealth of his business.

Bill Peel, the founding executive director of The Center for Faith & Work at LeTourneau University—the school LeTourneau started that now has some 3,000 students—wrote about how he came to that conclusion: "The decision to give away 90 percent of his personal income and stock in the company was the result of a previous decision—made when he was 30 and deeply in debt—to make God his business partner. Chastised by his missionary sister to get serious about serving God, LeTourneau was confused. Like most people, he believed that sincere dedication to God required that he become a preacher, an evangelist, or a missionary. He attended a revival meeting at church and gave in. Thinking he was headed to the mission field, he sought guidance from his pastor. After praying together, his pastor said, 'You know Brother LeTourneau, God needs businessmen as well as preachers and missionaries.' LeTourneau responded, 'All right, if that's what God wants me to be, I'll try to be His businessman.'"[49]

When financial success came years later, he believed this made him a debtor to God as well as his fellowman. His commitment to give away so much of his wealth was not so much a flash of generosity as much as a logical progression from his earlier decision to make God his business partner.

Experience Question: What changes do you need to make to become a profitable company?

Since he gave his business to God, it stood to reason that the profit belonged to God as well. He used to say, "It's not how much of my money that I give you God, but how much of His money does He want me to keep."

In an epilogue to R.G. LeTourneau's book, *Mover of Men and Mountains*, there is an evaluation of how LeTourneau viewed money and profit: "His attitude toward money is also unique. He does not view money as something to be accumulated for the satisfaction of looking at it, counting it each day to check its increase, nor as a measure of man's worth. He sees it only as a means to produce the machine that his mind has conceived or as a means to bring men to God."[50]

This grander view of profit will push the steward leader to not only strive for success but also for significance, and both are essential to hearing the words Well Done!

Find Creative Ways to Build Margin

Healthy companies find creative ways to build margin, which they can do through rising prices, lowering material or vendor costs, and reducing errors. Taking such steps means the bottom line increases. All of these are essential to be an excellent steward leader who creates profits with a purpose.

Work at it with all your heart, as working for the Lord.

A focus on excellence is always beneficial for a business. In Colossians 3:23, the Bible encourages workers, whatever they are doing, to "work at it with all your heart, as working for the Lord." Well Done leaders focus on business excellence by creating margin and profitability. Further, The Well Done leader will make the switch from being driven by profits to driving profits in order to accomplish a higher purpose.

A company of excellence has a keen focus on doing things right the first time. Good stewardship demands putting time, energy, resources, and effort to proper use through good decision-making, effective execution, and focused concentration so that projects and decisions do not have to be redone or undone. Excellence is essential for creating margin and higher levels of profitability. This kind of effort includes the following qualities:

Be Generous

Well Done leaders are generous. They strive to grow profits, not just for selfish purposes, but so they can also give to others. God calls for generosity in 2 Corinthians 9:6-7. "Remember this: Whoever sows sparingly will also reap sparingly, and whoever sows generously will also reap generously. Each of you should give what you

Generosity is a good business model.

have decided in your heart to give, not reluctantly or under compulsion, for God loves a cheerful giver."

Generosity should be considered more extensively than just the ability to give money. Steward leaders focus on all areas of generosity as they seek to build and grow their business. It is a wise method of leading.[51] And, while giving is one part of a growing company, it is not the only part. For companies and leaders to only give money would be to miss the core truth of profit with a purpose, which drives leaders to explore the value of generosity and embed these ideas throughout all aspects of the organization.

Generosity is a good business model. The *Journal of Organizational Behavior* released a research study that reported that a culture born through generosity improved companies' bottom lines.[52] The study examined ninety-five car dealerships that were similar in products and size and found that the dealerships with a generous culture sold more cars and had a higher level of customer service satisfaction.

Experience Question: How can generosity be used as an asset for your business? Why do you think that God asks His followers to be generous people?

Speaker and life coach Sharon Lipinski, the author of *365 Ways to Live Generously: Simple Habits for a Life That's Good for You and for Others*, wrote about the findings of this study. Evaluating it, in comparison to her other works, Lapinski wrote: "A company's culture is it's competitive edge, but creating one that facilitates productivity, employee engagement, and profit can prove challenging. The best way to transform your corporate culture is from the inside out, and data shows that the quickest way to get there is by inspiring a spirit of generosity at three levels."[53]

One of the best ideas for showing generosity is by doing what CEO Experience mentor, Scott Brunk did a few years ago. Scott is a third-generation CEO to a food distribution company called FoodPRO. The company started as a produce company almost 100 years ago and it has now grown to become one of the top five fastest-growing food distribution companies in the United States. FoodPRO has the company mantra 'Faith, Family, FoodPRO' and it seeks to keep its values in that order. To embody family and FoodPRO, Scott decided to be generous with one of the key next level leaders in his organization. The particular employee, Paul Mong, who was an afternoon delivery truck driver, had just completed seven years of error-free deliveries. Paul had delivered over one million items without a mistake to the customers of FoodPRO. When Paul achieved the million mark, Scott knew that it was time to give honor to whom honor was due and one of the best ways to do that was to surprise Paul with a brand new SUV. Paul is now well on his way to going another seven years without a mistake as he himself has set the goal of two million items delivered error free. Scott and FoodPRO were generous with Paul, and Paul has responded to the generosity of the organization.

One more second step comment:

Well Done leaders can impact both their company and communities when they strive to make a profit with a purpose. The ability to have a bigger "why" behind the company's growth and purpose is a profound shift for any business, especially for those that want to make a difference for eternity. Profit is essential for business success, but profit with a purpose is essential for eternal significance. Well Done leaders embrace the idea of profitability while executing a strategic plan to grow profits with a purpose.

Best Ideas: Write down two or three best ideas that you heard or learned from this chapter.

WELL DONE

Chapter 4

KNOW YOUR 'YESES' AND YOUR 'NOS'

When the leader becomes clear,
everything in the organization becomes clear.

"And do not swear by your head, for you cannot make even one hair
white or black. All you need to say is simply 'Yes' or 'No';
anything beyond this comes from the evil one."
Matthew 5:36-37

B e more decisive! One of the nation's most influential small business experts, author Frank Sonnenberg, laments abut what he sees as the passing of the era when keeping your word held special significance. People took pride in keeping their word and being of good character, with personal integrity, he says in his book, *Follow Your Conscience*. Because so many people knew each other's family, no one wanted to do anything that cast a shadow on their family's name; it was a time when parents instilled integrity in their children at an early age and viewed it as instrumental in achieving success.

However, while the world may have changed, he says the importance of integrity has not. Your word is your bond, and while we may not know everyone in our own town, the world is still smaller than we think, he adds. As an illustration, Sonnenberg suggests creating some bad news and seeing how quickly you learn this truism. Every time you give someone your word, he says, you are putting our honor on the line.

"You're implying that others can place their trust in you because you value integrity and would never let them down," Sonnenberg writes. "It goes without saying that if you don't live up to your word, you may end up tarnishing your credibility, damaging your relationships, and defaming your reputation. Most importantly, you'll be letting yourself down. You must answer to your conscience every minute of every day. . .When you operate with complete integrity, what you say will be taken at face value, your intentions will be assumed honorable, and your handshake will be as good as a contract. Most importantly, you can take great pride in the standards that you've set for yourself and sleep well at night knowing that your conscience is clear."[54]

Practice Clarity

The ability to say "yes" or "no" and then stand behind those words is a crucial aspect of success. Chick-fil-A founder Truett Cathy, whom I mentioned in chapter 1, discussed this fundamental principle when he wrote about his belief that the most common reason companies fail is a desire to grow faster than they can manage. This phenomenon can be particularly true with companies that make an initial public offering and find themselves staring at a pile of money. That gives them an overwhelming desire to grow, but growth must be digested as you go, Cathy said in *Eat Mor' Chikin*. While companies may set goals, if all goes according to plan, everything works out well, Cathy wrote, but if they have extended them-

> **The ability to say "yes" or "no" and then stand behind those words is a crucial aspect of success.**

selves to the limits of their finances and their talent, even a slight economic down-turn can force them to lay off employees to salvage things: "You don't build a good reputation by discharging people, but rather by developing people."[55]

Cathy applied the "yes" and "no" principle not only to opening stores but also to grow at the right pace to keep them open. He recalled how, when he brought Jimmy Collins on board as the chief operating officer, the founder told Collins that he wanted the COO not just to help open restaurants, but also to ensure that they stayed open. "I placed the greatest emphasis on 'stay open,'" Cathy wrote. "That sank in with Jimmy, and with everyone else who has come to work with us. I want everyone at Chick-fil-A to know that we don't build and open restaurants just so we can close them if they don't work out. We

Great decisiveness is one of the keys to influential leadership.

must be careful about how we build them, where we put them, and who we put in there to run them. Anybody can open a restaurant. All it takes is money. But keeping one open is what makes the difference."[56]

Great decisiveness is one of the keys to influential leadership. People cannot follow a person who does not know where they are going or why they headed in a particular direction. Jesus gave a secret to leaders when He taught: "And do not swear by your head, for you cannot make even one hair white or black. All you need to say is simply 'Yes' or 'No'; anything beyond this comes from the evil one" (Matthew 5:36-37).

> **Experience Question:** How can you mastering your "yeses" and your "nos" help your organization to succeed?

In these verses, Jesus spoke about the kind of clarity and decisiveness leaders need to engender in the belief of those who follow them. Otherwise, a leader can drift away and be subject to whatever direction the current might take them; then people will quit following the leader because they lose confidence in the direction in which the leader is going. More followers leave leaders because they lose confidence in the leader than for any other reason. Well Done leaders lead according to purpose, plotting their paths intentionally since they know that clearness in their courses will be reflected throughout their organizations.

Consultants Elena Botelho and Kim Powell studied the decision-making process of leaders, analyzing a database that included a sample of more than 2,600 leaders. Botelho and Powell combined that with thousands of hours of interviews and their two decades of experience advising CEOs and executive boards. Their groundbreaking research was featured in the Harvard Business Review and led to the book, *The CEO Next Door: The 4 Behaviors that Transform Ordinary People into World-Class Leaders.*

One essential habit they identified: was that the best leaders made fewer decisions than the other CEOs they studied. They wrote: "a powerful additional benefit of simple decision frameworks is that once they are embraced by the organization, CEOs can step back from the vast majority of the decisions that now can be made by their employees. And that is true of many of the best CEOs we see. Whatever their business, they are adept at triage. As problems and decisions cross their desk, they know which deserve real deliberation, which they should make a call and move forward on, and which should be passed to someone else to handle. They make fewer decisions."[57] In other words, the Well Done CEOs develop the habits and skills to say "no" effectively so they can say "yes" to the essential decisions only they can make. These CEOs know their "nos" because their "nos" make all the difference.

CEOs know their "nos" because their "nos" make all the difference.

Jesus taught his disciples the power of saying, "Yes" or "No." This power means leaders understand and know where they are going and what they are trying to accomplish. Well Done leaders show clarity by making their words mean something. They work hard to develop and build trusted relationships with their team by conveying to others that they can count on the leader's commitments.

Biblical Business Principle #4: Know Your 'Yeses' and Your 'Nos'
"And do not swear by your head, for you cannot make even one hair white or black. All you need to say is simply 'Yes' or 'No'; anything beyond this comes from the evil one." Matthew 5:36-37

Know your "Nos." Make great decisions based on core values. Find Your Yes. Live up to your word. Make your signature meaningful. Walk Away From Waits.

Know Your 'Yeses' and Your 'Nos'

Leaders gain their team's confidence when they are firm in their beliefs and boundaries. After all, saying, "No" is hard work. Leaders and business owners (especially entrepreneurs) are often wired with a "yes" gene. They believe they can do anything if they try hard enough. They say "yes" to themselves as they seek to build their business or accomplish some unseen task. While such a belief is essential, a 'no' boundary is also critical to balancing life in order to sustain the business. Learning to say, 'No' can be one of a leader's most beneficial habits, empowering that leader to maintain focus,

Learning to say, 'No' can be one of a leader's most beneficial habits, empowering that leader to maintain focus, enhance clarity, and establish healthy routines so they can lead for an extended period of time.

enhance clarity, and establish healthy routines so they can lead for an extended period of time.

Software executive Joel Trammell discussed the power of firm decision-making as a CEO in his book, *The CEO Tightrope*. He noted how no one could be an expert in all aspects of a business. However, the one thing a leader is responsible for is making a decision, Trammell says: "The buck stops at the CEO's desk. That is the job. If you don't like making decisions when you aren't sure of the correct answer, don't take a CEO job, because this might just be the biggest part of it. Many problems require a solution that impacts multiple departments, and only the CEO can make decisions across the organization."[58]

In my work with CEOs, and as a CEO myself, I have discovered the single most critical skill between successful and unsuccessful leaders is that the latter fails to grasp the art of saying, "no." Consider these essential steps to improving your ability to say "no" well.

1. Say "No" with grace

Every leader should be honored when others ask for our help since it demonstrates respect and confidence in the leader's ability. When a leader must say, "No," they should do so with grace, either by suggesting an alternative or thanking the person who asked while explaining why you are not able at this moment. Saying

"No" in the right way will keep the relationship intact and allow for later "yeses" when the "yes" can benefit both parties involved.

2. 2. Say "No," but know and explain the bigger "yes"

When a leader consistently repeats their top priorities, it creates accountability and conviction. Explaining the larger "yes" in your life will cement the need for you to complete your most important tasks. When the leader is clear, everything becomes clear. When the leader explains their passion for the project or vision that they are working on completing, then it helps other parties respect the leader's desire. The leader might also be able to turn their "no" into another person's "yes." The other person might hear about the vision of the leader and want to get involved with what the leader is doing.

In chapter 3, I mentioned R.G. LeTourneau, one of the first Well Done leaders who embraced biblical business principles for their business and found outstanding success. Told by his pastor that God needed people in business as well as preachers and missionaries, LeTourneau threw himself into the contracting industry. Before it was all over, he became a pioneer in timesaving techniques in construction. When he discovered his bigger "yes," it changed his life. Don't be afraid of your bigger yes, because in your yeses, you will find clarity and passion.

3. 3. Say "No" without regret

As a business leader, you have a tremendous task of building your business for success and significance. Your most important work is to honor God through your business and help it endure. Solomon spent seven years completing the temple. Moses spent forty years leading the people of Israel to the Promised Land.

Don't regret the "nos" that lead you to focus on completing the task that God has given you.

Nehemiah left his job as the king's aide to complete the difficult task of rebuilding the walls around Jerusalem. David spent years winning battles to establish his kingdom.

Other tasks are important, but what God has given you is essential for you to complete. Don't regret the "nos" that lead you to focus on completing the task that God has given you. Remember, Ephesians 2:10, which states that you are God's workmanship, created to do good works that God has prepared in advance for you to accomplish. Your success in life is about you completing the good works that you are called to do, not the good works that may appear to be rewarding or desirable, or that others ask you to do.

4.   **4. Say "No" to a "Yes"**

When you do say "Yes" to something new in your life or leadership, decide that you will say "No" to something in which you are already involved. This principle will ensure that you are not lengthening your list of obligations, but rather are replacing you're already "yeses" with a new "no."

Bill McDermott, CEO of the world's largest business software company, explains how to move from "no" to "yes" in his book, *Winners Dream: A Journey from Corner Store to Corner Office*. He wrote that people are most likely to change their minds when the world they once knew no longer exists: "A leader's challenge, then, is to explain why the old world went away, show people what the new world looks like, and get them excited to be part of it."[59] McDermott used this strategy to help usher in new initiatives, ideas, and innovations to help his company reach levels of profitability that seemed impossible just years before.

5.   **5. Say "No" By Evaluating Time and Capacity.**

One effective strategy that enables leaders to say, "No" is to schedule time for their "yes" list. When a calendar is full, the leader must stop saying, "Yes." Use your calendar and your time wisely. Your calendar should be a tool to help you say, "No." God established the number of hours during the day, and He does not expect you to do more work than you have time to complete.

The secret to success and the ability to accomplish a significant kingdom impact through your leadership might just come from your ability to master the "no." Tony Blair, the noted former prime minister of Great Britain, summarized it this way: "The art of leadership is saying no, not saying yes. It is very easy to say yes."[60]

> **Experience Question:** What are three ways you can become better at saying, "No" to others without offending them? Why is it essential for you to learn how to say "No" effectively?

Make Great Decisions Based on Core Values

Decision-making makes the difference. Great companies and leaders are built through a series of right decisions and choices that result in beneficial out-

The legacy of a leader is often determined by the choices and decisions that they make. comes and often determine the legacy of a leader. Studies have reported that up to 40 percent of new leaders fail in their new roles within the first 18 months because of the poor decisions and choices they made during this crucial launch time.[61] The legacy of a leader is often determined by the choices and decisions that they make.

Find Your Yes

Well Done CEOs and leaders need to embrace the importance of good decision-making. When leaders make better decisions, the company will get better. There are five critical "yes" decisions that every leader shows wisdom in making.

5 Critical "Yes" Decisions Every CEO Must Make

1. Say "Yes" to the Decision to Work Both "On" the Business and "In" the Business

Many CEOs fall into the rut of just working "in" the business and never make the leap to working "on" the business. Well Done CEOs understand the importance of getting off the crazy, day-to-day cycle to find a new direction, inspiration, or a specific strategy to move the business forward. This move can be seen through seemingly small decisions, such as hiring a personal coach, joining a mastermind, attending a conference, or going away for a personal retreat.

2. Say "Yes" to the Decision To Delegate and Trust Your Team

CEOs often try to do everything themselves; since many manage by control, they feel they have to control everything in the organization. However, this model can become a bottleneck to growth and success. Steel magnate Andrew Carnegie, one the most significant leaders of any generation, once wrote, "Teamwork is the ability to work together toward a common vision. The ability to direct individual accomplishments toward organizational objectives. It is the fuel that allows common people to attain uncommon results."[62] When a leader decides to trust their team, the possibilities of the organization become limitless.

Each month in the CXP *CEO Executive Retreat Guide*, there is a CEO Tool dedicated spot to what we call the "Three D's of a Steward Leadership." CEO

Experience asks leaders to consider their do, delegate, and decide actions for the month.

- "Do - What To." Leaders are to be people of action, called to do certain things regularly to move the company or organization forward.
- "Delegate - Who To." Each leader must consider tasks they should be delegating to others so they can focus on things only they can do. Delegation helps a leader to step back so that others in the organization can step forward.
- "Decide - Where To." The power of "yes" and "no" is that it gives the leader clarity on what will move the organization forward.

3. **Say "Yes" to the Decision to Develop a Habit for Personal Growth for Yourself and Your Team**

Many organizations stop growing because the leader stops growing. Lazy leaders focus their attention on improving their organization or their people, but never on improving themselves. They forget that they have blind spots and weaknesses that could be impacting the organization. Moreover, the people in an organization will rarely, if ever, lead at a higher level than the leader. In *The 21 Irrefutable Laws of Leadership*, John Maxwell calls this the "Law of the Lid." This best-selling author said: "Leadership ability is always the lid on personal and organizational effectiveness. If a person's leadership is strong, the organization's lid is high. But if it's not, then the organization is limited."[63]

Many organizations stop growing because the leader stops growing.

The Law of the Lid means that every CEO needs to decide to place a premium on personal growth by making it a personal habit. To make personal growth a habit translates into the development of a strategic plan and focusing on areas of their own improvement that will impact the company and their leadership performance. Well Done leaders continue to learn, grow, and develop throughout their lifetime.

4. **Say "Yes" to the Decision to Define Great Habits and Routines**

One habit every leader should develop is a great morning routine. The first moments of a day set the tone for the rest of the day. Every leader needs to decide on how to define a great morning routine. They need to know what they will say "yes" to first to so that they can say "no" to the other items that may stop them from accomplishing their purposes.

Leaders who aspire to be productive and effective start each morning by planning how to reach their maximum potential. Leaders who rush into the day without first considering where they are going and what they want to accomplish too often find themselves lost in the tyranny of the urgency. A good morning routine can consist of inspirational readings, reviewing strategic priorities, journaling, and vision casting.

Two authors have addressed the importance of such practices. In his book, *Becoming the Fulfilled Leader*, Todd Stocker—a pastor and popular speaker—says: "Your morning routine generates a 10X return for good or for bad. Make it good."[64]

Kevan Lee, an executive with a social media management platform, adds: "While there's probably not an ideal morning routine that fits everyone, we can learn a lot from the morning routines of successful people as well as from the research and inspiration behind starting a morning on the right foot."[65] One routine that is important for Well Done CEOs and leaders is a commitment to a morning devotional time with God. If God is the owner of the business, then it is a wise habit to set aside time to listen to His voice and discern His will for your life and your business.

5. Say "Yes" to the Decision to Discuss Your Vision Frequently and with Passion

Because life often becomes blurry, leaders tend to always look at what is new and different. When a leader is unclear, the organization becomes chaotic. With clarity from the leader, everything in the organization comes into focus. One way that a leader can bring clarity to the organization is through emphasizing vision. People will follow a leader who knows where they are going and why. Every CEO needs to decide to discuss their organization's vision frequently and with passion.

Leaders make thousands of decisions, but no decisions will be more important than these five decisions that every leader needs to make. The destiny of your company will be revealed in the decisions that you make. As the legendary management consultant and author Peter Drucker once wrote: "Whenever you see a successful business, someone once made a courageous decision."[66] It is also true that when you see a successful CEO, you see someone who has made the right critical decisions.

> **Win Activity: Find Your Yes!:** What do you need to be saying "Yes" to in order to make your business better? What do you need to say, "No" to in order to protect your business?
>
> 1. Yes -
>
> 2. Yes -
>
> 3. No -
>
> 4. No -

Say 'Yes' to What Makes You and Your Organization Better

When a person is emphatic about their "yeses," it can lead to enhanced passion and enthusiasm between the leader and their followers. Many leaders fall into bland grays instead of living in the bright and bold colors of leadership. They never discover those deep burning "yeses" in their life that steer them through difficult challenges of business and life.

Jesus is an excellent example of leading his followers to a "yes." In the story where Jesus meets Peter on the seashore, (John 21) he gets Peter to say "yes" to him three times. The last is the most essential because it forever changed Peter.

First, Peter said, "yes" to Jesus when Christ asked to borrow his boat. Exhausted because he had been out fishing all night long and disappointed because he had not caught any fish, everything in Peter was crying out: "no." When Jesus made a simple request so He could preach a sermon from Peter's boat, the disciple said, "yes."

Second, Peter said, "yes," when Jesus told him to cast down his nets. Though he questioned the request, Peter never said, "no." This story is a critical leadership moment to grasp—just because of a person questions or seeks more information about a decision; it does not mean they are saying, "no." Moreover, when Peter again said, "yes," he caught his biggest haul ever.

Third, Peter said, "Yes" when Jesus asked His disciples to follow Him. Peter left everything behind with this decision. Because his "yes" meant something, it changed his life.

Likewise, it is critical for the leader who wants to lead at the highest level to find their "yeses." Those things that so inspire the leader so much that they will not compromise or back down from accomplishing them.

Moses knew his "yes" when he led Israel to the Promised Land. Nehemiah knew his "yes" when he rebuilt the wall around Jerusalem. Esther knew her "yes" when she went before the king to save her people. Daniel knew his "yes" when he continued to pray despite the threat of punishment. Jesus knew his "yes" when He went to the cross. It is only when the leader discovers his or her "yes" will they be able to hear the words, Well Done.

Live Up to Your Word - Leave Behind Aspirational "Yeses"!

An essential component of knowing your "yeses" and your "nos" is to live up to your word. It is tempting as the leader, to make the mistake of committing to aspirational "yeses," which can sabotage the culture and ruin the confidence the team has in the leader. Aspirational "yeses" often come because a leader believes they can accomplish more than time permits; they have no margin in their schedule to complete a team's request. While aspiring to accomplish the request, they lack the time and ability.

Aspirational "yeses" are dangerous for the leader and the organization. It is far better to respond with a quick message of "yes" or "no" than to offer a half-hearted reply that sabotages the leader and the company. Doing so will cause a leader to lose credibility, dilute clarity, destroy confidence, and evaluate confusion. When a person does not follow through consistently, they lose credibility. Loss of credibility means a loss of leadership. Well Done leaders are credible leaders because they know what they can do, what they shouldn't be doing, and what they won't do.

Well Done leaders are credible leaders because they know what they can do, what they shouldn't be doing, and what they won't do.

One key damaging result of the aspirational "yes" is that leaders will destroy their own confidence. When a leader fills their days with aspirational "yeses," they begin to lose the confidence that they can accomplish things. Aspirational "yeses" will make the leader feel like a failure and point to their ineffectiveness.

Where people are present, confusion can quickly become present. When an organization adds personnel, it is more likely that many people will suggest many ways to accomplish tasks. The voice of the leader is important and essential to success. When a leader does not identify those things that are the most important for the organization to succeed, organizational confusion is the result. Many leaders and organizations are not bad people or corrupt organizations; they are just confused about the most important things.

One example of this is found in the Garden of Eden with Eve. Adam and Eve were the first business owners named in the Bible. They had a garden business and the specific tasks of naming the animals and caring for the plants. That changed when Eve became confused about her "yeses" and her "nos." When she became unclear, chaos reigned. As a result, confusion was elevated. She believed that she had the right to say "yes" to the fruit of the tree of knowledge, even though God had specifically told her "no" about eating the fruit from that tree. When a leader confuses their "yeses" and "nos" it causes confusion all throughout the organization.

> **When a leader confuses their "yeses" and "nos" it causes confusion all throughout the organization.**

Aspirational "yeses" can seem innocent enough, but they are deadly and will sabotage a leader's success. This concept of sabotage is one of the fundamental reasons that a leader should master the art of saying "yes" and "no."

Experience Question: What consequences are you observing in your organization because of too many aspirational "yeses?"

Make Your Signature Meaningful

One way a leader's word is important is through the use of their signature. While past business environments placed more emphasis on this than today, making your signature mean something is just as essential to success now. A leader's word and signature are two of the most important commodities leaders have at their disposal. Their signature on a piece of paper should have value behind it.

> **Experience Question:** As a leader, what changes would your team need to see to make your signature and your word mean something more than it is worth today?

An essential part of knowing your "yeses" and your "nos" is to fulfill your commitments, which includes your time commitments, such as meeting deadlines for projects or showing up on time for scheduled meetings. Leaders who are competent at maintaining their schedules grow in credibility in all aspects of their leadership.

Many leaders lead "fast," meaning that they work diligently to leave little space or time in their schedule between meetings or deadlines. The Well Done leader works diligently to count their hours so that they are using them effectively, not just adequately. They are also respectful of the time of others and the commitments that they make. The best leaders meet their deadlines, and they are aware of their scheduled appointments. They do their dead-level best to show up on time and to respect the time of others. These leaders are commitment keepers, and so their teams strive to keep their commitments to their leader.

Jesus was a leader that never led while out of breath.

Those who wish to lead their businesses according to biblical business principles can look to history's best leader: Jesus. He accomplished more in three years than most leaders accomplish in their lifetime. Jesus recruited and trained disciples, preached sermons, taught in the synagogues, healed people afflicted with a disease, performed miracles, and walked to many cities and villages. Yet, Jesus was a leader that never led while out of breath.

I find it fascinating that Jesus, who had such a short period of time to lead, accomplished so much. This fact becomes apparent when you read the Gospel accounts of Jesus and His ministry. Jesus never confused his "yeses" and his "nos."

The Son of God knew his "yeses" and his "nos" with great clarity. Every day in his ministry, He knew explicitly what He was supposed to be doing and why He was supposed to be doing it. Even though Jesus had a great deal to accomplish in a short period of time, He was clear about His activities and his priorities. Jesus was not teaching when He was supposed to be healing. He wasn't praying when he was supposed to be performing a miracle. He wasn't spending time with His disciples when He was supposed to be with the crowds. He was exactly where He was supposed to be, at the right time. He knew His commitments, and never wavered from them.

One prime example of the clarity of Jesus was the day that He raised his friend, Lazarus, from the grave. Everyone else thought He was late. After all, Lazarus had been dead for three days. In fact, when Jesus arrived at Lazarus' house, Mary and Martha, the sisters of Lazarus, reprimanded him for being late. They were upset that Jesus did not get there before their brother died. They expected Jesus to be there to heal Lazarus or at least to provide comfort to them. However, Jesus was not late at all; He was right on time. He showed up three days after His friend's death to accentuate the miracle of raising Lazarus from the dead while foreshadowing His own death and resurrection. Jesus had a purpose for His time and His actions. He stayed with His purpose even when those closest to Him did not understand His actions or His decisions.

Walk Away from Waits

Leaders like having plenty of options when deciding on paths to take in business. Although options are beneficial when considering choices to make, slowing down the process of decision making can sabotage business success. Why? It creates confusion. It is far better for a leader to reach a "yes" or "no" decision than to fall into the trap of waiting. Waiting can cause business leaders to become indecisive. This indecisiveness is especially harmful if a leader wants to encourage their team members to make decisions rather than let decisions only happen under their watch.

Experience Question: When do you find yourself saying "wait?" What steps do you need to take to walk away from waits?

I highly recommend that leaders be wary of waiting if they hope to lead an organization effectively. I wrote an article for Forbes, where I explored why waiting is often the wrong choice.[67]

Leaders must not wait too long to make their next business decisions. Examine how waits hurt Well Done leaders.

1. Waits can weigh down the organization with uncertainty and unclarity. Leaders must provide clarity to the organization on priorities and values. It is only when the leader knows where they are going and why they want to get there that they can inspire people to follow their lead. When a leader falls into the habit of waiting on decisions or projects, it creates confusion among the team about top priorities. Leaders and CEOs should frequently communicate with team members the top priorities of the organization — be it profit, product development or even customer service, and explain in as much detail as possible how those priorities impact every level of the organization.

2. Waits can weaken the leader's impact. It's easier for a leader to say "wait" as opposed to "yes" or "no." However, this only weakens the leader's voice. Leaders must be crystal clear on the boundaries they are setting for their organization when they give a clear no and must be bold in their passion for answering yes.

3. Waits can deter productivity. Waiting can cause a leader and team to worry about all the projects and tasks that are not getting done. Alternatively, it can cause a team to feel weighed down with other projects and activities that are not essential to business success. Revisit your decision to wait, either by rejecting and ignoring a task ("no") or by acting upon and moving forward with a task ("yes.") Establish clear boundaries around how many "yes" projects your team is working on at any given time. In the same way, establish a boundary around the number of "waits" that are on your "waitlist." When your organization has reached its capacity, it's time to move projects and tasks to the "no" column so that they do not slow down the progress of the "yes" tasks that your team is committed to completing.

4. Waits can work against momentum and the ability to move forward. "Yes" is a momentum maker; "wait" is a momentum killer. When a

person has an idea, and they bring it to you, the leader, the last thing they want to hear are phrases such as "Yes, but" "Not now," or "Maybe later." Give your employee a yes or a no rather than a "wait." "Wait" kills the momentum and enthusiasm of a team that is working toward a solution. Communicate to your team that you always want to say yes to their ideas and solutions but that they must first develop a solution and approach.

When you become a "yes" or "no" leader rather than a "wait" leader, you will lead your organization to a higher level of focus, and your team will accomplish more tasks.

When you become a "yes" or "no" leader rather than a "wait" leader, you will lead your organization to a higher level of focus, and your team will accomplish more tasks.

> **Experience Question:** What "yes" or "no" decision do you need to make in order to move your business forward?

One last second step comment:

Any good steward leader who wants to lead his or her business according to Christ's principles should show the same kind of rock-solid commitment. Leaders will have others question their decisions and choices. Many times those closest to the leader are the ones with the most prominent voices that can distract or persuade the leader to move from clarity to uncertainty. Effective leaders strive for clarity in all of their decisions and priorities at all times with everyone in the organization. When the leader knows their "yeses" and "noes," they lead more effectively and they are well on their way to becoming the kind of the leader who will hear the words, Well Done!

Best Ideas: Write down two or three best ideas that you heard or learned from this chapter.

WELL

DONE

Part II
The Parables of Jesus

Chapter 5

MAKE THE MOVE
FROM OWNER TO OVERSEER

*The most significant change you can make in your life and business
is the move from owner to overseer.*

*"His master replied, 'Well done, good and faithful servant!
You have been faithful with a few things; I will put you in charge
of many things. Come and share your master's happiness!"*
Matthew 25:21

You are not the owner! When living the principle of stewardship instead of ownership, few people shine more brightly than Stanley Tam, the founder of United States Plastic Corp., whom I mentioned in Chapter 3. One of the early leaders of the faith at work movement, Tam legally reassigned ownership of his business to God. Ironically, the story began when he went broke in photographic silver reclamation and turned to faith to revive his business.

His son-in-law—current US Plastics CEO Wesley Lytle—recalls: "He said, 'God, if you'll bless this business, I'll honor you in any way that I possibly can,' with that he started over again, with doing exactly what he was doing before, but now his purpose had changed. Instead of being a goal of getting personally rich, it was a goal of: how could he honor God?"[68]

The book Tam wrote in 1969, *God Owns My Business*, remains in print after fifty years, with an updated edition released in 2013. He has made such an impact during his life that in 2015 visitors came from as far away as Costa Rica to celebrate his 100th birthday. Over the years, Tam has overseen the use of more than $140 million of corporate profits for mission work. In his book, he writes about seeing himself like the tail attached to the end of a kite.

"As long as I'm attached to the kite I can't help but succeed," Tam says. "I must keep clean, obedient, and to do this I make it a point every day and often several times during the day of committing myself anew to the Lord . . . Throughout the day I quietly commit to the Lord whatever comes up in my activity. I ask Him for guidance when I have problems and thank Him for help when I work out answers to those problems. It isn't necessary to get on one's knees or to recite a specific prayer. All God asks is for our minds and our motives to be in assent to His will, acknowledging His power, and this can be a moment's thought, even an attitude of the heart."[69]

Experience Question: If you embrace the belief that God owns your business, how would that change the way you manage or lead the business that God has given you to steward?

Biblical Business Principle #5: Make the Move from Owner to Overseer
"His master replied, 'Well done, good and faithful servant! You have been faithful with a few things; I will put you in charge of many things. Come and share your master's happiness!'" Matthew 25:21

Become a Steward Leader. Strive for Excellent Oversight. Move From Doing It Alone to Doing It With Others. Be Ready to Give an Answer. Seek to Please the Master.

I have been working with Christian CEOs and business owners for over a decade. When I have the conversation about how they view themselves and who truly owns the business, I can almost see a literal weight lifting from their shoulders. Until they embrace the truth that they are only a steward of the business, they carry all of the weight and responsibility of the business—and it's a heavy burden. When they think they must make all of the decisions and be responsible for everything that happens in the business, it's too heavy. Making the shift from ownership to stewardship allows them to welcome God into the conversation and to consider what He would want them to do in the business. This shift helps the leader to embrace their true identity as a steward.

Make the Move from Servant Leader to Steward Leader

Steward leadership is the most effective kind of leadership, the kind that represents an essential shift for Christian business owners. Moving from an ownership mentality to a stewardship perspective, as Stanley Tam did, is a critical shift for a leader. As I wrote in a recent blog for the Biblical Leadership website:

"Christian CEOs understand that God is the owner of the business, and their responsibility is to do their best at stewarding the resources God provides. This shift can bring a significant blessing to the Christian leader. When leaders become aware that they are no longer the owner, they can release the burdens of ownership, decision making, and business responsibilities. They can shift their primary focus to what God is asking of them, meaning they work to bring glory to their Father who is in Heaven (who is the real owner of the business). This shift to make decisions based on stewardship releases the human owner from the responsibilities of ownership."[70]

One of the most memorable parables that Jesus ever told was a parable about moving from ownership to overseer. This parable is the topic of frequent discussion in Christian business circles, where it is known widely as the "Parable of

Talents." This story of Jesus appears in Matthew 25:14-30: *"Again, it will be like a man going on a journey, who called his servants and entrusted his wealth to them. To one he gave five bags of gold, to another two bags, and to another one bag, each according to his ability. Then he went on his journey. The man who had received five bags of gold went at once and put his money to work and gained five bags more. So also, the one with two bags of gold gained two more. But the man who had received one bag went off, dug a hole in the ground and hid his master's money. After a long time the master of those servants returned and settled accounts with them. The man who had received five bags of gold brought the other five. 'Master,' he said, 'you entrusted me with five bags of gold. See, I have gained five more.' His master replied, 'Well done, good and faithful servant! You have been faithful with a few things; I will put you in charge of many things. Come and share your master's happiness!' The man with two bags of gold also came. 'Master,' he said, 'you entrusted me with two bags of gold; see, I have gained two more.' His master replied, 'Well done, good and faithful servant! You have been faithful with a few things; I will put you in charge of many things. Come and share your master's happiness!' Then the man who had received one bag of gold came. 'Master,' he said, 'I knew that you are a hard man, harvesting where you have not sown and gathering where you have not scattered seed. So I was afraid and went out and hid your gold in the ground. See, here is what belongs to you.' His master replied, 'You wicked, lazy servant! So you knew that I harvest where I have not sown and gather where I have not scattered seed? Well then, you should have put my money on deposit with the bankers, so that when I returned I would have received it back with interest. So take the bag of gold from him and give it to the one who has ten bags. For whoever has will be given more, and they will have an abundance. Whoever does not have, even what they have will be taken from them. And throw that worthless servant outside, into the darkness, where there will be weeping and gnashing of teeth.'"*

When Well Done CEOs and leaders listen and take the words of this story to heart, a subtle shift takes place in how they lead and run their business. They move from pleasing themselves to pleasing the Master. They make a move from making all the decisions about what is the right thing to do, to making decisions about what is the right thing to do to please the Owner of all things. I often call this shift a shift from ownership to overseer. Becoming a good steward is a good principle on which to build a great business.

Win Activity: Overseer Defined: What characteristics or attitudes would you want people in your organization to possess as an overseer of their department or area?

1.

2.

3.

4.

Practice Excellent Oversight

It is essential to clarify what the shift looks like when a leader moves from ownership to overseer. Business ownership is easy to identify; every decision and action stems from what the owner thinks and feels. Stewardship is a shift to make decisions based on the ideas and concepts that one day every person will have to give an account for all of his or her decisions and actions before the one who truly owns the business. Moving from ownership to stewardship includes several key steps. The steward leader has the following responsibilities:

1. Overseers understand that God owns ALL of the business

Steward leaders recognize that everything they have comes from God and should be considered for His purposes. This fundamental shift releases the burdens of business. The steward leader/owner no longer must carry the weight of every decision, choice, and consequence. The leader is released to work with all of their might while understanding that the end result is left to the Owner who owns all things.[71]

King David penned these words in Psalm 24:1: "The earth is the Lord's, and everything in it, the world, and all who live in it." When the leader recognizes that it all belongs to God, then the leader can hold all things in proper perspective. Every steward leader must wrestle with whether they genuinely believe that it is God's business or theirs. When it is God's business, it can impact both the now and eternity.

"Anything we try to hang on to here will be lost," says best-selling author Randy Alcorn in his book, *The Treasure Principle*. "But anything we put into

God's hands will be ours for eternity. If that doesn't take your breath away, you don't understand it! If we invest in the eternal instead of in the temporal, we store up treasures in Heaven that will never stop paying dividends. Whatever treasures we store upon Earth will be left behind when we leave. Whatever treasures we store up in Heaven will be waiting for us when we arrive."[72] The benefit of a shift to steward ownership is the legacy of impact can last for eternity. How a steward owner acts today will impact forever.

2. Overseers understand that they have to give an account for ALL of their decisions

Owners often answer to no one, but stewards give account to the heavenly Owner. The steward owner is challenged to make better decisions because they understand that someday they will have to give an account for all that they did as they stewarded the business they were given to lead. This knowledge keeps the steward owner sharp and helps this leader maintain the right perspective. In fact, of all the people in the organization, the one that will be held accountable the most is the leader. Therefore leaders must always be ready to give an account for all of their decisions and choices.

Well Done owners consistently ask themselves the question, "If I had to give an account to God today for my decisions and actions in the business that I steward, would He say to me, Well done?" This question can be an arbiter for decision-making and value-building. Many owners can be tempted to make decisions that are not in the best interest of the business because they never have to give an account of their actions. When this shift of thinking takes place in the mind of a leader, they understand that they will have to account for all of their decisions.

> **Well Done owners consistently ask themselves the question, "If I had to give an account to God today for my decisions and actions in the business that I steward, would He say to me, Well done?"**

3. Overseers understand the importance of engaging all people under their care

The steward leader believes they have been placed in the business with a purpose to accomplish. They are not satisfied with just doing a task. Instead, they want to use all of their gifts and abilities to accomplish the task with excellence. The steward leader intends to please the Master. They understand precisely what the Master wants and use all of their resources to complete the task before the Master returns. They want to be seen as an excellent servant. Thus, the steward leader treats every person with respect, and they utilize every talent they have been given to produce results for the Master.

The steward leader acts as a servant leader with the people under their care. They work to ensure that each person on the team feels engaged. The leader removes obstacles that hinder the team member from completing their tasks with excellence. The leader knows their team, and they call out the best in each team member with the full awareness of the team member's role in the organization is essential for the overall success of the company.

4. **Overseers understand that they must use ALL resources wisely**

One key aspect of stewards is that they are not owners, but overseers of resources at their disposal. These resources include money, time, people, and tools or equipment. In the parable of the barns, the overseer was to give an account of how well they handled the blessings given to them by God, who left the owner in charge. How a leader handles resources will speak volumes about their values and ultimate purpose.

"As Christians, we have a mission which our Lord expects us to accomplish in the here and now of this present age," writes Hugh Whelchel, the executive director of the Institute for Faith, Work & Economics in his book, *How Then Should We Work? Discovering the Biblical Doctrine of Work.* He adds: "The stewardship of all we have been given is what we are called to do while we wait for our Savior's return; this is what we were made to do."[73]

Steward leaders do not accept the lack of performance from any aspect that they oversee. These leaders understand that their primary responsibility is to see that everything they manage is used to its highest level of performance.

5. **Overseers understand that they are called to reach full capacity for ALL things under their care**

Steward owners lead businesses that are bigger than just one person or idea. A multitude of people with a variety of approaches will bring success to a company in the marketplace. Steward owners who build a sustainable and scalable business invest in attracting and developing good talent so that the business becomes bigger than just the owner. Owner-driven and owner-led companies usually die with the owner. Owners who find and gather the right team of people around them builds lasting corporations. This attitude is an excellent business principle because it is a biblical notion.

> **Experience Question:** Are you leading your company to reach full capacity? What change do you need to make to better use all of the resources at your disposal?

Move from Doing It Alone to Doing It with Others

Every leader needs to have others question their decisions and others to make decisions on the things that the owner questions.[74] Leaders make a multitude of choices; many end up making the wrong ones when they try to make those decisions alone. The fundamental truth is that when leaders make better decisions, their companies get better.

The fundamental truth is that when leaders make better decisions, their companies get better.

If one person is making all the decisions, then the organization will be hindered by the limits of that person's thinking.

An essential action of growing and developing a company is finding the best people. Growing companies grow people. Smart businesses focus on finding and retaining the best talent. When companies miss this central principle, everything suffers. Companies that focus on capacity make a shift to help their team members reach their full potential. "Capacity Conversations" can prove to be more valuable than performance reviews as they communicate that the organization desires to help each team member reach their peak performance.

A "Capacity Conversation" is conducted between a leader and a team member where they examine how aligned the team member's performance is to the full use of the capacity of their talents, gifts, and abilities. The team members' tasks are reduced to no more than four key areas of focus. The team member then rates themselves on their current capacity in each area of job performance. The leader also gives the team member a rating of how well they feel the person is reaching their capacity. The conversation then continues to determine how much more the team member can strive to accomplish in the coming twelve months. Concrete steps are established so that both parties are clear about how to use more of the team member's talents, abilities, and gifts. The Strengths Finder assessment tool is an excellent resource to use as a part of this exercise. Also, a spiritual gifts test can be a helpful resource for a team member to help them to assess how they were wired and what gifts they possess and can use to reach fulfillment and to help the business succeed.

The wisdom of others can be powerful. Every great leader in the Bible had at least one advisor, and every leader built a team. Many business leaders try to do things all on their own. However, oneness is never full capacity. Steward owners believe in the power of others and understand that no great company was ever built only by one person.

> **Experience Question:** Where are you trying to lead alone, and you know you and your company would be better if you were leading with someone else?

In his book *Leadershift*, leadership expert John Maxwell writes, "one of the first and most important shifts anyone must make to become a leader is from soloist to conductor. You can be a successful person on your own, but not a successful leader."[75] Even though they hire talented people, many business owners sabotage the scalability of their companies because they continue to operate as soloist. The soloist leader never embraces decision-making as a team and never employs the concept of helping others develop an ownership mentality throughout the business.

Well Done leaders understand the value of moving from acting as a soloist CEO to becoming a steward CEO. The steward CEO embraces the truth that God brings people into the organization for a variety of purposes and reasons. These leaders strive to embrace team decision-making, the engagement of team players, and the importance of growing and developing their people. Max De Pree, the former business executive who pioneered the idea of an inclusive corporation where all voices are heard, wrote in his best-selling *Leadership is an Art*: "Life is more than just reaching our goals. As individuals and as a group we need to reach our potential. Nothing else is good enough. We must always be reaching toward our potential."[76]

Be Ready to Give an Answer

Overseers know that one day they will have to account for every action they take. In the parable of the talents, when the owner returned, each leader had to give an accounting of what they did while the leader was away. Two of the leaders were ready to do so, but one failed miserably. This situation reflects the defining difference between an owner and a steward: the owner does not believe they are responsible for giving an account, while a steward is always ready to provide an answer for the way they do business.

> **Experience Question:** As a leader, do you have reasons for the decisions that you make, and are you comfortable with sharing with your team the reason you made the decisions you made?

David Green, the CEO and founder of Hobby Lobby, has been an excellent example of boldness and being prepared to answer for the business decisions he makes. David led Hobby Lobby in a lawsuit against the Affordable Care Act because he believed that it violated what he thought was good stewardship. However, David has practiced this perspective for years in all aspects of the business. The book *More Than a Hobby*, he wrote: "I am a merchant who believes and respects Jesus Christ. To say that I should walk out of church on Sunday at noon and then stuff everything I've heard and practiced into a dark closet for the next six days is not realistic, or even desirable. Customers had better hope that I treat them according to the moral teachings of my faith! They don't have to agree with me on all religious matters. They don't have to embrace the same Savior I embrace. But, surely there's nothing wrong with my holding him up for public consideration."[77]

Green understands that biblical business principles are not only good for business; they are essential to hearing the words "Well Done." Since God wants to be involved in every area of our life, every person will have to give an account for every decision they made in life. Every person will have to give an account for how they lived and the choices they made — including every Christian business owner.

In Romans 14:11-12, the apostle Paul reminds the recipients of his letter in Rome: "It is written: 'As surely as I live,' says the Lord, 'every knee will bow before me; every tongue will acknowledge God.' So then, each of us will give an account of ourselves to God." Paul was encouraging every person who would read this letter to remember that God will hold every person accountable for the actions they took and the decisions they made while on this earth.

Seek to Please the Master

The best stewards seek to please the master in all that they do. Good employees genuinely want to please the leader by doing what the leader desires. Apostle Paul further explained this concept in his second letter to the Corinthians: "So we make it our goal to please him, whether we are at home in the body or away from it. For we must all appear before the judgment seat of Christ, so that each of us may receive what is due us for the things done while in the body, whether good or bad" (2 Corinthians 5:9-10).

> **Experience Question:** If you had to give an account to God today for your decisions and actions in the business that you steward, do you believe that you would hear God say, "Well done?" What changes do you need to make in order to hear those words?

One characteristic of Well Done employees is that they work to please their leader. These excellent workers seek to see the company in the same way that the leader sees it. They want to understand the vision that the leader is trying to create. They prioritize their tasks and projects based on how the leader would prioritize them. They make the leader's problems their problems, and they do not make their problems the leader's problems. They work

One characteristic of Well Done employees is that they work to please their leader.

to implement the goals of the leader, and they value what the leader values. In everything that the team member does they work to please their leader. Business owners can identify excellent employees quickly.

In this same way, the owner of a business should strive to become an outstanding employee as they seek to please their leader, God. Well Done leaders understand that they are to strive to please God with all that they do, knowing that one day, God will take back ownership of all the things that He has given to them. At the end of their life and as they stand before their maker, they will be evaluated by one measure: How much did they please the owner of all things?

One last second step comment:

Business owners are not excluded from the truth of these verses about ownership versus stewardship. Business owners and steward leaders must be ready to give a response to why they did the things they did. Moreover, they should be ready to tell how those decisions measured up to the values and principles God establishes in the Bible. This would include such realities as to how they managed and spent their money, treated their employees, and served their customers.

While a shift from owner to overseer is not a simple task, it becomes easier to understand why this shift is so significant and essential for businesses seeking to honor God. As respected professor, theologian, and author Wayne Grudem says in his book, *Business for the Glory of God*: "When we are responsible stewards, whether taking care of our toys at age four or managing the entire factory at the age of forty, 'if we do this work as unto the Lord,' God looks at our imitation of his sovereignty and his other attributes, and he is pleased. In this way, we are his image-bearers, people who are like God on the earth, whether we own few possessions or many, and whether we own a small business or a large one."[78]

May that be true of you, no matter what the size of the company or organization you oversee. After all, God is watching, and one day will require a report from the stewards of His resources. Every engaged leader seeks useful information on how well the business is performing. The committed leader also seeks to know how individuals in the business are performing. These leaders call people to give an account for their work and their effort. Reporting is only a fearful prospect for individuals who are not performing well. Good performers are never bothered by giving a report or update on what they do or don't do.

Good performers are never bothered by giving a report or update on what they do or don't do.

The poor performers in God's eyes are those who see themselves as the only owner of their business. These individuals cannot give proper recognition to the One who created all things, including their company. These owners do not make space for God in their business, and therefore God is not recognized in His proper position. For the leader who has decided to become an overseer rather than an owner, they are well on their way to hearing the words, Well Done!

> **Experience Question:** How often do you say the words, Well Done to your team? What benefits would your company receive if you built a Well Done culture?

Best Ideas: Write down two or three best ideas that you heard or learned from this chapter.

WELL

DONE

Chapter 6

TRUST THE LAW
OF SOWING AND REAPING

*The harvest you are reaping today is
from the seeds that you planted yesterday.*

*"Still other seed fell on good soil, where it produced a crop—
a hundred, sixty or thirty times what was sown."*
Matthew 13:8

Plant what you want to reap! Hobby Lobby is one of the more notable American business success stories. It started with the small seed of David and Barbara Green taking out a six hundred dollar loan in 1970 to begin making miniature picture frames at their home. In August of 1972, they opened their first Hobby Lobby. The modest three hundred square foot store in Oklahoma City did $3,200 in retail sales by the end of that year. David Green left his supervisory position with another company in 1975 to open a second outlet in the city. The year after that, he opened another one in Tulsa. Today, its 850-plus stores and more than 37,500 employees make Hobby Lobby the largest privately owned arts-and-crafts retailer in the world.[79]

David Green understands the law of sowing and reaping: you must plant seeds in order to get the right results. In his book *More Than a Hobby*, Green noted that no one could pick winners all the time. Thus, the Hobby Lobby model set a goal to maintain a designated margin on an entire category of products.

"The average buyer is overseeing some 3,000 SKUs (Stock-keeping units) and spending around $20 million a year," Green said. "They know that if the whole cluster of SKUs delivers its margin target at the end, everything is fine. This frees them to take risks. They know their mandate: 'Get the very best value you can for the customer.' If this means bringing in something we've never carried before, that's fine as long as it belongs in a Hobby Lobby environment. If this means taking an expensive trip to Thailand or Slovakia, so be it. We don't quibble about travel budgets. A few thousand dollars on airfares and hotels is nothing coming compared to the high-potential products with great margins that can be found along the way."[80]

David and Steve Green have embraced the principle of sowing and reaping throughout the Hobby Lobby model. These owners have sown seeds of trust with their employees and their customers by providing exceptional products distributed with the right margins.

Proven Laws

A leader can embrace the laws of life. After all, they have been proven through time; because they are tried and tested, and they prove profitable. Leaders appreciate truths because they know that truths can be trusted. When a leader finds a key principle that generally works in all situations and all times, it allows the leader to trust the process. One such law or truth is the law of sowing and reaping. I have found that this principle is essential to mastering life and the challenges of business.

Jesus taught on this principle in the "Parable of the Sower." He told a story about a farmer who planted seeds that fell on different types of soil. Although the ground provided different returns, the leader in this parable reaped an abundant harvest from the few seeds that fell on the good soil. The good seed matched with the good soil brought a bonanza; as Jesus put it: "Still other seed fell on good soil, where it produced a crop—a hundred, sixty or thirty times what was sown" (Matthew 13:8). The power of this principle appears in this single verse. One seed planted in the right place has the potential to produce up to a hundred-fold return. One good seed can produce a Hobby Lobby-sized harvest.

Although the parable that Jesus taught was designed to teach about evangelism and discipleship, the application of this principle applies well to how leaders should think about the decisions, actions, and choices that they make related to their business. Well Done CEOs know and trust the law of sowing and reaping to grow their business and their impact. Second Corinthians 9:6 says, "the point is this: whoever sows sparingly will also reap sparingly, and whoever sows bountifully will also reap bountifully." The New Living Translation put it this way: "Remember this—a farmer who plants only a few seeds will get a small crop. But the one who plants generously will get a generous crop." (NLT)

Remember this—a farmer who plants only a few seeds will get a small crop. But the one who plants generously will get a generous crop.

The truth is that a person will never reap a harvest from seeds that are never planted. Furthermore, to receive the highest level of return for every seed that is planted, it must be placed in fertile soil. Daniel J. Martin, president of the prestigious Christian school, Seattle Pacific University, explores the concept of the soil as it relates to business in his book, Rich Soil: Transforming Your Organization's Landscape for Maximum Effectiveness. Martin wrote that "rich soil connotes healthy and fertile soil—soil that has the right blend of nutrients to produce exponential returns."[81]

Biblical Business Principle #6: Trust the Law of Sowing and Reaping
"Still other seed fell on good soil, where it produced a crop—a hundred, sixty or thirty times what was sown." Matthew 13:8

Sow bountifully. Be generous with your seeds. Plant daily. Be continually trying new things. Don't be afraid to start small. Practice patience.

Well Done leaders would be wise to understand a few essentials of sowing and reaping since each of these facts apply to leading a successful company and ultimately hearing the words: Well Done. The law of sowing and reaping will both challenge the leader to sow better and encourage the leader to plant continually, even when a harvest does not immediately appear on the horizon. This principle is especially helpful in the areas of sales and marketing but can be applied in many areas in the business.

> **Experience Question:** Where have you seen the principle of sowing and reaping proven true in your life and your business?

3 Facts About Business Sowing and Reaping

1. Every Business Should Plant Widely

One fundamental component of the parable of the sower is the location of where each seed fell. It is prudent to pay attention to what and where a business is planting its seeds. Two key questions steward CEOs should consider is (1) do they have good seed? And (2) are they planting that seed in good soil? Good seed could be seen in relation to the products that a company sells and the people that they employ to deploy their services. Only a good seed in good soil will produce good crops. Well Done CEOs focus their businesses on how to develop a better seed and plant it in better soil. A better seed might come in the form of hiring better people or in building a better product, and better soil is finding the best markets to share their products and services. This best seed and soil mentality will allow the leader to build their business on a solid foundation.[82]

For you to plant widely, your products need to be the best, and you need to be effective at identifying your ideal customer. Further, you need to know how to reach those customers effectively. The better businesses get at planting; the more likely the businesses will reap a good harvest. As noted author Robert Louis Stevenson says: "Don't judge each day by the harvest you reap, but by the seeds you plant."[83]

Don't judge each day by the harvest you reap, but by the seeds you plant.

In his best-selling book EntreLeadership, syndicated talk show host and business author Dave Ramsey discusses planting widely. Commenting about starting a business in the chapter, "Don't Flop Whoppers," he writes: "The Bureau of Labor Statistics found that the average worker will have ten different jobs by age forty. If there is that much change and movement in the marketplace, you need to make sure your business direction incorporates that. The whole marketplace can move under your feet very quickly, and your passion and calling can keep you at the cutting edge of change. If your business is simply a set of mechanics that produces profit, you will never see the change coming, you will never embrace the change, and you will never ever lead the change."[84]

The principle of planting widely was why I decided to launch the "7 Pathways to Well Done" that I mentioned in chapter 3. CEO experience desires to help one million CEOs hear the words Well Done. I wanted to focus on planting seeds with CEOs instead of making CEOs fit into my model. The sower must plant many seeds for the right seed to fall on the right soil in order to produce a robust crop.

The sower must plant many seeds for the right seed to fall on the right soil in order to produce a robust crop.

2. Every Business Should Fertilize Willingly

Protecting good seeds is an important task. Well Done leaders focus on keeping their best people and updating their best products to ensure that those products stay relevant for customers and consumers. In planting, fertilizing adds value to the seeds. Many businesses have a good seed, but then, they do not work hard to ensure their growth. Fertilizing in business comes in terms of customer service and follow-through. Every steward leader should consider where the business needs to protect the seeds that have been planted. Stewardship companies need to nurture ideas, protect company values, promote quality in everything that they do, and excel at servant leadership as they seek to help those who purchase their products and services.

Kingdom impact through a business can happen more effectively when the company builds deep and lasting relationships with customers and employees. Customer and employee retention is key to protecting good soil. Some conversations about faith will only take place when a person has had many situations in which he or she has been able to observe your faith in action. Don't discount the idea of protecting good seeds.

3. Every Business Should Weed Wisely

To effectively produce a good crop, weeds must be removed. Weeds in business will come in the shape of distractions, division, and discouragement. Steward leaders who want to reap a harvest will consider what obstacles they must remove to obtain a productive crop, especially since weeds tend to be the easiest plant to grow.

College President Martin notes: "organizational weeds can develop across the entire organizational landscape or within certain programs or divisions. When the company is distracted by these weeds, it is easier to lose sight of the mission, and the operations become so watered down that success is nearly impossible."[85] Sometimes the weed can come in the form of a misaligned employee or a misplaced project. Whatever it might be, don't be afraid to remove the weeds from your business.

When the crop is ready, reaping—or closing the deal—is essential. Reaping is receiving blessings of the hard work in planting. It is a good evaluation of how well a business is in planting and growing. When a company is not reaping the right results, the leader must evaluate the planting process. However, when the time of harvest has come, the business must do everything in its power to reap the results of their hard work. To leave results, undone is to make all the prior efforts useless.

When a leader embraces the truth of sowing and reaping, it will shape every decision and every action in the organization. Leaders who sow wisely act differently than leaders who don't understand this principle. Too many leaders become so focused on the "now" they can't see the "tomorrow." Well Done leaders understand that in order to lead tomorrow, they must do the work of improving today. If a leader does not improve, they become right-now leaders instead of best-now leaders. The best-now leader sows seeds feverishly, knowing the seeds they plant today will reap a harvest tomorrow.

The best-now leader sows seeds feverishly, knowing the seeds they plant today will reap a harvest tomorrow.

So what does it look like to understand and embrace this principle? Consider and implement the following ideas.

Be Generous with Your Seeds

Well Done leaders know that the harvest they are reaping today comes from the seeds that they planted yesterday. Another part of the Bible reminds us that we will reap what we sow. Therefore, sow bountifully and be on a constant lookout to reap your harvest. Remember the admonition of 2 Corinthians 9:6 that whoever sows sparingly will reap sparingly.

The more seeds you plant, the better your chances for success. Seeds are to be used, not kept; only a seed that is planted can reap a harvest. Only ideas explored can be implemented. Only products that are developed and produced can be purchased. Every steward leader needs to examine how well they are managing the seeds under their care.

> **Seeds are to be used, not kept; only a seed that is planted can reap a harvest.**

These seeds can come from both customers and employees; most often, the seeds come in the form of ideas of how to improve their product or service.

The law of sowing and reaping will encourage Well Done CEOs to embrace the art of generosity. The farmer knows that in order to reap an abundant harvest, many seeds must be planted. Becoming generous with what God has given to the leader will help the leader find favor and receive a more robust crop.

Plant Daily

During the sowing season, the farmer plants daily, knowing that every day is essential. Since planting is a daily process, no day should be missed. Every day of planting is critical for the long-term success of the crops. The same is valid for business. If you stop planting, you can be sure that you will stop reaping Every day of planting in the business is essential to the long-term success of the business. Every day, the people of the business must be planting the right seeds by doing their tasks with excellence and energy.

For the Well Done CEO, it is essential that they plant seeds for God's kingdom as well as for company growth. Leading a business by the Biblical Business

Principles means that the leader will use them every day to guide decisions in their organization. The leader will teach and train their entire workforce to apply the principles for impact in the most significant way possible. This kingdom thinking inspires the organization to not only be successful from the world's point of view, but also from the viewpoint of heaven.

One way to plant daily is to use your business as an opportunity to share your values and your faith. Putting pictures on the wall with Scripture verses or leaving a Bible on your desk or in your showroom is a daily planting in which you may never know how the seed will take effect in the lives of those who come into contact with your business. I have developed a tool at CEO Experience, called "31 Days to Kingdom Impact." It is a practical, step-by-step daily planting guide on how to use your business for kingdom impact. You can go to www.ceoexperience. com to download the tool and start planting kingdom seeds in your business.

Continually Try New Things

It is tempting for business leaders not to trust the principle of sowing and reaping. Unfortunately, such people tend to plant too few seeds. The seed metaphor is an explanation of being open to new ideas and exploring ideas of innovation. When a steward CEO believes that they do not have to be open to new ideas, they begin to see their potential shrink. The call for the Well Done CEO is to be a lead innovator and change agent; Jesus was one of the most disruptive leaders who has ever lived.[86]

In the parable of the sower, the one who planted the seeds found four kinds of soil. In Matthew 13:4-8, Jesus taught:

"As he was scattering the seed, some fell along the path, and the birds came and ate it up. Some fell on rocky places, where it did not have much soil. It sprang up quickly, because the soil was shallow. But when the sun came up, the plants were scorched, and they withered because they had no root. Other seed fell among thorns, which grew up and choked the plants. Still other seed fell on good soil, where it produced a crop - a hundred, sixty or thirty times what was sown."

In other words, many seeds were planted, but only a portion of the seeds produced. In business, leaders may have to explore numerous ideas to find the right product or solution to a problem. A steward leader must challenge the company to think outside of the box to find new possible solutions - ones that would never have been discussed or discovered had the leader not pushed for creative and innovative thinking.

> **Experience Question:** How open are you to new ideas and innovative changes to your company? Could you be missing a new seed that will produce a good harvest?

In his excellent book, *Business Secrets from the Bible*, Rabbi Daniel Lapin explores this concept in a chapter entitled "As Painful as Change Can Be, It Often Contains the Seeds of Growth." Lapin ends with this charge: "The lesson is that change, while scary and stressful, can carry the seeds of growth and good fortune. This is as true in business as it is on the battlefield. We must remain true to our purpose but accept that change will happen, and adjust our plans, behavior, and business tactics so that we may not lose sight of our underlying purpose. Embrace change and you may find fortune where you thought there was only misery."[87]

A review of the soils mentioned in the parable of the sower is a useful paradigm for leaders to consider as they explore new products, services, and solutions. Every seed will fall into some kind of soil. I have renamed them because it becomes easier to identify and understand which idea falls into which of the four categories: stony, shallow, sticky, or super soil.

The Stony Soil: Some seeds fell on the path and never reached the soil. These seeds represent ideas that are considered but never implemented. Leaders consider many ideas and possibilities, but should only invest in those that could prove to produce some level of a harvest. Steward leaders should measure how many new ideas are being discussed in the organization each month. When companies stop creating new ideas, they will be left behind.

The Shallow Soil: This soil allows a seed to take root, but the roots are not deep. Some ideas in business have merit, but they are not the ultimate solution that will produce for your company. Often, a CEO or business leader will find out quickly if their idea has merit because others will see the result of their decisions immediately. Others will discourage them from continuing to invest where no harvest can be reaped.

The Sticky Soil: Some ideas will be accepted and implemented, but they will still not produce much of a harvest. The thorny soil is painful, but still necessary because sometimes, what a business needs the most is a good failure. Steve Jobs began a big project in 1978 that he expected to produce a harvest: the creation of the Apple Lisa Project. His vision was to build a personal desktop computer that everyone could use. The Macintosh, as it is known today, is a series of personal computers that consists of the MacBook Pro, the MacBook Air, and the Mac. However, this phenomenally successful series was only developed because of the seven years of failure that Jobs and the Apple team experienced through the Lisa Project.[88]

The Super Soil: Some ideas are game-changers. The Wright brothers started their journey for flight in Dayton, Ohio, in 1896. The brothers imagined that they could use materials from their bicycle shop to create a plane that could fly. Seven years later, in 1903, they traveled to Kitty Hawk, North Carolina, and flew the first powered flight, which lasted just twelve seconds. Before they left, they had flown more than 700 powered flights with their glider.[89] They planted seeds for seven years before they reaped a harvest that would lead to the innovation and industrialization of a nation.

> **Experience Question:** What weeds are stopping your seeds from producing? What could you do to remove the weeds that are choking your plants?

Be open to new ideas. The world needs fresh thinking and new solutions. Steward CEOs should be on the front line of innovation as they plant many seeds in many different soils until they find the ground that will produce an abundant harvest.

Win Activity: Seed Planting: What seeds should you be planting today in the hopes of reaping a harvest tomorrow?

1.

2.

3.

4.

Don't Be Afraid to Start Small

This Biblical Business Principle should encourage every Well Done entrepreneur not to be afraid to start something with a small seed, which can later provide a plentiful harvest. Sometimes leaders are scared to start small because of a fear of failure or of wasting time and resources. However, small starts can lead to big breakthroughs.

> **Experience Question:** How could your business plant more seeds today so as to ensure that you reap a bigger and better harvest tomorrow?

One example of this is from a Well Done CEO, with whom I have worked for almost a decade. Joe Connolly is the president of Pro Wood Finishes in Rockville, Maryland. Joe has led a good distribution business for nearly 40 years. He loves his customers, and he also loves God. During a CEO Retreat Day, members discussed how to have a more significant impact for God through their business. One planted the seed of an idea that Joe decided to implement. Pro Wood Finishes has a showroom where contractors can view different shades of color for finishing jobs as well as purchase other building and remodeling products. As a result of discussion at the retreat, Joe decided to put Bibles in the showroom of his business, free to any customer who wanted one. He went to a nearby bookstore and purchased five large study Bibles to give away.

Sensing God led him to put out the Bibles, Joe had no idea what customers would think about the Bibles or do with them. Shortly after putting up the display with a sign stating, "Free Bibles," he returned to the showroom to see all five had disappeared. Surprised and inspired, Joe decided he needed to order a box so more people could have access to the Bible. Soon the next set of Bibles had been taken, and then another and another. Finally, Joe expanded his impact by putting out Spanish Bibles and children's Bibles. Pro Wood Finishes has now given away more than a two **Every business has the potential to do big things when they are not afraid to start small.** thousand Bibles, less than twenty miles from capital of the United States. That is kingdom impact. Joe's ability to start small will allow him to hear the words, Well

Done, when he gets to heaven. Every business has the potential to do big things when they are not afraid to start small.

> **Experience Question:** How could you use your business to plant seeds for God's kingdom daily?

Practice Patience

After the farmer has planted, he waits for the harvest. Patience is essential in farming—and in business. Many leaders make the mistake of sowing good seeds, but then moving on too quickly and not being patient as they await the harvest. Patient leaders are excellent leaders because they understand that the harvest will come at the right time. So as they wait, they prepare to reap the harvest.

In his book, *Leaders Eat Last*, British-born organizational consultant Simon Sinek discusses the importance of patience when it comes to developing trust in leadership: "Our world is one of impatience. A world of instant gratification. A world ruled by dopamine. Google can give us the answer we want now. We can buy online and get what we want now. We can stand and receive information instantaneously. We don't have to wait a week to see our favorite show; we can watch it now. We have become accustomed to getting what we want when we want it. This (perspective) is all fine and good for movies and online shopping, but it's not very helpful when we are trying to form bonds of trust that can withstand storms. That takes time, and there is no app for that."[90]

Having a good view of tomorrow inspires the leader to know what to do today.

Patient leaders are inspirational because they have a deep sense of belief that the seeds that they have planted will produce a good harvest. Patient leaders are visionary because they not only see today; they understand how what they do today can impact their tomorrows. Having a good view of tomorrow inspires the leader to know what to do today. One of the most critical leadership traits is knowing when to wait and when to act. Sometimes the best thing you can do for your business is wait for the seeds that you have planted to come to harvest.

Experience Question: In what ways could mastering the principle of sowing and reaping to help both your internal team and your customer become more effective and impactful?

One last second step comment:

The principle of sowing and reaping has been tested and has been proven reliable. No business can escape the tenants of this principle, nor should they try. The principle is the key to success and will help a leader hear the words Well Done if it is embraced and practiced.

The Well Done leader sows seeds into their life and into the life of the business, knowing that the tomorrows of the business depend on the work of today. These leaders plant and keep planting until it is time to work at bringing in the harvest. When the harvest comes, the time for celebration is at hand.

Sowing and reaping leaders use all of their time today to prepare for what is next. The most effective leaders embrace this principle by setting aside time to get away to learn and improve themselves. These leaders sow seeds in their own personal development. Well Done leaders understand the leader they were yesterday will not be able to lead effectively tomorrow unless they improve today.

Well Done leaders understand the leader they were yesterday will not be able to lead effectively tomorrow unless they improve today.

Best Ideas: Write down two or three best ideas that you heard or learned from this chapter.

WELL
DONE

Chapter 7

BELIEVE AND ASK
FOR THE IMPOSSIBLE

People can do the impossible when someone believes it is possible.

"Jesus looked at them and said, "With man this is impossible,
but with God all things are possible."
Matthew 19:26

No matter what the circumstances, God's people have always believed in the impossible: Daniel in the lions' den, Gideon against an army that vastly outnumbered his, young David facing down nine-foot-tall Goliath, or Paul surviving attacks designed to erase him from this earth. Such tales only sound easy in the retelling. In the midst of battle, whether against a physical army, a powerful ruler, or a great recession, faith can be in short supply. That's why they call it faith.

While we can always look to biblical heroes, there are plenty of modern-day saints whose faith can also inspire. One example is the late Paul Kuck, founder of Regal Marine Industries. In 1973, Kuck faced a challenging moment in his life and business. His boating business once looked like a sure bet in an area that was booming thanks to the growth of the new theme park Walt Disney World. But in this difficult moment, it now appeared that Regal Marine looked like it might not survive.

The Arab oil embargo had quadrupled the price of oil, leading to nationwide gas rationing, a two-year-long stock market slide, and a severe reduction in Regal's staff—from thirty-five down to six. His stomach in knots, Kuck penned a letter to God that still hangs in the corporate offices. It explained that he was releasing his business and making it God's business. He believed that God could make the difference, and if the company were to be successful, he needed God to do the impossible. Paul saw no other way forward.

"My dad would tell the story that he was giving it over to God, but he wasn't giving him much," said Duane Kuck, Paul's successor as president and CEO, in a 2017 interview.

"It's not always easy, but we try to think of it in terms of a stewardship relationship vs. an ownership relationship. I think that the 1973 moment was my parents' acknowledgment of an act of surrender. From that, we made it through that hard time and several hard times since. Our perspective was shaped by that act of surrender."[91]

From that moment, the direction of Regal Marine changed forever. Today, the company is known for its high-quality, "best-in-class" yachts and boats, and its integrity in dealing with customers and clients. Amazing things can happen when a leader allows God to lead, even though it doesn't always mean smooth sailing. From its low point of six, by 2006, Regal's staff numbered 1,000. Then came the Great Recession, and it shrank to 400 before rebounding to 600. Through it all, the Kuck family has believed in a God who is faithful regardless of circumstances.

A God Sized Vision

A God-size vision for an organization can change how a steward leader thinks and dreams. Everything great in life starts with a dream. The world is better when people dream big and believe that impossible things can happen. All leaders should challenge themselves and their teams to ask "what if?" questions to expand their belief. Well Done leaders will use their imagination to see the world in new and different ways.

> **Experience Question:** How big is your vision? How would you feel to see God interact with your company in a way that could only be described as a God thing?

In Matthew 19:26, Jesus makes a powerful proclamation reminding His disciples of the power of belief. The disciples are intrigued about a situation they see as impossible, a rich person entering God's kingdom, given the standard their Master has just outlined. However, Jesus gives a powerful affirmation when He speaks to them: "Jesus looked at them and said, ‹With man this is impossible, but with God all things are possible.'"

That is an excellent principle on which to build a life and a business. Jesus speaks to the power of belief because the faith-driven entrepreneur believes that with God, all things are possible. People really can do the impossible when someone believes that it is possible.

In another story that Jesus told, he explains how this principle can change how a person views the impossible situations in their life. In Luke 18:1-8, Jesus engages his listeners in a story about a poor widow who has lost everything. Through this story, Jesus encourages his followers to understand and embrace the power of

People really can do the impossible when someone believes that it is possible.

believing in the impossible. Listen to how the Bible records this story. *"Then Jesus told his disciples a parable to show them that they should always pray and not give up. He said: "In a certain town there was a judge who neither feared God nor cared what people thought. And there was a widow in that town who kept coming to him with the plea, 'Grant me justice against my adversary.' "For some time he refused. But finally he said to himself, 'Even though I don't fear God or care what people think, yet because this widow keeps bothering me, I will see that she gets jus-*

tice, so that she won't eventually come and attack me!'" And the Lord said, "Listen to what the unjust judge says. And will not God bring about justice for his chosen ones, who cry out to him day and night? Will he keep putting them off? I tell you, he will see that they get justice, and quickly. However, when the Son of Man comes, will he find faith on the earth?"

The widow in this story had nothing to offer except her ability to believe that God could do the impossible. Every day she went before the judge with the belief that one day, the judge would listen to her request. Daily she asked, and every day she believed. In the end, what once seemed impossible became possible. Through this parable, Jesus reminds every Well Done CEO that what

What seems impossible today can become possible tomorrow when the leader believes it possible.

seems impossible today can become possible tomorrow when the leader believes it possible.

Biblical Business Principle #7: Believe and Ask for the Impossible.

"Jesus looked at them and said, "With man this is impossible, but with God all things are possible." Matthew 19:26

Dream Big Impossible Dreams. Set Huge Impossible Spiritual Goals. Stretch yourself and your team. Find new ways to look at old problems. Embrace belief. Create Win Walls. Pray Big Prayers and Expect Bigger Answers.

When a CEO and business leader embraces this principle, they are released to live the vision that God has given them for their business. After all, God is the God of vision, and He wants His people to be visionary. In his book, Visioneering, megachurch pastor Andy Stanley talks about how if God has a vision for what you are to do with your allotment of years, you had better get in on it.

"What a tragedy to miss it," Stanley says. "Missing out on God's plan for our lives must be the greatest tragedy on this side of eternity. Granted, this world offers a truckload of options when it comes to possible visions to pursue. But you were tailor-made, carefully crafted, minutely detailed for a selected divine agenda.

It is what you were created and re-created for. God's visions for your life are the things that will give your life impact beyond this life."[92]

The fact that God has a plan gives hope and encouragement to every leader. Every day, entrepreneurs and faith-driven leaders face impossible situations in which they need a vision, a plan, or a dream. These leaders have to deal with a variety of conditions that seem impossible to solve from the lens of human thinking. This "impossibility principle" challenges leaders to think more broadly, act more boldly, and believe bigger than if they were only to consider what they are capable of accomplishing.

Jesus's ministry was an example of believing in the impossible. The Redeemer who had been prophesied for generations was upon that generation. While the Israelites believed a Savior would come, they were not sure of the timing. Jesus spent His time on earth trying to convince people to believe that He was the Messiah—the "Chosen One."

Since Jesus knew all that was possible, He taught His disciples to believe in the impossible. It was impossible to think that someone from lowly Nazareth could be the Messiah. The same idea applies to the disciple Peter that he, a fisherman, would preach on Pentecost and save 3,000 souls. The same concept applies to Paul, the greatest persecutor of the early Christians, that he would become the most prolific writer of Scripture, authoring nearly half of the New Testament. No one foresaw that Jesus could take twelve ordinary men and change the world. What was once considered impossible is now eminently believable.

Likewise, in today's business world, it sometimes seems impossible to believe that following God's principles can be profitable: 1) to believe that God has equipped, trained, and commissioned men and women with leadership gifts to make a difference in the **All of these things that once seemed impossible are now possible with God.** marketplace. 2) that thousands of CEOs gather each month to discuss how to apply biblical principles to their business so that in Heaven they can hear the words: Well Done; or 3) that God can use a company for kingdom impact to save thousands of lives. All of these things that once seemed impossible are now possible with God.

Dream Big Impossible Dreams

People prefer to associate with leaders and organizations that embrace big visions. A fatal flaw for leaders that can cost them the trust and commitment of their team is not having a dream or a vision worth working toward or one that can clearly be communicated. David Novak, the former chairman and CEO of YUM Brands, writes about this principle in his book, Taking People with You. Novak sees that one essential element for effective leaders is to ask themselves: What can I do to show people my will to succeed?

"What can I do to inspire in them the same belief that this can be done?" Novak says. "Nobody follows Eeyores. Remember the donkey from Winnie the Pooh who always thought it was going to rain? Imagine him trying to get people on his side and believing they could climb a mountain. People want to follow leaders who believe they are capable of doing great things that ignite that same belief in others. To be that type of leader, you have to choose a 'can-do' mindset."[93]

A passage from Ephesians 3:20,21 is an application of the biblical business principle Jesus taught in Luke 18:27. Ephesians 3:20,21 states that "now to Him who is able to do immeasurably more than all we ask or imagine, according to His power that is at work within us, to Him to glory in the church and in Christ Jesus throughout all generations, forever and ever! Amen." All Well Done leaders should challenge themselves to supersize their thoughts and their beliefs. One example is Bill McDermott, the CEO of SAP, the world's business software leader. In his book, *Winners Dream*, he talks about facing a challenging time when his wife, Julie, was receiving treatments for cancer. McDermott drew inspiration from childhood to meet that challenge: when his younger brother died, his mother told him he would always have a guardian angel on his shoulder.

Ephesians 3:20,21 states that "now to Him who is able to do immeasurably more than all we ask or imagine, according to His power that is at work within us, to Him to glory in the church and in Christ Jesus throughout all generations, forever and ever! Amen."

"And whenever things got a little rough at home or at the deli or at school, she'd remind me, 'Bill, don't worry, you have a guardian angel,'" he writes. "I grew up believing that I did, and over the years, with all the good fortune I'd had, there was a part of me that continued to believe an angel had a least something to do with all of it. At this moment, in the hospital and at work, when I need to stay strong for my family and my company, it feels good to believe in something greater than all of us. So I choose to have faith that Julie will be healthy again, and that there is a reason we are here. I trust in that angel, and myself."[94]

The power to believe in the unseen is a fantastic leadership trait. For many years I have led a workshop on becoming a high performing leader. One thing I ask participants to do is to think of the best leader they know and then write down the person's characteristics or traits. Then, we put all of our lists together to form a more extensive list of the most essential attributes of a leader. These compilations are interesting and insightful.

However, what is left off the typical list is even more intriguing. I have found that through the years, the characteristics that do not make the list of leadership traits are the most important traits to consider. One of the traits often overlooked that pertains to leadership is the ability to dream or imagine.

Dreaming – A Way to Set Better Goals

There are several reasons God asks spiritual leaders to dream. Leaders who practice dreaming will find several benefits for themselves and their teams.

Dreaming helps the leader to set better goals. As Pamela Vaull Starr, a poet and writer who made her mark in the twentieth century, once said, "Reach high, for the stars lie hidden in your soul. Dream deep, for every dream precedes the goal."[95] To set better goals, the leader must dream bigger dreams, and have a burning desire to see the impossible become a reality. CEOs and business owners should consider developing a dream list of impossible things you hope to accomplish during your lifetime.

> **To set better goals, the leader must dream bigger dreams, and have a burning desire to see the impossible become a reality.**

> **Experience Question:** What is the last dream that you remember having? Do you find it easy or difficult to dream about the future of your life and business?

Maybe God has given you the ability to do something that has never been done before. Don't shy away from the impossible.

Moses had an impossible dream that one day his people would be released from slavery; God made that dream a reality.

Nehemiah had an impossible dream that the walls of Jerusalem would be rebuilt; God made that dream a reality.

Abraham had a dream that he would be a father; God not only made that dream reality, but He also supersized it.

Dreaming helps the leader see a brighter future. The best leaders are visionaries who imagine a better future for themselves and their companies. The likes of Steve Jobs and Bill Gates are on a long list of such leaders. One of my favorites is Walt Disney, who once reminded his team: "If you can dream it, you can do it. Remember that this whole thing started with a dream and a mouse."[96] Well Done leaders should always consider what brighter future they are trying to create.

Dreaming helps the leader pursue a bolder potential. Dreaming will bring out the best in a team. Having big dreams will call people to think more creatively, challenge the status quo, and inspire harder work. Dreams call on people to work at their highest level. It is easy for leaders and business owners to settle for a small portion of people's potential. Well Done leaders are called to see bigger and ask for more.

Dreaming helps the leader to serve a bigger cause. One of the reasons dreaming is so important is because it enlarges the leader and prompts them to think larger than themselves. I love to ask leaders: "What if? What if something new could be done? What if you could solve one problem? What if you create this new product?" Every leader

Well Done leaders challenge their people to find solutions instead of making excuses.

should find a quiet place and ask themselves a series of "what if?" questions that are larger than themselves. The best leaders also lead their team through this same exercise. Well Done leaders challenge their people to find solutions instead of making excuses. They lead their team to have big beliefs rather than shrinking to the bare minimum.

Dreaming is hard work. All of us have the potential to dream big dreams. Every person can ask, dream, and imagine a bigger and bolder life. It all starts with dreams. Don't neglect this essential leadership trait. When you dream, you will become a better leader.

Create the HISG - Huge Impossible Spiritual Goals

Many businesses have no higher goal for their business than to just be in business for the next week. An essential part of believing and asking for the impossible is setting goals that seem impossible to reach. For Well Done CEOs, this includes over-arching spiritual goals their businesses can accomplish. Well Done leaders create huge impossible spiritual goals.

Good to Great author Jim Collins wrote about the importance of the BHAG—Big Hairy Audacious Goal—for business.[97] Christian companies should practice the art of the "HISG": Huge Impossible Spiritual Goals. These are the kind that only God can accomplish. Having a vision provided by God and then seeing Him fulfill the vision gives you the freedom to trust God to do the impossible.

A few "HISG" goals that I have seen Christian leaders accomplish include expanding a local business into an international enterprise, seeing a large number of salvations take place in or through the business, and developing of a non-profit ministry to help support a cause that the business owner cares about.

Imagine getting to heaven and standing before the throne of God, and He asks you what goals you set for Him or His kingdom, but all you can recount are business goals you set for yourself. Such a leader would never hear the words Well Done. God wants to reward the courageous in faith who have the desire and ambition to allow Him to do what He alone can do in the business. When a leader makes room for God to show up, He always does.

Imagine getting to heaven and standing before the throne of God, and He asks you what goals you set for Him or His kingdom, but all you can recount are business goals you set for yourself.

Win Activity: HISG: What dreams would you like to accomplish for God through your business if you really believed that everything was possible?

1.

2.

3.

4.

As you pursue these HISGs (Huge Impossible Spiritual Goals), here are some suggestions that may make the path a bit smoother:

Stretch yourself and your team

Huge impossible spiritual goals can be scary. Many leaders shy away from establishing clear goals and key performance indicators for their company. Because they lack a strategy for success, they don't want to face failure.

However, an essential reason a leader should establish such goals is that it stretches them and their team to do more and accomplish more than they could ever do without them. Goals should be established in every area of the business and life. To hear Well Done, a leader must grow in the areas of leadership, followership, energy, health, compass, mind, business, and relationships. If anyone of these is weak, it weakens the leader and causes the organization to leak leaders. Weak leadership will cause the organization to leak leaders.

Weak leadership will cause the organization to leak leaders.

When a leader establishes goals and focuses on them, they will turn into wins. When a leader starts winning, they will focus more on winning, as will their teams. Winning leads to momentum, and momentum leads to success.

Find new ways to look at old problems

CEOs who cover new ground will challenge the team to step outside their comfort zone to find new solutions to old problems. Jesus was the most significant disruptor and innovator of all time.[98] He established new rules, new behaviors, and new values. He went on to teach His team that "no one pours new wine into old wineskins" (Mark 2:22). The best leaders should ask their team to continually explore new solutions, new ideas, and new possibilities. Well Done CEOs and their teams should become the best innovators in every field.

> **Experience Question:** What "What If" question do you need to ask your team to answer?

Each month in the CXP CEO Retreat Guide, I have leaders review a tool called the "Question Quadrant." It is designed for the leader to do an environmental scan on what God is doing in their life or business and what is happening in the world around them. CXP leaders are disciplined to learn how to focus on what is changing in their world and to identify where they have had to stretch themselves to meet the demands of their life or business. When leaders can identify changes that need to be made quicker and faster, they are more equipped to move themselves and their businesses forward compared to a leader who ignores the changes around them. A clueless leader will often fall behind the organization or the leader who sees the change and embraces it.

Learn the "Art of the Ask"

Jesus was a master at asking questions. The reason was to help people look at things in a new way. Jesus wanted people to see what He could see. Leaders who ask questions instead of barking commands will inspire their teams' thinking and engage team members to grow in their belief of the impossible.

In his book, *Good Leaders Ask Great Questions*, leadership expert John Maxwell notes that asking questions is a great way of preventing mental laziness and moving ourselves out of ruts. "If you begin a task with certainties, you will probably end in

Leaders who ask questions instead of barking commands will inspire their teams' thinking and engage team members to grow in their belief of the impossible.

doubts," he advises. "But if you are willing to begin with doubts, you will likely end in certainties. Perhaps that's why someone once said, 'The future belongs to the curious. The ones who are not afraid to try it, explore it, poke at it, and turn it inside out.'"[99]

> **Experience Question:** How can you get better at learning the art of the ask? What questions do you need to be asking in your organization or business?

Create Win Walls

Leaders who lead to Well Done will focus on what is working and will build on the momentum that has been created. CEOs and leaders can often become discouraged and burned out when all they focus on in their organization is what needs to be corrected or fixed. The leader must acknowledge those areas and work to improve the organization, but a leader who leads well will also focus on the successes or "wins" that the organizations have achieved.

Jesus told a compelling story in Luke 17:11-19, in which he healed ten lepers and instructed on the importance of praise and gratefulness. This interaction is an essential story for business owners to read and embrace. Here is how the story is recorded in the Bible: "Now on his way to Jerusalem, Jesus traveled along the border between Samaria and Galilee. As he was going into a village, ten men who had leprosy met him. They stood at a distance. and called out in a loud voice, "Jesus, Master, have pity on us!" When he saw them, he said, "Go, show yourselves to the priests." And as they went, they were cleansed. One of them, when he saw he was healed, came back, praising God in a loud voice. He threw himself at Jesus' feet and thanked him—and he was a Samaritan. Jesus asked, "Were not all ten cleansed? Where are the other nine? Has no one returned to give praise to God except this foreigner?" Then he said to him, "Rise and go; your faith has made you well."

Jesus asked an insightful question to the one leper that returned: "where are the other nine?" The point of this interaction with Jesus is that there is power in praise and wins. Wins build momentum and energy in the life of the leader and in the organization. An important prayer for the leader to pray is the prayer of gratefulness for what the owner of the business and life has done in the life of the business. Well Done CEOs never forget to give praise to the One who does the hard work in the business.

Listen to that question again; where are the other nine? Jesus had just completed the most significant event that would ever happen to them in their lifetime. He had cured them of a disease that had made them outcasts to society and even to their own families. Jesus had healed them of an impossible problem for which there

Jesus likes to celebrate successes and wins.

was no cure or pathway for improvement. I don't think Jesus is frustrated with them for them wanting to see their family or friends; however, I do think that this passage reminds the reader that Jesus is longing for his people to see all the ways He is doing significant things in their life and world. Jesus likes to celebrate successes and wins. Jesus gives victory, and He wants his followers to have grateful and thankful hearts for all that He is doing.

When leaders turn their attention from what needs to be working, to what is working they start to build momentum in their organization. At the CXP CEO Retreats, we help leaders focus on wins through the use of a Win Wall. This wall is an opportunity for a leader to look back over the previous thirty days and write the wins that they or their organizations have received or achieved. When a win is celebrated, it is more likely to be repeated. To stop and focus on what is working can often lead to big breakthroughs. Wins give inspiration and often motivate individuals to vision cast into the future to believe that they can accomplish new wins in the days ahead. Well Done leaders do not forget where their wins come from, and they pause long enough to thank the one that can give new wins in the future. Dreaming leaders are Well Done leaders.

Pray Big Prayers and Expect Bigger Answers

Of all the tasks that steward CEOs engage in daily, one of the most essential is talking with the true Owner of the business. In prayer, the Owner can provide belief, encouragement, wisdom, and direction during all seasons.

Jesus made it a habit of going away by Himself to pray. Mark 1:35 records: "Very early in the morning, while it was still dark, Jesus got up, left the house and went off to a solitary place, where he prayed." If that was true of Him, why should it be any different for any CEO? I have actually found that my business experiences can enhance my spiritual life. More than once, I have been driven to prayer from the situations that I had to face in business.

Knowing how to pray is an important start for effective prayer. The Well Done CEO will focus on prayers that align with the company's purpose and mission. There are a few critical prayers for those who wish to honor God with their business.

A Prayer of Effectiveness: Any reader of the Parable of the Talents can attest that God is concerned with work that produces results. Leaders and CEOs can quickly become distracted with the day's fires and miss out on the work that God has specifically designed for them to complete. The prayer of effectiveness ensures that the leader keeps in mind the most critical tasks and projects that will propel them to hear the words: Well Done, in their business and eternity.

A Prayer of Release: Leaders like to maintain control of all things, but steward leaders understand they have received oversight, not ownership. An important prayer for faith-driven leaders is a prayer of release. It must be prayed often in the life of the business. The model is Christ's prayer in the Garden of Gethsemane, whereas He faced the unimaginable task of going to the cross—He prayed, "not my will, but yours be done." (Luke 22:42)

A Prayer of Favor: Christian businesses have the potential to be the "best in class," whatever the industry or trade. J.C. Penney led his department store chain to become the nation's largest department store chain. Truett Cathy led the Chick-fil-A franchise to become a leader in fast food even though he closed the stores one day a week.[100] Leadership sage Maxwell is a former pastor who has become one of the most widely known in his field. To date, he has written nearly 100 books, which have sold more than twenty million copies and often reach the New York Times bestseller lists.

> **Experience Question:** How do you feel about the favor of God? Have you ever asked God for favor? Why or Why Not?

These are just a few examples of leaders who received favor in their desired field. Jesus makes a powerful statement about the prayer of favor in Matthew

7:11: "If you, then, though you are evil, know how to give good gifts to your children, how much more will your Father in heaven give good gifts to those who ask him!" God is not afraid to give favor to those who are bold enough to ask and trust Him for the gifts that He alone can provide from heaven. Don't be afraid to ask God to expand your company beyond your wildest imagination.

A Prayer of Increased Insight: It takes wisdom to run a business, so another prayer steward CEOs should focus on is asking for knowledge and increased insight in the many decisions that must be made to lead an effective and successful business. As James writes in James 1:5: "If any of you lacks wisdom, you should ask God, who gives generously to all without finding fault, and it will be given to you." God wants his children to seek out His wisdom so they can make better decisions.

Stanley Tam illustrates the truth of this Scripture in his book, God Owns My Business, which is still in print fifty years after its release. He talks of how—when he needed money for U.S. Plastics—he didn't ask God to send down green manna from the skies or for a handout from a well-heeled Christian businessman: "On the contrary, I've asked God to show how I could upgrade the effectiveness of our business operations so we could generate the needed capital. In other words, I have asked Him to illuminate my mind and guide our business decisions, and He has wonderfully answered this kind of prayer thousands of times. My theory is that God has given each of us a brain and expects us to use it. There are laws in business just as in anything else, and if we use our heads in harmony with those laws, we stand a good chance of success."[101]

The business leaders who recognize that they do not know all things, but that they work for the One who does, will take a huge step towards success when they are motivated to tap into that knowledge. Asking questions is an excellent process, and asking the God of wisdom to provide it is always a good prayer.

In his first book, *About My Father's Business*, entrepreneur Regi Campbell—who has been the CEO of four companies—explored how any faith-based person can impact the marketplace through identifying and praying for the people around them. He called it the IMAP grid (where you identify the faith level of every person you influence at work), a tool that will give you a kingdom focus each day. He suggested, before starting the workday, to put your IMAP in front of you and pray for the people on that grid. Whether you pray for them randomly, or the As one day and the Bs the next, is your choice.

"However, praying for the people in your sphere of influence every day is a 'must do,'" Campbell wrote. "Ask, 'Lord, which of these people do I need to pray for today?' And then pay attention to the name or names He draws your eye to. Ask, 'Father, which of these people do I need to touch today?' Be ready to jot down the name He draws your attention to. Ask, 'Lord, what would You have me do for (whomever He has directed your attention to)?' You see, there's a huge difference between coming up with some grandiose plan for leading someone to Christ and this daily approach. That's what being about my Father's business is all about—getting daily orders and following them. One person, one day, one step at a time."[102]

> **Praying for the people in your sphere of influence every day is a 'must do.'**

For every faith-driven leader to hear the words, Well Done, they must be about their Father's business in bringing the people under their care into the knowledge of Jesus and the possibility of salvation. Therefore, one of the essential tasks of any leader is to pray for, and with, their people daily.

In Ephesians 1:17-21, Paul wrote about the idea of perception of this prayer for the church of Ephesus: "I keep asking that the God of our Lord Jesus Christ, the glorious Father, may give you the Spirit of wisdom and revelation, so that you may know him better. I pray that the eyes of your heart may be enlightened so that you may know the hope to which he has called you, the riches of his glorious inheritance in his holy people, and his incomparably great power for us who believe. That power is the same as the mighty strength he exerted when he raised Christ from the dead and seated him at his right hand in the heavenly realms, far above all rule and authority, power and dominion, and every name that is invoked, not only in the present age but also in the one to come."

In other words, Paul was asking God to give the leaders of that generation eyes to see what He wanted them to understand so that they could act like Him. Spiritual leaders in the marketplace must pray for open eyes to see not only the business opportunities that are before them but, even more importantly the spiritual opportunities that will provide an eternal return.

A Prayer of Gratefulness: Leaders can often sabotage their success because they only focus on what is not working in their business. This type of leader spends their time and their energy on putting out fires and fixing problems. Although every Well Done leader will solve problems and fix issues, they understand that they also must focus on the good things that are happening in the business. I like to call these good things wins. When a leader celebrates a win, it is more likely to be repeated. A leader who knows their wins can build energy and excitement and find the momentum that can lead to breakthroughs.

> **When a leader celebrates a win, it is more likely to be repeated.**

> **Experience Question:** Which of the five types of prayer that every leader should pray is the prayer that you need to be praying in this season of your life and business?

One last second step comment:

Too many leaders today think too small. Leaders need to dream big. People can do amazing things when someone believes in them. When a leader believes in the impossible, then all things become possible. Well Done leaders are visionary, and they can see into the possibilities of the future. They know that impossible things can happen because they serve a big God that longs for His people to do things that matter. Sometimes these things can start with simple asks and simple prayers that align the leader's heart and attitude with the One who knows what is really possible. Well Done leaders believe and ask for the impossible.

Best Ideas: Write down two or three best ideas that you heard or learned from this chapter.

WELL
DONE

Chapter 8

BUILD TO THE 4TH GENERATION

Your destiny unfolds in the future,
but it is shaped by the decisions that you make today.

"Therefore everyone who hears these words of mine and puts them into
practice is like a wise man who built his house on the rock. The rain came
down, the streams rose, and the winds blew and beat against that house; yet
it did not fall, because it had its foundation on the rock."
Matthew 7:24-25

Although founder Mary Kay Ash has been dead for nearly two decades, who hasn't heard of Mary Kay®, one of the most ubiquitous cosmetics brands in the world? If you haven't been to a home party, you likely have a spouse who has, or you have at least heard of them. According to the company's website, Mary Kay® products are sold in more than thirty-five markets worldwide by more than 2.4 million independent beauty consultants.

An energetic woman who established her business in an era when few married women with families worked outside the home, Mary Kay built her enterprise on a solid foundation - and she was not shy about sharing the faith that helped build it. As the company's website says:

> "As a committed Christian, Mary's faith was always foremost in her daily life and was the guiding source of wisdom behind her business success: 'My priorities have always been God first, family second, career third. I have found that when I put my life in this order, everything seems to work out. God was my first priority early in my career when I was struggling to make ends meet. Through the failures and success I have experienced since then, my faith has remained unchecked.'"[103]

In a 1997 interview with Religion News Service, Ash attributed her company's tremendous success to the choice to "take God as our partner."[104]

When entrepreneurs and business owners build their businesses with the right perspective—and on a solid set of principles—they are built to stand the test of time. They reflect the character of God, the Creator who helped Adam and Eve form the first business in the Garden of Eden. His ways are better than the world's best thinking. By using His principles, His followers have built nations and thriving organizations and developed innovative products and services. God has made everything and everyone, so He knows how things work best. He knows how to build something that lasts.

God gave insight into this four-generational thinking when He interacted with the people of Israel after their disobedience in building the Golden Calf. The Golden Calf was temporary. It lasted only a few days or possibly months before it was destroyed. The people who built the Golden Calf thought only about their immediate needs. In contrast, God throughout the Bible thought about the coming generations. In Exodus 34:4-7, God speaks these words to his newly formed nation.

"So Moses chiseled out two stone tablets like the first ones and went up Mount Sinai early in the morning, as the Lord had commanded him; and he carried the two stone tablets in his hands. Then the Lord came down in the cloud and stood there

with him and proclaimed his name, the Lord. And he passed in front of Moses, pro-
claiming, 'The Lord, the Lord, the compassionate and gracious God, slow to anger,
abounding in love and faithfulness, maintaining love to thousands, and forgiving
wickedness, rebellion, and sin. Yet he does not leave the guilty unpunished; **he pun-**
ishes the children and their children for the sin of the parents to the third and
fourth generation. *'''*

Catch the vision of what God is doing here. He states that His punishment will continue into the third and fourth generations. In genealogy, the typical generation is a 20 to 25-year time span. Therefore God is saying to His people that He is doing something that could last up to 100 years. Now in contrast, God also reminds His people that His blessings long outlast his punishments. In Deuteronomy 7:9 God gives this promise about His favor, "Know therefore that the Lord your God is God; he is the faithful God, keeping his covenant of love to a thousand generations of those who love him and keep his commandments."

> **"Know therefore that the Lord your God is God; he is the faithful God, keeping his covenant of love to a thousand generations of those who love him and keep his commandments."**

Wow, a thousand generations. God has a long view. A thousand generations could last up to 25,000 years. The point that needs to be made is that God wants people to have a long view.

The Bible mentions this four-generation idea again in the book of Job. In the very last verses of the book, God is renewing his blessing to Job and confirms that Job will have twice as much as he had before he lost everything because of his faithfulness in staying obedient and pure during his most difficult moments. God records these words about the life of Job. "After this, Job lived a hundred and forty years; he saw his children and their children to the fourth generation. And so Job died, an old man and full of years." (Job 42:16,17)

Job had a four-generation blessing. God wanted Job to be able to tell his story to his children and their children to the fourth generation. The Well Done leader is not a short-sighted leader. The Well Done leader is a leader who builds something that can bless future generations. This principle is especially important for business owners since most businesses never make it past the first generation.

The Well Done leader is not a short-sighted leader. The Well Done leader is a leader who builds something that can bless future generations. This principle is especially important for business owners since most businesses never make it past the first generation.

> **Experience Question:** What changes would you make if you made the shift to generational thinking rather than just short-term thinking?

Without a solid foundation, buildings will not stand. The same is true for individuals and companies. Businesses that stand the test of time, despite ever-changing economic cycles and market fluctuations, are worthy of admiration and emulation. CEOs who wish to make a difference should not waste time building things that will not outlive them. Building on the right foundation will help your business endure the storms of market changes, fickle customer tastes, and differing employee expectations. It is only a solid foundation that can last in the midst of changing markets.

Jesus practiced the principle of building something that would long outlast Him. The Lord was not in the "building now and forgetting about tomorrow" mode. Instead, Jesus built on the todays to ensure the tomorrows came. A key to building a great business is to rely on the right foundation so that, amid changing times, the company will continue to stand tall and make an impact for God's kingdom.

Jesus built on the todays to ensure the tomorrows came.

Homebuilders and contractors lay the foundation of a building with the future in mind—not just for the day, but for a multitude of years to come. In the same way, leaders who rely on a solid foundation make decisions today that will make an impact for years to come. In other words, your destiny will unfold in the future, but it is shaped by the decisions you make today. Therefore, to build on a solid foundation so that your business will last, it is best to make decisions today with tomorrow in mind.

Biblical Business Principle #8: Build to the 4th Generation
"Therefore everyone who hears these words of mine and puts them into practice is like a wise man who built his house on the rock. The rain came down, the streams rose, and the winds blew and beat against that house; yet it did not fall, because it had its foundation on the rock."
Matthew 7:24-25

Build on a solid foundation. Prepare for tomorrow by making the right decision today. Become a value-driven organization. Work on big, seven-year-long projects. Commit to strengthening the foundation.

The Parable of the Rock

In Matthew 7, Jesus tells a business parable to His followers. As with all His parables, it contained implications for life and business:

"Therefore everyone who hears these words of mine and puts them into practice is like a wise man who built his house on the rock. The rain came down, the streams rose, and the winds blew and beat against that house; yet it did not fall, because it had its foundation on the rock. But everyone who hears these words of mine and does not put them into practice is like a foolish man who built his house on sand. The rain came down, the streams rose, and the winds blew and beat against that house, and it fell with a great crash" (Matthew 7:24-27).

These words stress the importance of examining the strength of one's foundation. Well Done leaders follow the example of the wise builder who built his house on the rock.

Notice that there are two types of builders in this parable. One builder built on the rock, and the other leader built his house on the sand. Well Done leaders build on a firm foundation, while worldly leaders follow the popular, prevailing theories, the changing sands, or fads of the day and thus build on a faulty foundation. It is not terrible to pursue new ideas or concepts, but they should be measured against principles that have stood the test of time. If a new concept complements an existing standing principle, then it is worth pursuing, but if the new idea goes against what has been proven right, then the organization might be building on a sandy foundation.

Only businesses erected on a solid foundation will last. Every company has an opportunity to build on the right foundation. Companies and leaders can examine the successful organizations and leaders that have spanned the landscape of business over the last two-hundred years and find the commonality of those businesses that have not only lasted but excelled. What I discovered in my examination and study of such leaders is that the ones that have endured for long periods have built on the solid foundation of Christian principles and perspectives.

> **Win Activity: Foundational Principles:** What foundational principles are you building your life and business around, on which you will not compromise? List those principles below.
>
> 1.
>
> 2.
>
> 3.
>
> 4.

Build on a Solid Foundation

Solid foundations are built on principles that are as enduring and strong as a rock. As more than one scholar has observed, the rock analogy is used extensively in the Bible.[105] In Matthew 21:42, Jesus compares Himself to a stone the builders rejected. This parable and the concept of rocks mentioned in Scripture make great guideposts for leaders seeking to build on the right foundation. Rocks have a connotation of strength and steadfastness, which is why, before wise builders proceed, they make sure they are building on a rock-solid foundation.

> **Experience Question:** How would you describe the foundation of your business? What solid biblical principles have you built your business on that you know will stand the test of time?

Well Done leaders follow sound principles. Principles lead to purpose, which, in turn, leads to power. Wise leaders make principled decisions with conviction; the best leaders know who they are and what they believe. Now, both builders in the Matthew 24 parable were decision-makers and capable of building a house. However, one made a decision based on principle, while the other followed perceptions. Principles are always better than the perceptions of the moment since principles have been tested and proven, serving as a type of North Star that guides and directs regardless of the season. As former CEO and Harvard Business School professor Bill George says in his book, True North: "Anyone who follows their internal compass can become an authentic leader."[106]

Well Done leaders continue leading with persistence. Since rocks are hard, the house with its foundation on rock withstood the storms of rain, floods, and winds. The house built on a foundation of sand fell when it was inundated with storms. Some things are destined to stand, and some things are destined to fall. Those things built on a solid foundation will stand the test of time. Even in the worst of storms, the house built on rock will stand.

Many storms face a Christian leader, but none are too big for the Well Done leader to overcome and withstand. Jesus tells this story to His disciples because He wants His followers to demonstrate the kind of intelligence that can withstand difficult, stressful situations. The leader who has made decisions based on rock-solid principles can stand tall even in the worst of storms.

Well Done leaders lead by developing and preparing strong plans. General Dwight D. Eisenhower, whose World War II success led him to the presidency, once said: "In preparing for battle I have always found that plans are useless, but planning is indispensable."[107] Great plans lead to great growth. Unfortunately, many businesses have no grander plans than to stay open until tomorrow. One of the leaders in this parable planned ahead by looking past the current situation to anticipate changing weather patterns. Jesus is reminding His listeners to trust God with their plans and measure them against the principles God has given to move them in the right direction. To move forward successfully, the wise leader spends time

Many businesses have no grander plans than to stay open until tomorrow.

planning what the future will look like, so they are prepared when opportunities present themselves.

The theme of planning resonates through God's Word. Note the clarification that Jesus gives to His disciples at the beginning of Matthew 7:24 about those who are wise: "Everyone then who hears these words of mine and puts them into practice." In other words, people who do them. Those two words are essential for success; not everyone who listens to this parable is wise. Not every leader leads with wisdom. The wise builder is one who not only hears the words, but puts them into action. The wise leader makes good plans and then diligently carries them out. The wise leader practices the principles that make a difference, following good habits and making good choices that will make a difference today and tomorrow.

> **The wise leader practices the principles that make a difference, following good habits and making good choices that will make a difference today and tomorrow.**

Companies that put this principle into application like ServiceMaster, which has now been in business for over 90 years, will build on a solid foundation. According to its website, ServiceMaster was founded as a moth-proofing company in 1929 by Marion E. Wade, a former minor league baseball player. Wade, who operated his new business out of his home, had a strong personal faith and viewed individual employees and customers as worthy of dignity and respect. Based on the foundational principles of its owner, the company has gone on to achieve both growth and success.

Prepare for Tomorrow

Don't waste time building things that won't stand the test of time. Building on the right foundation will help your business withstand the storms of market changes.

Godly things last. Every business has a life cycle, with a certain number of days or years it is designed to last. According to the Small Business Administration: "More than half of small businesses survive for five or more years, and about a third of them survive for more than ten years."[108]

Experience Question: How long is your vision? What would your company look like if you looked an extra seven years ahead?

However, in God's scheme of things, such enterprises are meant to last longer. Too many companies only exist for the short-term, with no long-term plan in mind. Kingdom companies build for today with tomorrow in mind. As a futurist, Jesus is calling all steward leaders to lead with the future in mind. He made decisions that impacted everyone's tomorrows, especially the one to go to the cross—a decision that had many tomorrows in mind.

In the same way, CEOs should seek to lead a value-driven business, where they reach decisions based on their core values, and with tomorrow in mind. As various experts remind us: Having ethical values in business is key to creating a successful organization. Having a good sense of values will help the leader and everyone throughout the organization make better decisions.[109]

Staying true to the core values of the organization will help the organization, and its people remain faithful to the founder's purpose.[110] Every company should measure its success by its progress toward faithfully fulfilling the organization's fundamental values and mission.

Become a Values-Driven Organization

A key to building a great business is to act with integrity—doing the right thing at all times—in all situations. Faith-driven leaders can find inspiration for such a stance in Proverbs: "Let your eyes look straight ahead; fix your gaze directly before you. Give careful thought to the paths for your feet and be steadfast in all your ways. Do not turn to the right or the left; keep your foot from evil." (Proverbs 4:25-27) Businesses that demonstrate integrity are built on the type of solid foundation that will last for generations. Companies that lack this are built on slippery ground that can crumble at any time, which is why we have seen high-flying, multi-million-dollar corporations suddenly crash into bankruptcy.

The right decision is always right. When a company makes a series of right decisions, it has a better chance of succeeding in this generation, as well as making it to the next, and the next after that. Decisions made with only short-term thinking in mind often lead to a short lifespan. Values-based decisions help a company endure. They demonstrate the kind of light that Jesus said His followers should be in the world:

"You are the light of the world. A town built on a hill cannot be hidden. Neither do people light a lamp and put it under a bowl. Instead, they put it on its stand, and it gives light to everyone in the house. In the same way, let your light shine before others, that they may see your good deeds and glorify your Father in heaven." (Matthew 5:14-16)

Well Done leaders know that the right foundation is vital to success in this world and is of significance in the world to come. Christian principles and values form a stable platform on which to build a business. The tallest buildings have the strongest foundations. Principles taught in the Bible have stood the test of time; Christian companies and non-Christian companies have proved this alike.

> **The tallest buildings have the strongest foundations.**

Many consumers in America respond well to Christian businesses and Christian business principles; a 2011 survey by the Barna Group reported "that 43 percent of consumers would be more likely to buy from a particular brand if it was managed according to Christian principles. Thirty-seven percent said they would be more likely to buy from a particular brand if it embraces and promotes the Christian faith. Only 3 percent of respondents in each question said that they would be less likely to support the brand."[111]

Glorifying God Through Business

Businesses can move to a new level of business success and kingdom impact when Christian CEOs and leaders teach their employees how to embody principles of faith and Christianity in their work. Well Done CEOs understand the value of Christian principles, and they are not afraid to share with their team principles that work in both life and business. In October of 2018, the Barna Group released a study of what faith looks like in the workplace. It reported that "encouragingly, working Christians say they hold to standards and virtues of professional integrity that represent the Church well. They are rooted in a conviction that Christians should act ethically (82 percent), speak the truth (74 percent), and demonstrate morality (72 percent). On an even more spiritual level, respondents say working Christians should make friends with non-Christians (66 percent), withstand temptation (59 percent) and do excellent work in an effort to bring glory to God (58 percent)."[112]

Christian workers should be the highest performing workers in the marketplace because they embody the values and principles of success and significance. Further, non-believers who embrace biblical business principles can work at a high level, even if they don't understand where the values they embrace originate. CEOs and business leaders who wish to help their employees both at work and in life will become serious about giving their team members the education of values that will help them to perform better in their current occupation and then in any further occupation that they endeavor as they go through their life. The CEO or leader that neglects to teach Godly values to their team members will not glorify God in and through their business.

> **Experience Question:** When are you most tempted to compromise your integrity in making decisions in your business?

Many successful businesses have been built on Christian principles. Well Done leaders who embody Christian values and concepts make better decisions, engender lasting relationships, and inspire higher levels of trust among team members and vendors. Christian principles work, and more businesses would experience higher levels of growth if all their employees understood and embraced biblical business principles as they fulfill their responsibilities in the workplace.

> **Experience Question:** Would you say that all of your employees act in alignment with the core values of the organization?

Work on Seven-Year Projects

Building on a solid foundation today means having the opportunity to build again tomorrow. One way to embody building on a solid foundation is to practice building long-term projects that take a long period of time to complete. One way to communicate this idea is to work on seven-year projects.

Although seven-year projects are challenging for leaders and organizations to commit to, every leader should consider them. Prolonged projects can pro-

Prolonged projects can provide powerful payoffs.

vide powerful payoffs. When a company can select the right project in which to invest time, resources, and manpower, the payoff is that the investment will propel the company to become a leader in its field - the kind that becomes known as a differentiator in the marketplace. Companies that commit to prolonged projects can realize several key benefits, even if the project is a failure.

Seven-Year Projects Help Leaders and Companies Become Resilient

Persistence and commitment are vital to building a successful company. Most companies become successful through prolonged hard work and discipline as they focus on the right habits. There are few overnight successes.[113] Companies benefit when they develop the muscle of persistence through resilience. Prolonged commitment to a seven-year project in one area of a business can help the leader build persistence in many areas of the company. Extended projects help organizations become persistent organizations.

Seven-year projects help leaders and companies find a variety of solutions that can lead to new and better products

When organizations focus on solving a problem, they discover that in looking for one solution, they often find many answers. Long-term projects help companies to practice finding and implementing many possible solutions. Inventors and creators whom breakthrough to become highly successful often expend tremendous energy in research and development before they develop the solution that leaves a lasting legacy. A long-term project can help teams and leaders learn valuable lessons and find many solutions to a problem, which can lead the team to discover a critical solution: the kind of solution that will lead to peer or customer recognition. Many solutions lead to finding the main solution.

Adam Grant discusses this idea at length in his best-selling book, *Originals*. In the chapter titled, "Blind Inventions and One-Eyed Investors," he writes this about the power of practice for finding original ideas: "If originals aren't reliable judges of the quality of their ideas, how do they maximize their odds of creating a mas- **Many solutions lead** terpiece? They come up with a large number **to finding the main** of ideas. Dean Simonton, Professor of Psy- **solution.** chology at UC-Davis, finds that on average, creative geniuses weren't qualitatively better in their fields than their peers. They simply produced a greater volume of work, which gave them more variation and a higher chance of originality."[114]

Imagine a world where the masterpieces of the greatest inventors did not exist. If the genius inventor had given up after just a few attempts, the world would be a lesser place. God challenges steward CEOs to be focused on long-term projects that provide long-term value.

Seven-Year Projects Challenge the Company to Develop Products of Value

Quick solutions and products are not always the best ones. Architect Frank Lloyd Wright gives excellent insight into this truth in his statement: "You can use an eraser on the drafting table or a sledgehammer on the construction site."[115] Author and therapist Wayne Muller, who founded "Bread for the Journey"—a network of grassroots community development philanthropists—echoes this thought: "In the soil of the quick fix is the seed of a new problem because our quiet wisdom is not available."[116] Prolonged projects challenge team members to use their most creative and outside-the-box thinking. Best-thinking practices often lead to better products. When companies only engage in short-term thinking or quick solutions, they rob themselves of their full potential and the potential of developing products built with longevity and excellence in mind.

Seven-Year Projects Change the Focus from "Yes" to "No"

Great companies get great at saying, "no." When companies have decided on their "yes" projects, it helps them develop the discipline of saying, "no." To focus on a prolonged project, project owners and leaders must develop the discipline of rejecting potential distractions. A long-term project that is clearly designed, and

An extended focus can help to produce better products and solutions.

one in which the team is highly engaged, leads to a prolonged focus. An extended focus can help to produce better products and solutions.

The leader of an organization is tasked with setting a vision and placing a premium on the right projects and priorities. Leaders who work hard on the right projects help lead good companies to great success. The leader who never settles on the right priorities never receives the benefit of prolonged projects. Every leader should consider the size of their projects and whether the project is significant enough to inspire and motivate the team for an extended period of time. The right project in the hands of the right people can provide value to the company for many years.

> **Experience Question:** What seven-year projects are you working on in your business? What benefits can you see for your company if you would commit to longer projects?

Strengthening the Four Foundations of a Business

I encourage CEOs to take quarterly retreats to examine the four fundamental foundations of their business: 1) vision, 2) business strategy, 3) business operations, and 4) kingdom impact. These four areas are essential to building a successful organization for the long haul. It is the leader's primary responsibility to measure success in each of these four areas and to ensure that the team that follows them has the tools necessary to further expand upon the leader's strategy and goals.

1. **Vision: (This Answers the Question of: Where to)**

Vision is not only knowing where you are going, but also understanding why you want to go in that direction in the first place. Leaders are measured by their vision and how well they communicate that vision to others. A vision must be revisited frequently to ensure the organization is moving in the right direction. Every leader must communicate with clarity, where the organization is going, and why it is going in that direction.

Jesus had a very clear vision of what He had to do, and when it had to be done. His followers were able to follow Him because they knew where He was going and the values that He upheld. When the leader is filled with a vision, it engenders inspiration from the followers. Well Done leaders have a clear vision, and they walk towards their vision.

Every year leaders should set aside time to recapture their purpose and to make sure that they have clarity on where their vision is taking the organization. A leader's personal vision can help to shape the vision of the organization. When the leader becomes clear, everything in the organization will become clear. Well Done leaders become clear about their vision so that they can drive clarity in those they lead.

2. **Business Strategy: (This Answers the Question of: What's Next)**

Businesses with high integrity are built on a solid foundation; people like doing business with companies they can trust. Employees like following leaders they can believe in and in whom they can place their confidence. A solid foundation in business is essential for long-term success. Employees must act with integrity and always do what is in the best interests of the company they serve. Leaders should lead in such a way that it inspires their teams because they lead with compassion and honesty. As Proverbs 11:3 says: "The integrity of the upright guides them, but the unfaithful are destroyed by their duplicity."

One way that businesses that hope to last should strengthen their foundation is through recruiting and hiring well.[117] Companies that hire well, focus on both the effectiveness and the integrity of an individual. Every Well Done leader should look to attract competent, talented individuals who possess high integrity.

3. **Business Operations: (This Answers the Question of: What Is)**

Focusing on the fundamentals can prove beneficial and essential to more significant growth and strategic planning. Having ethical values in business is key to building a successful organization. A good sense of values will help the leader and everyone throughout the organization to make better decisions. Staying true to the organization's core values will help the organization and help its people remain faithful to the founder's purpose. Every company should measure its success on the fundamentals of its values.

Integrity means that we know the truth and act accordingly. Leaders with high integrity are not afraid of the truth. Instead, they allow it to guide their decisions and outcomes. Businesses with high integrity act with truthfulness in all interactions with customers, suppliers, and peers. Leaders are called to see and know what is really happening in the business. Aloof leaders, or leaders who turn their heads to avoid knowing what is really happening with their products, employees, or customers, will never build a successful company.

4. Kingdom Impact: (This Answers the Question of: What Endures)

One pillar for companies to examine is the impact they are making in their community and in the lives of their employees and customers. Well Done leaders should always consider a review of their company's kingdom impact. It would be a terrible thing for a Christian CEO to build a great company that lasts for hundreds of years, but when they get to Heaven find they made little impact on the kingdom of God. Christian companies must do better. If non-Christian companies can work to improve the environment, participate in community causes, and impact otherworldly issues, how much more should that inspire the faith-driven leader to strive to make an impact for the kingdom of God?

One last second step comment:

The question for every leader to examine is: On what foundation are you building your business? Companies must examine the core values of the organization and establish a healthy company culture where honesty and integrity are both elevated and practiced in daily decisions. It is a beautiful thing when a leader leads a company with integrity and a strong moral compass. However, one person with integrity does not ensure the success of an entire enterprise. For companies to endure, the leader with integrity must inspire others to follow a clear set of values that penetrate every aspect of the business and that are supported in every decision that is made throughout the organization.

Only companies built on a solid foundation will stand the test of time. Well Done leaders should have a vision of creating an organization that lasts at least one hundred years. A long view by the leader will help to blunt a short-term decision made by the team. When companies last and grow because they have been built well, they reflect the glory of God. I pray that every Well Done leader and entrepreneur will have the vision to create something of significance that lasts for generations. The organization that is built well is one way for the leader to hear the words Well Done. Well Done leaders work to build their organization to the 4th generation.

Best Ideas: Write down two or three best ideas that you heard or learned from this chapter.

WELL DONE

Part III
The Practices of Jesus

Chapter 9

KNOW THE ORDER OF THINGS
AND WORK THE ORDER

When a leader understands the order of things,
things become easier to understand.

"But seek first his kingdom and his righteousness,
and all these things will be given to you as well."
Matthew 6:33

I began this book with a review of Chick-fil-A and its explosive growth in the past dozen years. To recap, it has tripled in size, to become one of the nation's largest fast-food chains, and created a loyal customer base thanks to its Second Mile customer service and its policy of living out founder Truett Cathy's biblical beliefs in actions as well as words.

That is the shorthand version of its success. The path to success has been paved with obstacles, setbacks, and vociferous criticism by those who don't like the company's core values. Chick-fil-A may be one of the country's most profitable enterprises, but nearly forty years ago, it went through some serious financial challenges. The problems sent directors into an extended conference to determine what this business was all about—its primary reason for existence.

Former chief marketing officer Steve Robinson, who now runs his own consulting business, recalls this time of great clarity in *Covert Cows and Chick-fil-A*. In his memoir about his thirty-four years with the chicken chain, Robinson tells of executives having to determine their order of things. At the end of two days of intense discussion and multiple drafts, debate, and prayer, the group had written a purpose statement to express the reason for their existence: To glorify God by being a faithful steward of all that is entrusted to us and to have a positive influence on all who come in contact with Chick-fil-A.

"The Holy Spirit had orchestrated something we had not even planned to do," Robinson writes. "We had captured in words how Truett had already been leading the business. We all had been attempting to live his model, and now we had a statement to help us and those who followed us. We were not a 'Christian business,' but rather a business where owners and leadership aspired to apply and live out biblical principles. In 1982, at our moment of deepest financial crises, we stepped back and determined why Chick-fil-A existed. We embraced that purpose and were sobered by it. We were all a part of leading a unique business, to say the least."[118]

Amid a difficult and trying time, Chick-fil-A found their order of things, and began to work their order which helped them to not only endure during the problematic moment but to strive after the moment had passed. It is essential for any leader who seeks to hear the words Well Done to press into knowing their order and working their order so that they ensure that they are doing the right things when the right things are to be done.

Win Activity: Knowing Your Order: Think of something in your life that is unclear. What would be your order of importance to defining clarity?

1.

2.

3.

4.

Seeking God First

Jesus had the practice of knowing His order and working His order. In Matthew 6:33, Jesus gave His followers a critical principle to follow when He said, "But seek first his Kingdom and his righteousness, and all these things will be given to you as well."

Jesus was reminding his followers of their first priorities. He understands that it is easy to confuse order and become distracted by things that are urgent at the moment but not essential for long-term success. One mistake that many leaders and CEOs make is becoming confused about the proper order of activities and tasks to move the business forward.

The first three words of Matthew 6:33 are quite instructive: "But seek first." An essential business-leadership practice is to focus on the crucial things that are often deemed "first things." When a leader knows what is first, they can determine and begin to work the order of other things. When a leader understands the order of things, things become easier to understand.

When a leader understands the order of things, things become easier to understand.

Therefore, Well Done leaders do not become confused about the order of things. They know what is first, and they allow what is first to take priority in their lives and in their businesses.

> **Experience Question:** Matthew 6:33 reminds Well Done leaders to seek first God's Kingdom. How could you acknowledge God and His Kingdom more in your life and business?

Order is important. Jesus never wavered on the order of things. He knew that which was most important. Jesus knew His mission, and He knew what He needed to accomplish and when He needed to have it accomplished. As a result, He knew how to place actions, priorities, decisions, and tasks in an order that helped Him to fulfill His ultimate purpose. Jesus was driven by passion and was able to get things done. He preached, healed, debated, and trained all on His mission because He knew His order of importance each day that He lived.

Order is important. Jesus never wavered on the order of things.

Many businesses become confused about the order of things because they do not have a leader who knows the order or will communicate how to work the order for the success of the business. Successful businesses find innovative and creative ways to communicate the order of importance in their company. Mission BBQ is one example of how a smart company reminds both customers and employees of their order as an organization. Founders Bill Kraus and Steve "Newt" Newton named their BBQ franchise Mission BBQ because they had a mission to honor the military and the values of the country. A unique way that they remind their teams and customers about the order of their organization is at noon, each and every location has every employee and customer stand and sing the National Anthem. This one act, which happens daily, reminds everyone who enters this company about the order of why this company was founded and what is important to them as they seek to expand and grow.

Jesus never wanted his followers to forget their order. Jesus would later explain, in Luke 14:25-33, an essential application of knowing the order of things and working that order. He used a business story to highlight the art of discipleship, one that taught His followers that He and God's kingdom must come first on their priority list. This passage reads:

"Large crowds were traveling with Jesus, and turning to them he said: 'If anyone comes to me and does not hate father and mother, wife and children, brothers and sisters—yes, even their own life—such a person cannot be my disciple. And whoever does not carry their cross and follow me cannot be my disciple. Suppose one of you wants to build a tower. Won't you first sit down and estimate the cost to see if you have enough money to complete it? For if you lay the foundation and are not able to finish

it, everyone who sees it will ridicule you, saying, 'This person began to build and wasn't able to finish.' Or suppose a king is about to go to war against another king. Won't he first sit down and consider whether he is able with ten thousand men to oppose the one coming against him with twenty thousand? If he is not able, he will send a delegation while the other is still a long way off and will ask for terms of peace. In the same way, those of you who do not give up everything you have cannot be my disciples."

This parable is about a lifetime commitment to Jesus. Jesus is reminding His followers that it is of no benefit in starting a relationship with Him if they are not willing to be committed to Him for a lifetime. This parable also has many applications to business, but one of the most essential is the importance of making an order of things that can easily become disordered.

It is not good business to start a project that you could not finish. Likewise, it is not wise to start acting or producing when you have no way of determining what the process is and how the process is completed. The Bible gives clarity to how God sees the order of things. His order must be followed to ensure success.

Experience Question: How would you describe first things versus second things?

Four First-Things for Business

1. God Should Always Come First

The encouragement of Matthew 6:33 is to seek God and His kingdom, above all else. God promises when you honor Him first, He will not hold back on all the things that you need. A promise that any Well Done leader can count on is that by giving up, you get ahead. When you release control of your life and business to God, God will walk with you each step of the way—and through each decision you make. Christian companies should put God first in how they conduct their business, how they treat their customers, and the quality they use to build their products or offer their services. God should be able to look into any business and be pleased with the work that is conducted there.

> **God should be able to look into any business and be pleased with the work that is conducted there.**

2. Your Family Should Know They are More Important than Your Business

Many families of business owners suffer because the business takes priority over everything. Nearly fifty years ago, Harry Levinson—then a clinical professor of psychology in the department of psychiatry at Harvard Medical School—wrote an article for the Harvard Business Review discussing conflicts in family business-es.[119] That article has been reprinted multiple times because the conflicts that he discussed in 1971 are the same issues that families deal with today. The rest of the family often feels neglected by their leader and left out in comparison to the business. A business owner should always convey to their family that the family is more important than their work. When that order gets confused, life simply begins to fall apart.

For years, I have taught leaders and CEOs to treat their spouses and families with the same care they would their most important customer. I tell every CEO with whom I work: "My wife is my number one customer because she will be with me for fifty years. She has the authority to cancel any meeting at any time. I will answer every call from my wife, no matter who else I am meeting with or what else I am doing." I never want my wife to doubt her place in my life—a model I believe is good for other CEOs and leaders to follow.[120] Likewise, families should always rank above the business, never doubting your order of what is most important.

3. Without Your Customers, You Do Not Have a Business

Customers are essential to a business' success and sustainability. In the modern era, I think many businesses have forgotten this fundamental principle. Companies once believed and taught that the customer is always right. Today, it is still essential to train every employee in the necessity of serving customers and practicing the Golden Rule in relationships. Businesses should make it a priority to love their customers and serve them passionately. Says Harvey Mackay, the founder of Mackay Mitchell Enterprises, said: "No business can stay in business without customers. How you treat—or mistreat—them determines how long your doors stay open."[121] Customers should always be the first thing for businesses and business leaders.

4. The Business Needs to be Bigger than the Steward of the Business

Many businesses aren't any bigger than the leader, and as a result, they get in trouble. If everything in the company is dependent on the owner, when the owner stops doing those things, the business stops. Well Done leaders build companies that can continue even when the leader is not able to continue. Companies should be better when the leader is involved in the business, but businesses should be able to continue to perform even when the leader is not in the company.

Consultant John Burley, whose firm advises companies on strategic growth planning, mergers and acquisitions, and other

Companies should be better when the leader is involved in the business, but businesses should be able to continue to perform even when the leader is not in the company.

matters, addressed the topic of building a business that is bigger than one person in an article for Inc. magazine.

"If the customer 'feels like' they are doing business with the owner, then does the business really have any customers at all?" Burley asked. "That's a strong statement, but when buying a small business, you are often buying the business's ability to produce a certain amount of cash flow in the future. If the owner is gone and all the customers were doing business with the owner, can you really count on that future cash flow? Here's the challenge to overcome. Most small businesses are successful because of a successful entrepreneur. When you talk to the customers they don't say, 'I use ABC company down the street' they say, 'I got a guy who handles that.' Their guy might be the CEO of the company that's actually servicing them, but in their mind, it's 'I use Bob, he's great.' The problem is, nobody wants to buy Bob."[122]

Successful companies must be built bigger than the owner if they hope to succeed and overcome the "Bob" problem. Every successful business is built in such a way that it is larger than one person. Business owners need to develop their business so that they can go away when necessary to get vision, insight, and direction, and still have a business to continue to grow and develop.

Steven Covey teaches this principle in his best-selling *Seven Habits of Highly Effective People*, which is still in print after more than thirty years. He writes that effective management is putting first things first. While leadership decides what "first things" are, it is management that puts them first, day-by-day, moment-by-moment. Covey says: "Management is discipline carrying it out. Discipline derives from disciple–disciple to a philosophy, disciple to a set of principles, disciple to a set of values, disciple to an overriding purpose, to a superordinate goal or a person who represents that goal."[123] Indeed, focusing on the right things in business is a key to success. Understanding transformational biblical business principles that help to build a significant business is the first step towards knowing the order of things.

Biblical Business Principle #9: Know the Order of Things and Work the Order

"But seek first his kingdom and his righteousness, and all these things will be given to you as well." Matthew 6:33

Strive for clarity. Seek first the principles of God and His kingdom. Know your priorities. End Second Things. Build Great Processes. Practice the art of first fruits in all aspects of your life and leadership.

Strive for Clarity

When the leader is clear, everyone and everything in the organization becomes clear. The fundamental flaw of troubled leaders is a lack of clarity, which fosters uncertainty. Well Done Leaders must be clear about what success looks like, both for the organization and for every person who works in the company. The clearer the leader can be about where they are going and the dreams they hope to accomplish, the more power and influence they achieve. They will gather people around them to help accomplish their mission and purpose. However, those leaders who lack clarity will always struggle to gather influence and effectiveness.

When the leader is clear, everyone and everything in the organization becomes clear.

The best way for a leader to gain clarity is through embarking on a retreat. It is only when a leader can step away from the business that they can see the business with a clear set of eyes. Leaders that never stop to consider where they are going continue to lead the way they have been going, whether it leads them to where they want to go or not. The very first act in the ministry of Jesus was when Jesus stepped into the wilderness for forty days to connect with God and to clarify the order of His ministry.

Seek First God's Principles

Jesus encourages steward leaders to practice God's thinking in every area of life, and that includes their business. God's principles are good principles, ones that stand the test of time. They prove beneficial in multiple situations and with all kinds and types of leaders. Since God's biblical business principles have been verified and tested, many successful CEOs and companies have used these principles to grow thriving enterprises.

God's principles are good principles.

> **Experience Question:** What godly principles do you believe are essential to your success in life and business?

Order can lead to success. When you know what your order is, it empowers you to work with focus and energy, elevating the most important tasks to the right order. Well Done leaders are clear about their priorities and know how to make difficult decisions in trying times to set their business up for success. Clarity is essential for good leadership.

J.C. Penney used the Golden Rule to build the largest department store chain in the world. Truett Cathy used the Second Mile Mentality to grow a fast-food chain to the third-largest fast-food chain, even though Chick-fil-A generates its profits in six days instead of seven. David Green, the CEO of Hobby Lobby, stood on his principles of knowing the order of things as he decided to honor God with His business despite facing overwhelming pressure from the world to "fit in" and go along with politically-correct ideologies. Stanley Tam used the principle of moving from owner to overseer as he was the first CEO who released ownership of his company to God.

In the parable of the builder, the builder who doesn't finish the task is not a Well Done leader. Jesus points to the ineffectiveness of the leader who starts a project without being able to finish it. The leader who starts but cannot complete is not clear on the order of things and how things must be done. This kind of leader never sat down to consider and examine the entire project to understand if they could see it through to completion. Every project has a process, and the wise builder will know the steps of the process to ensure that the project will be complete and successful. They can communicate the steps clearly, and they get buy-in from their team to do the steps and tasks in order to bring the project to a successful conclusion.

Second Things Must Never Become First Things

Leaders must put an end to second things. The idea of knowing your order and working your order has proven dependable and beneficial for leaders of every generation. Leaders often struggle with deciding on what items are the most important. Many days in the life of a leader, the urgent takes priority over the planned. Leaders can be swayed to focus their attention based on the immediate needs of their teams. Although it is always important to be responsive to them, the leader must never forget to focus on what they believe will move the organization forward.

Management consultant and best-selling author Peter Drucker addresses the necessity of keeping priorities in order in his influential tome to leaders, *The Effective Executive*, writing: "Effective executives know that they have to get many things done—and done effectively. Therefore, they concentrate—their own time and energy as well as that of their organization—on doing one thing at a time, and on doing first things first."[124]

Because of this tug of war, Well Done CEOs would do well to remember Ephesians 2:10, "For we are God's handiwork, created in Christ Jesus to do good works, which God prepared in advance for us to do." In this verse, the apostle Paul reminds his readers of the importance of their calling. Paul states that God has a plan that He is working out in their life and that He goes before them to create works that He wants them to accomplish. God's desire for busy executives is not that we are so busy that we miss out on the joys of life. Jesus had the potential to be the most active person who ever walked on the face of the earth, and yet He never hurried. He was precisely where He was needed, when He was needed, and did what He was required

> **For we are God's handiwork, created in Christ Jesus to do good works, which God prepared in advance for us to do.**

to do. Could it be that as leaders, many get exhausted not because they have too much to do, but because they have never discovered their primary calling and focus in life? Exhausted leaders usually are ones that have never identified or committed to knowing their order and working their order.

Second Things that Often Become First Things

A place to start for each leader is to discover your "second things" which are those tasks and responsibilities that are important, but not essential. First, let's define the term "second things." As we begin to understand what takes priority in your life and business, you must have a boundary to delineate the leading priorities versus those things that rate lower. "Second Things" can be defined as activities that do not support the betterment of the mission of the organization or your calling as a leader. "Second Things" are activities, decisions, and tasks that confuse a leader from knowing and working on the first things of a business. "Second Things" are not necessarily bad or wrong things; they are just not "First Things."

Leaders are called to push the organization forward. Leaders have the responsibility to focus all of their energy and efforts on the tasks that will make a difference for the organization. Many times these are the things in the organization that only a leader can do. These tasks cannot be delegated. Great leaders understand the difference between being busy and being productive. They are keenly aware of both their own personal mission statement and how their personal calling and gifts should be used to enhance the performance of the organization they have been called to lead.[125] Second things can become first things too quickly, which is why CEO Experience offers an annual Vision Masterplan for CEOs, helping them clarify what specifically they are called to accomplish in the year ahead to move their organizations forward. To further define this:

Second Things are actions that serve no purpose in elevating the organization's values.

Deliberate actions are critical to a leader's success. Far too many leaders get frantically stressed because they spend all day trying to solve others' problems instead of focusing on elevating their own organization's potential. Leaders must be adamant about setting healthy boundaries around their time and energy. Leading an organization is too important to waste time on things that have little impact or benefit.

Second Things are alignments you make with others because you want them to like you, but they serve no purpose for the greater good.

Business owners and CEOs are often sought after to help guide community organizations. This flood of requests for help isn't minutiae. After all, good leaders are committed to helping their communities. However, Well Done leaders don't just automatically commit to something without a more significant cause that is motivating them.

"Second Things" are agreements that should not have been given in the first place.

In an article for *Forbes*, career coach Ashley Stahl outlines three reasons to say, "No" more often, commenting that successful people know how to do just that. She writes that "saying yes to others can have a powerful impact on your career, your reputation, your professional growth—but saying no—especially when it's uncomfortable to do so—is one of the most powerful steps you can take in your personal growth."[126] Many leaders have to learn to say "No" after they have experienced the damaging effects of always saying "Yes." Indeed, science is now showing that saying "No" improves productivity and mental health.[127]

Many leaders can get overextended and overcommitted because they have a heart that desires to help. However, the most helpful thing is to be focused and to commit only to those things that the leader can excel at completing. Well Done Leaders should examine their choices and behaviors to ensure that they are not involved in second things. When a leader becomes unfocused and unclear, the organization will do the same.

> **Experience Question:** What boundaries could you establish around second things so that they never become the first things in your organization?

Build Great Processes

Well Done Leadership is about first things: priority points that leaders can leverage to help the organization achieve breakthroughs.

Every business would like to be profitable. As Peter Drucker once said: "Profit for a company is like oxygen for a person. If you don't have enough of it, you're out of the game. But if you think your life is about breathing, you're really missing something."[128] In other words, Drucker is suggesting that a great company needs profit, but business is not just about making a profit.

> **Experience Question:** What processes in your business need better organization or clarification in order to be accepted and embraced by all employees?

Unfortunately, in today's business climate, it is not easy for companies to make a profit. One business owner I work with once quipped when someone asked what he did for a living: "I run a great business, but for three years I ran a nonprofit and did not know it."

That is why the first fundamental in business includes building reliable processes to ensure profitability. The key to profitability lies within a business's core processes." After years of working with business owners, I have discovered that profitable enterprises embrace five fundamental processes.

> **The key to profitability lies within a business's core processes.**

1. **An Effective sales process**

The number one critical process of every business is the sales process. Many companies create excellent products but have no idea how to sell. Sales is an essential part of the success of any business. The sales process should include answers to fundamental questions:

- Who is our ideal customer?
- What are the critical sales steps from introduction to close?
- How long does the typical sales cycle take?
- What is the usual sales amount?

2. **An Engaged customer experience process**

Smart companies focus on profit plus customer experience. Good leaders develop an engaging and inviting customer experience. Great customer experiences will bring repeat customers, which is necessary to create a sustainable business. One simple starting point is to identify your Net Promoter Score. A Net Promoter Score is a business survey that gauges the level of customer satisfaction with a company after a customer experience. Customers will receive a number on a scale of one to ten, with the number signifying those who promote the business through referrals to a detractor of the company who tells others not to do business with the organization.

3. An Equipping training process

Since the market is always changing, smart companies become learning companies. Companies that are going to lead into tomorrow will focus on developing and equipping their team today. In a 2015 survey by the Human Capital Institute, 74 percent of companies noted that creating a learning culture was an upcoming priority.[129] This survey points to the fact that growth-minded business owners understand the need to improve. When your people improve, your company improves.

4. An Empowered goal setting process

Goals inspire action and effectiveness. In their book, *The Strategy-Focused Organization*, Harvard Business School professors Robert Kaplan and David Norton note: "only 7 percent of employees fully understand how they can help achieve company goals."[130] During a presentation at a 2015 goals summit, the first hosted by BetterWorks to discuss OKRs (short for Objectives and Key Results), CEO Kris Duggan said that companies that do goal setting quarterly are 3.5 times more likely to be top performers in their industry.[131] Great companies who are led by Well Done leaders set and achieve goals.

5. An Easy and repeatable purchasing process

Every company must create an effective purchasing process. Since today's consumer has many buying options, a quicker, easier path to purchase your product or service is essential. This process should include methods to handle customer complaints and steps to turn customers into your "brand champions."

Successful companies are built with successful processes. The late William Edwards Deming, widely acknowledged as the leading management thinker in the field of quality, once said:" If you can't describe what you are doing as a process, you don't know what you're doing."[132] Create and perfect these processes to reach profitability.

Practice the Art of First-fruits

One aspect of understanding the order of things is learning the art of "first-fruits." This concept is a biblical principle. It draws its name from Old Testament times, when people gave the first of their harvest as an offering to God, in recognition of Him providing the conditions to produce the harvest. As Proverbs 3:9-10 says: *"Honor the Lord with your wealth, with the firstfruits of all your crops; then your barns will be filled to overflowing, and your vats will brim over with new wine."*

The idea: God should come first in your wealth, your priorities, your time, and your purpose. Since God wants to be first in all things, the wise steward leader will make God first in everything. One way that many steward CEOs practice this principle is by tithing through the business. Nick Nicholaou, the president of Ministry Business Services Inc, outlines methods for tithing through the business in an article titled, "Tithing Considerations for Business Owners."

"Many business owners want their business to be a 'tithing business,'" Nicholaou says. "The best' first fruits' model (calculating based on gross earnings) is to have the business tithe 10 percent of its book net income before taxes. This calculation should include all forms of income. . . . The goal is not to live by a strict rule, but rather to live a life reflecting the generosity we received from our Lord. He challenges us to tithe and live generously towards his works."[133]

Noted author Randy Alcorn—whose *Money, Possessions, and Eternity* is still selling after three decades in print—reminds steward leaders about the importance of first fruits in *The Law of Rewards: Giving what you can't keep to gain what you can't lose*. In the book, Randy writes, "God keeps an account open for us in heaven, and every gift given for his glory is a deposit in that account. When we give, we withdraw funds from our earthly account to have them credited in our heavenly account. . . . we are the eternal beneficiaries of our giving. The money God entrusts to us is eternal investment capital. Every day is an opportunity to buy up more shares in his kingdom."[134]

> **Experience Question:** How can you embrace the idea of first-fruits in your company?

One last second step comment:

Leaders will experience great clarity when they know the proper order of things and follow that order. Whether in business or life, priorities make all the difference. Therefore every Well Done leader should know their order and work the order.

Best Ideas: Write down two or three best ideas that you heard or learned from this chapter.

WELL

DONE

Chapter 10

IMPROVE YOUR TEAM TO IMPROVE YOUR ORGANIZATION

When your people get better, your organization gets better.

"Come, follow me," Jesus said, "and I will send you out to fish for people.'
At once they left their nets and followed him"
Matthew 4:20

One of my favorite pictures in my office was taken in 1921. It shows four noted American leaders gathered in western Maryland for a camping trip: famed inventor Thomas Edison, Firestone Rubber founder Harvey Firestone, automaker Henry Ford, and President Warren Harding. One reason I like this picture so much is that it serves as a valuable reminder of the importance of having the right team.

In the winter of 1914, Ford started a tradition of camping with Edison—an idol of Ford's as the auto magnate was growing up—nearly every year to brainstorm ideas, share new insights, offer mutual encouragement and support, and inspire each other to greatness. Many other business and industry leaders joined these camping trips during their decade-long duration. A 2013 article, released on the 150th anniversary of Ford's birth, called it "perhaps fitting" that a pioneer of automobile travel and the developer of the first patented motion picture camera played the quintessential buddy roles straight out of a road-trip movie, while other famous Americans comprised the supporting cast.

"Renowned naturalist and best-selling essayist John Burroughs, a septuagenarian who resembled Rip Van Winkle with his long white beard, joined the industrialists on their tour of the remote Everglades," writes Christopher Klein about that first trip. "The three men shared a love of the outdoors, although where Burroughs saw a pastoral stream, his fellow travelers saw an untapped source of waterpower. The following year, it was tire and rubber magnate Harvey Firestone who joined Ford and Edison on a tour of California after the men attended the Pan-Pacific Exposition in San Francisco."[135]

After Burroughs passed away, Harding took his place. Not only has the photo of that first year of the newly elected president with the group inspired me, so has the area in the picture. Motivated by the image of their camping trip, I later traveled to the location and spent the night in a tent to replicate the occasion (I think it is always good for leaders to go to places that inspire them.) One reason I wanted to visit that campground was that it represents a firm statement about the power of having the right team around you.

Leading Leaders

No great leader ever led alone. The most exceptional leader, Jesus, modeled the process of developing an organization bigger than himself. He set the example of developing a robust, healthy organization by building a team that could produce results with him and, when necessary, lead without him. That contrasts with many business leaders. One crucial mistake many that many business owners make is not developing

No great leader ever led alone.

a capable team. Leaders will often grow the organization as large as they themselves can take it, but never grow it beyond their own abilities.

> **Experience Question:** When do you feel the loneliest in your leadership? How does it impact you to know that Jesus never led alone?

The wisdom of others can be powerful. Every great leader in the Bible had at least one advisor. Spiritual leaders understand the wisdom of listening to many voices to discern the one that matters most. God never intended for leaders to lead by themselves. Instead, He calls people to walk along beside the leader to help accomplish the purposes that God has called the leader to complete.

Business leaders and entrepreneurs often try to disprove this principle, but they do so at their own peril. Many business leaders try to do things on their own: hence, the familiar saying, "It's lonely at the top." The reality is that it is only lonely at the top if you are trying to lead in isolation. Steward leaders believe in the power of others. Those Well Done leaders who embrace the principle of growing the company by growing their team, never lead alone.

One way of growing your organization is by developing of a second-in-command. Every #1 leader needs a #2, and then a #3, a #4, and so on. Leaders can reach new heights and experience breakthroughs when they build a quality team around them. Growing companies have discovered that leaders lead better when they have a second in command; leading an organization by one's self can be frustrating and extremely disappointing.

Although many leaders instinctively know they should lead with others, on a practical basis, this can prove difficult and so frustrating they can easily "throw in the towel." It may seem so much easier to lead alone than to invest time and effort in trying to build a team. However, part of the design for great leadership is for the empowering leader to invest, influence, and engage with others.

Biblical Business Principle #10: Improve Your Team To Improve Your Organization
"'Come, follow me,' Jesus said, 'and I will send you out to fish for people.' At once they left their nets and followed him." Matthew 4:20

Find the right and best people to bring around you. Make people your top prior-
ity. Learn from everyone. Spend time with a wise team of mentors. Learn faster
by learning from others. Ask questions and listen. Seek counsel. Model Follower-
ship. Find passionate and reliable people.

Leaders who learn from others learn faster. It is better if you have a team around you to inspire you and help you build something bigger than you can build by yourself. Find your passion and add passionate people to your team. They not only perform better, but I believe that one passionate person is worth four "regulars." Passionate people are reliable; they embody ownership of problems, and they seek to complete work in a manner consistent with how their leader would want the work to be done. Passionate people have found their purpose. When a leader or leaders find the gifts and passions of their people and discern how to release those passions, the company will enjoy higher productivity.

Leaders who learn from others learn faster.

> **Experience Question:** Why do you think that, as His first act of ministry, Jesus selected the twelve disciples? What can modern-day faith-driven leaders learn from that?

The Search for the Right People

As I've already mentioned, Jesus built an organization instead of relying solely on His own efforts. His first official act was to call and develop His team. He understood that the quality of His team would determine the quality and success of His organization. The future of the church would be in the hands of the men that he selected. This truth is why Well Done leaders follow Jesus' example as they seek to build their team.

Find the right and best people to bring around you

Well Done leaders should not miss this essential truth of team performance and team effort. God wants leaders who can call and develop a healthy and growing team. Best-selling author and organizational consultant, Dr. Randy Ross, writes about the importance of thriving relationships—in work and life—in his book

Relationomics. In it, he notes that in the end, you can have all the money you've ever desired, a successful career, and good physical health, but without loving, healthy relationships, life will feel incomplete.

"The next time you find yourself scrolling through Facebook instead of being present at the table, stop and engage with those around you," Ross writes. "If you're considering staying late once again at the office instead of being home for dinner with the family or getting together with a friend, then stop and reconsider. If you begin to treat people as assets to the organization rather than valued individuals who are worthy of your time and attention, then reassess your leadership. If you find yourself hiring with little commitment to the long-term growth and development of team members, then revamp the system. If you begin to feel as though leadership is a solo endeavor, then slow down and spend more time cultivating connectedness with others."[136]

Jesus handpicked twelve key people who had specific gifts and talents. No two of His disciples were alike. They led and thought differently from each other, and yet each proved essential to the success of leading the church after Jesus left this earth. Leaders who can develop the next generation of leaders in their company will find several benefits in growing their people.

A key benefit of a leadership team is the more profound friendships that will likely evolve among its members. Leaders grow in their impact when they move from leading employees to leading friends. Jesus called his disciples his friends (John 15:15).

Another compelling benefit of having a great team is that it allows the leader to take breaks to achieve balance in their own lives. Leaders benefit from responsible people in their organizations. By nature, most leaders have a deep drive to create a better company but are often frustrated by a lack of time, a lack of people, or a lack of resources to help make their plans a reality. Those who develop a team draw inspiration, encouragement, and the ability to stay positive from their team.

Finally, a leader enjoys enhanced accountability from a group of leaders. Even top corporate leaders need someone to hold them accountable. There is a temptation for every CEO is to become isolated. When no one holds a leader accountable, the person can be tempted either to make decisions that will hurt the organization or to make no decisions at all. Leaders lead better when they have people on their teams who always speak the truth and are willing to challenge them.

Pastor and leadership mentor Terry A. Smith—author of *The Hospitable Leader*—pushes leaders to become hospitable by welcoming others into their business or other settings. He writes that "every leader who wants to accomplish good purposes must be aware of what the climate of the organization we serve is saying. Though words are part of this environmental reality, sometimes the overall atmosphere of a place speaks so loudly that people can't hear what we actually say."[137]

Practice Mentoring

Many #1 leaders can find it challenging to identify a #2 leader. People at the top of the organization can often lead in isolation because of the doubts, fears, and bad beliefs that shape their thinking about themselves and their people. Leaders can be especially susceptible to wrong thinking and bad beliefs. Bad beliefs are often formed around a sliver of truth that doesn't reflect the whole picture. Embracing these false narratives often leads to ineffective results

Also, leading a team can be hard work, which can inhibit a leader from building a team. Yet by practicing the art of mentoring, coupled with focus, CEOs can grow their team and their effectiveness. Entrepreneur and leadership coach Christine Comaford addresses the importance of identifying leaders and matching them with the right tasks in her 2013 bestseller, *Smart Tribes: How Teams Become Brilliant Together*. She writes that "more often we see Chaos Culture play out because roles are not clearly defined or we have the right people— great people—doing the wrong thing. The more people are mismatched or unclear about their roles, the more chaos we find in an organization or in that particular part of the company."[138]

Failing to mentor others and investing in the development of a "Next Level" leader can be a serious mistake. In order to develop an organization, people must be developed. There are a few concepts that often hinder leaders from taking this step. Among the statements that leaders who lead in isolation make are:

In order to develop an organization, people must be developed.

"No one can do it like me!"

The belief that no can do it like the leader is a misguided belief. Often, business owners and entrepreneurs learn every part of their organization before releasing any areas to others. The benefit is grasping how all parts of the business fit together. The drawback is when the leader limits potential progress because of an unwillingness to release tasks that someone else could do better. Every organization functions at a higher level when people are allowed to excel in their areas of giftedness and abilities. Although leaders can lead well in many areas, no leader excels in every area.

Jesus was a one-of-a-kind type of leader, yet He understood that for His organization to succeed, He had to find others who wanted to lead like Him. They could never lead exactly as He led, but they could lead like Him.[139] Today's leaders who lead like Jesus still lead better than those who attempt to lead according to their own ideas and principles. Every CEO and owner can learn to lead like Jesus led.[140]

"I am the only one who can do it!"

Another misguided belief that hinders the development of leaders is insisting on doing each task, so it is done "the right way." Executives can be very particular about how they want projects completed. They often worry that others will never treat their companies, products, or customers the way they want them handled. This attitude prompts the leader to lead alone. Great organizations learn how to communicate values and priorities, even when the founder is no longer in leadership. To become a transferable company, the company must learn how to create a culture of effectiveness among a variety of people. When businesses depend on one person to do important tasks, they risk not being able to complete them. When a leader releases their team to complete tasks and make decisions in new ways, innovation thrives, and the organization often improves.

"It is easier for me to do it!"

Leaders will not invest in developing their team when they doubt that they have the time or resources to help the #2 leader become and act like a #1 leader. This philosophy sabotages a leader into thinking they don't have time to do the things that will make a difference for the future of the organization. These leaders

These leaders become "right now" leaders instead of "best now" leaders.

become "right now" leaders instead of "best now" leaders. This action almost ensures that the organization will die with the leader.

Leadership is always about focusing on what is best for the organization today and in the future. Remember, as I said in chapter 6 on trusting in the law of sowing and reaping, leaders reap a harvest today from the seeds they planted yesterday. There is no better time to grow a leader for the future than today. Better to have a leader today than the hope of one tomorrow.

"They will do it, and then they will leave!"

Fear demotivates a leader who believes if they invest time and training in a leader for the future, that newly equipped leader will leave for a better position in some other organization. There is wisdom in changing one's leadership perspective from "losing" people to "lifting" people. Empowering leaders always desire to raise their people through training, encouragement, and experience.

"They will do it and then give me more work to do!"

Some leaders let worry be their guide, fretting they will never have enough time to implement all the ideas of their next level leader. Some executives think that bringing someone into a new place of leadership will just cause more work for themselves. However, with a long-term view of leadership and impact, the wise executive knows that the right people doing the right things in the right way will make a huge difference. In the short term, a new leader may cause more work, but in the end, two hands doing the work will reduce the leader's load.

According to a 2014 *Forbes* article, the single biggest issue facing small businesses in China is that they have no hope of succession. Fifty percent of small and family-owned businesses report that they have no one who is aspiring to take over the leadership of the organization. This family business issue is not just a dilemma for China. A majority of small, family, and solo owned businesses have never taken the time to develop and train a successor.[141] To truly have business success, leaders should focus on raising the next generation who will continue to help your business make an impact long after you have quit leading. To develop these people may just be your most significant work.

> **Experience Question:** What bad beliefs have you allowed to stop you from developing the next generation of leaders in your organization?

Learn faster by learning from others, especially mentors.

Leaders who lead at the highest level find people who will be at their side to help them to think intentionally about their next steps. When leaders have people they trust to make decisions and lead well, it enables them to spend their time working "on" their business and not just "in" their business. As Proverbs 15:22 teaches, "with many advisors comes success."

However, leaders can invest time and energy in supporting their team and then find they have no one to encourage them. The idea of support is why identifying that #2 leader is so important for the #1 leader. A person who walks with the CEO at a high level can speak encouraging words at just the right time to help the leader keep going.

Great leaders are life-long learners. They are teachable and remain curious and humble. Learning leaders accept that they have not learned enough, achieved enough, or accomplished enough. They get up every day with a mindset of discovering something new. Learning leaders learn from people in every walk of life; they also learn from their mistakes and failures. Leaders who prioritize learning, acquire knowledge faster so they can lead further.

Great leaders are life-long learners.

> **Experience Question:** Do you have a mentor? What is the single most important leadership lesson you have learned from someone else?

Four Learning Habits of Effective Leaders

A key business advantage is the speed at which teams can innovate, produce, and deliver products and services to customers. Speed is a differentiating factor in any industry. Exceptional leaders embrace the concept of learning faster, which results in moving their organization forward. After working with CEOs for almost two decades, I have discovered four learning habits that effective leaders use to learn faster.

1. **Absorb wisdom from the mistakes of others.** One practical way to learn faster is to learn from others' mistakes. Intelligent leaders understand that it is far better to learn from the mistakes of others than to make all of those mistakes themselves. They also understand that learning this way can save thousands of hours of grief and frustration. Remarkable leaders are also not afraid to learn from their mistakes. They realize that mistakes make instructive and excellent teachers.

2. **Acquire knowledge from the experiences of others.** Smart leaders utilize the experience of others. They look for mentors who can give them insight and perspective into a variety of areas in their lives and businesses. Well Done leaders recognize that the best use of time is to be around others who can help them learn faster. A leader who does not learn from the experiences of others will never learn any faster than what they can learn on their own.

3. **Assimilate information from the practices of others.** Effective leaders put themselves in a variety of learning circumstances. They read books, listen to audiobooks, attend conferences, join CEO groups, hire a business coach, and take personal retreats. They utilize every opportunity available to improve themselves and their companies. Learning leaders are intentional about the number and quality of educational experiences they are involved in regularly.

4. **Apply new ideas from the success of others.** Execution, the act of doing, is the key to enduring knowledge. Smart leaders not only learn; they also apply. The best leaders understand how to put significant ideas into practice once they are acquired.

Consultant Peter Drucker, whom I've quoted several times in this book, once proposed an essential management principle for leaders: "A manager is responsible for the application and performance of knowledge."[142] The real secret is not to apply everything you learn, but to apply the most valuable information that will provide an essential difference in future performance.

In today's marketplace, change seems to occur at lightning-fast speed, making it essential for leaders to learn faster and apply knowledge systematically. Leaders who learn faster will ultimately lead further.

Model Followership

Followership is essential to good stewardship. To lead an organization well, a leader must learn how to not lead in all areas. Well Done CEOs learn how to step back so that they can move forward. A leader who excels at followership will learn how to follow God and listen to His voice because ultimately God is the owner of the business.

Good leaders also know how to propel their team forward. Every great leader should learn how to become a great follower. Well Done leaders learn when they should follow their teams so that the team can accomplish more than the leader could ever do alone.

One example of this attitude is found in John 3:30. In that verse, the reader is given insight into the attitude of John the Baptist as he steps back to elevate Jesus and his ministry. John the Baptist simply states, "He must become greater; I must become less." To lead well, leaders must learn how to follow well. The Well Done leader who practices stewardship is intentional about learning to lead by following.

To lead well, leaders must learn how to follow well.

Great leaders practice good "followership." This decision by leader allows others to lead in their area of giftedness. Leaders can practice followership through effective delegation—one of successful entrepreneurs' most potent tools. Productive leaders know how to utilize their people and their time in a way that helps them focus on essential tasks.

They also value the capacity to use all of the strengths and skills of their people to accomplish astonishing achievements. Former President Theodore Roosevelt once declared, "The best executive is one who has sense enough to pick good people to do what he wants to be done, and self-restraint enough to keep from meddling with them while they do it."[143]

Every successful leader would agree with President Roosevelt's insight. However, many entrepreneurs rarely practice effective delegation, as shown by a survey from a recent leadership retreat. Eighty-five percent of seasoned executives who attended reported they hardly ever delegate. It is no wonder why so many leaders race around starved for time while their most talented people feel unchallenged by their work.

> **Experience Question:** Where do you practice "followership?" How can you encourage your team to lead you?

Four Ways to Get More Done with Delegation

Entrepreneurs who learn the art of delegation will perform at a higher level than their peers who won't or don't delegate. Every entrepreneur should practice delegation. Leaders will never hear the words "Well Done" until they know how to bring others along on the journey. Richard Sheridan, the CEO of Menlo and the author of the book *Joy, Inc, How We Built a Workplace People Love* writes about how to step back so that others on your team have the opportunity to step forward.

"Often the most important leadership moments occur when we by stepping out of the way and letting the team take over. Accept that something has gone in a direction that you did not expect and perhaps, don't even fully support. You then must have the patience to see that the team is learning from this experience and that its own leadership talents are developing in these moments of mistake making."[144]

Every leader needs to empower their team effectively to reach their maximum performance. To delegate effectively, practice these four principles.

1. Let your team know you trust them

Delegation is not only ideal for leaders, but it also becomes a perfect conduit for their teams to grow individually and collectively. Legendary inventor and educator Booker T. Washington once said, "Few things help an individual more than to place responsibility upon him, and to let him know that you trust him."[145] Effective leaders must examine when they last entrusted their team with a critical project or task. If they see significant gaps in their delegation, likely, there are also substantial gaps in conveying their beliefs to their team members.

Mission BBQ empowers their team members in each location through what they call their Empowerment Statement. This statement is read twice a day to all their teammates as a reminder of Mission BBQ's belief in their team members and to inspire team members to act in alignment with the values of the organization. The Mission BBQ Empower-

You are trusted and empowered to use your good judgment to do whatever you feel you need to do to Take Care of Our People.

ment Statement says: "You are trusted and empowered to use your good judgment to do whatever you feel you need to do to Take Care of Our People." This statement is read twice a day to each person on the team, and it conveys the owners' belief that everyone in the organization can act and lead like the owners would act and lead.

2. Release responsibility and authority

Entrepreneurs are often more inclined to assign responsibility than authority. Leaders who delegate tasks without authority will end up with the responsibility for the completion of the task. Proper delegation means transferring it entirely. When team members are given final authority to make decisions, the chances they will bring completed work and solutions back to the leader increases.

3. Delegate meaningful work

One mistake leaders find themselves doing is assigning tasks nobody wants to do. Smart and effective leaders delegate meaningful tasks to teach their teams. Best-selling author and management professor Sydney Finkelstein talks about this truth in his book, *Superbosses*. He says these bosses are great leaders because they are the consummate delegators and thus can continuously and rapidly propel their protégés to new heights.

Finkelstein writes that they relinquish "a degree of authority and oversight that would make many ordinary bosses cringe . . . with so much responsibility on their shoulders and a clear sense of accountability, not to mention the trust of their superboss, protégés come away feeling a sense of their own power and worth, as if they are more like partners than subordinates."[146]

4. Praise the efforts and results of your team

While it is good to delegate effectively once, it is beautiful when it becomes a natural part of the company culture. Moreover, it is transformational to always empower people effectively. Every leader can start down the path toward consistent delegation when they praise both the effort and the results of their teams who have accomplished assigned tasks. Entrepreneurs should envision what it could mean to their organization if they can consistently, effectively delegate.

In The Energy Bus, 10 Rules to Fuel Your Life, Work and Team with Positive Energy, Jon Gordon writes "The best way any leader can demonstrate their love for their team is to help each person discover their strengths and provide an opportunity for that person to utilize them. When you create a system that provides a way for your people to shine you not only bring out the best in them but in the rest of the team and the company as well. If you really want to love your team, help them do what they do best."[147]

Up to the Challenge

Effective and consistent delegation might be the most laborious task for a leader, but it is also the most beneficial. Every entrepreneur and business professional should look to improve their leadership by enhancing their delegation skills. The following four tips are a must for effective delegation and can deliver incremental growth for everyone involved.

Always Be Recruiting

People can either make or break a business, so hiring the right people is essential. A bad hire can drain cash flow and devour hours of the leader's time and energy that are too valuable to waste. Every startup and small business will become better when they intentionally attract and hire better personnel.

Here's a look at five qualities to look for when you need to hire your next "A-player":

Trustability: If you don't think you can trust a person, they will never be able to succeed. Trustability is all about finding people who exhibit character. While competency and education are also important, employees can acquire training and experience for a position that is unfamiliar to them.

A person's character is the essence of who the person is at their core, which usually doesn't change. That is why it is essential to start with people of high character. Every organization benefits from having a good set of interview questions and other tools to help discern trustworthiness.

Reliability: Is this person reliable? Being a person the leader can count on, is one of the essential traits of a great team member. Leaders must know they can count on a person to do the tasks they are responsible for completing. When a leader does not believe their team is reliable, they will either do the task themselves or find another person who can.

Teachability: As your people progress, your business improves. Teachability is an essential characteristic of growing leaders and companies. Legendary basketball coach John Wooden once said: "It is what you learn after you know it all that counts."[148]

When individuals have a teachable disposition, they have endless opportunities to improve themselves and thus their organization. Wise leaders hire and reward people who focus on self-improvement and personal development.

Likability: Teams spend a tremendous amount of time together during working hours. One essential quality to look for in an A-players is likeability. Others should want to work with them to accomplish various tasks. Likability adds energy to an organization.

Sustainability: High employee turnover damages the progress and success of any organization. A vision to reduce turnover and create workplace consistency is why it's vital to evaluate all prospective new hires in terms of their longevity (i.e., how long they believe a person will stay with the organization).

> **Experience Question:** What fundamental values are essential for the people that you are looking to add to your team?

Startups and small businesses do not have the luxury of time or money to continually hire and replace departing, or poorly performing employees. When you find a person you believe will stay with the company for an extended period of time, you know that you have found a strong candidate.

Well Done leaders focus on finding and retaining the best talent. When companies miss this crucial principle, everything else suffers. Focus on the best qualities and characteristics of potential hires, and you will position your company to grow, scale, and achieve next-level business success. When your team gets better, your business will too.

> **Win Activity: Your Team:** Who do you need on your team for your organization to take the next step forward? List those people below.
> 1.
>
> 2.
>
> 3.
>
> 4.

One last second step comment:

Every organization gets better when the people in the organization get better. That may seem like a simple statement, but it is an essential statement for every CEO and business owner to embrace and apply. Jesus spent three years helping his disciples to get better. He invested in his team, knowing that the future of his organization and ministry depended on it. For leaders to ignore their people or to ignore their culture is at their own peril. CEO Experience mentor, Vaughn Thurman, who owns and leads a dynamic software company named High Gear which specializes in a no-code workflow, states it this way: "When a leader loses their culture, they lose their company." Vaughn is correct. The culture is made up of people, and the people in an organization must never be lost. Companies will never succeed when the people in the organization are not succeeding. Therefore Well Done leaders know it is essential to improve their organization by improving their people.

> **When a leader loses their culture, they lose their company.**

Best Ideas: Write down two or three best ideas that you heard or learned from this chapter.

WELL DONE

Chapter 11

DO THINGS TODAY THAT IMPACT TODAY AND TOMORROW

Kingdom Companies Should Become Conversion Companies.

"Store up for yourselves treasures in heaven, where moths and vermin do not destroy, and where thieves do not break in and steal. For where your treasure is, there your heart will be also"
Matthew 6:20-2.

In the early days of Wealth Building CPA, Ebere Okoye must have rolled her eyes at times, just thinking of her Washington, DC-area company's name. Ebere started her CPA firm out of necessity, not desire. Yet after years passed, she had no wealth nor profits. At times she even doubted she could provide detailed financial planning and advice on tax issues and investment strategies, especially to real estate investors.

However, Ebere made a key pivot in her fortunes when she decided to make a difference for eternity. Looking back over the years, she realized that God had placed her in business for a purpose. Awakened to this spiritual reality, she released ownership to God. When she did, God blessed the business. A significant step came in tithing from the gross profits. "I put God on payroll, and I expected Him to show up," she told me.

One way this entrepreneur invests in eternity is serving and caring for her clients. That includes an "eternal perspectives" letter she sends to those dealing with tough issues. In addition, she often sends chaplains to meet with them. The letter contains a deeply personal message, relating how a relationship with Christ helped her through difficult times.

This Kingdom impact and customer care aren't just talk to her; she lives her faith. One time a client had to cancel a meeting because of emergency surgery. Not only did Ebere's team dispatch an "eternal perspectives" message to her, but they also sent flowers to the hospital. When the customer received them, she immediately called, thankful that someone had cared enough to notice when was facing a delicate operation. She concluded by choking back tears as she told of how, in almost sixty years, no one had ever sent her flowers.

To Ebere, a customer has more significance than a financial payoff for services rendered. Her character reflects the teachings of Christ, who had the habit of making a Kingdom impact everywhere He went. He reminded His disciples He was moving their lives to a level of significance—not because of the job they were to do, but because of the way they were to do the job they had been given.

The way we do our jobs and serve the public reveals the state of our hearts and where our real treasure lies. As Jesus says in the Sermon on the Mount: "Do not store up for yourselves treasures on earth, where moths and vermin destroy, and where thieves break in and steal. But store up for yourselves treasures in Heaven, where moths and vermin do not destroy, and where thieves do not break in and steal. For where your treasure is, there your heart will be also." (Matthew 6:19-21)

Experience Question: When in business, have you trusted in God's plan even when it did not make sense?

Biblical Business Principle #11: Do Things Today that Impact Today and Tomorrow

"Store up for yourselves treasures in heaven, where moths and vermin do not destroy, and where thieves do not break in and steal. For where your treasure is, there your heart will be also" Matthew 6:20-21

Invest Wisely. Make Bold Risky Spiritual Decisions. Shine Your Light. Produce Godly Fruit. See Spiritual Opportunities. Acknowledge Christ before Men. Trust God and His Direction.

Towns and cities deteriorate when investments in them slow down or stop. In the same way, companies face difficulties when the leader and key people in the organization forget to make the right investments in the company. "Investment" is another term for treasure. Leaders are called to lead with passion, and to give their all to see their investment produce a good return. A Well Done leader must make investments wisely to ensure those investments will last for eternity.

> **A Well Done leader must make investments wisely to ensure those investments will last for eternity.**

Business leaders are called on to make numerous investments. A leader must make wise use of the company's resources to make the right investments in the business, its people, and its infrastructure. They bring growth as they set the direction of development. Neglect of a business often means it is doomed to shrink and ultimately die.

> **Experience Question:** What are the most essential investments that you are making in your business?

Invest Wisely

With his reputation as the wisest man in history, King Solomon is worth listening to, especially when it comes to his comments on work and profit. Solomon reminds his readers that work without purpose is meaningless. Reflecting on the riches and other things he had accumulated in life, Solomon writes:

"I hated all the things I had toiled for under the sun, because I must leave them to the one who comes after me. And who knows whether that person will be wise or foolish? Yet they will have control over all the fruit of my toil into which I have poured my effort and skill under the sun. This too is meaningless. So my heart began to despair over all my toilsome labor under the sun. For a person may labor with wisdom, knowledge and skill, and then they must leave all they own to another who has not toiled for it. This too is meaningless and a great misfortune. What do people get for all the toil and anxious striving with which they labor under the sun? All their days their work is grief and pain; even at night their minds do not rest. This too is meaningless" (Ecclesiastes 2:18-23).

In this hard but truthful passage, Solomon chronicles the absolute worthlessness of work. To work for work's sake or monetary profit is worthless. To work for a worthy cause - namely, God's kingdom, is worth it.

> **To work for a worthy cause - namely, God's kingdom, is worth it.**

Starting a business can seem admirable and desirable. Running a business is hard work. Business owners and CEOs can get disillusioned with such demands. At some point, it can get comfortable for an executive to stop putting all of their heart into the business. When a leader quits giving their all, the people will soon follow.

It is vital to give the business all that it needs in a proper perspective. This principle is why stewardship of a company is so essential. A leader should not try to shoulder all the company's burdens, but they must retain the tenacity of giving their all at all times.

The Big Payoff

One question CEOs often ask me is where they should spend their time and energy. The latter is a difficult one to answer because of the scope of business. Investments in the right products and critical infrastructure are essential to success. Above that, I encourage every leader to invest in the areas that Jesus invested as He sought to grow His organization.

1. Invest in people

Jesus was a people person. He called twelve disciples to walk alongside Him so he could equip them to run the organization after He returned to heaven.

Every business should be in the people business, focusing on the customer and developing internal team members who work directly with the customer.

I challenge every leader to select three key people in the organization to mentor and work with each year. When a leader chooses critical people to invest in, it helps the mentee and the organization. Regi Campbell explores this concept in his book, *Mentor Like Jesus*, writing that Jesus modeled His faith transparently, living out His life in front of His mentees: Campbell writes, "They became like family to Him. They saw how He applied His faith, how He struggled, how He handled stress, and how He handled dying. Jesus taught along the way of life. He was practical yet spiritual. Jesus helped His guys with practical situations . . . everything from taxes to workplace issues, from goal setting to family relations. He was far more practical than hypothetical. They discussed the law for sure, but Jesus taught from His knowledge and experience."[149]

It always helps build an organization when a leader communicates values, case stories, and principles they follow. For leaders of faith, a mentoring relationship can have a spiritual impact on the person in whom the leader has invested their time and resources.

2. Invest in wisdom

Many leaders are wise. However, God demands that Well Done leaders continue to grow in wisdom. Every Well Done CEO should have personal growth plans for themselves and their next level leaders. A growth plan can consist of things such as mentors, places to see and go, books or journals to read, and experiences to enjoy.

Again, Solomon expresses wisdom on this topic: *"Listen to advice and accept discipline, and at the end you will be counted among the wise."* (Proverbs 19:20) Wisdom is an essential demarcation for the faith-driven leader. It is always wise to listen to others and learn what they have learned.

3. Invest in personal development

Many companies stop growing because the leader stops growing. Growing leaders and growing people grow companies. A leader should always be growing, which is why every business and spiritual leader must

Growing leaders and growing people grow companies.

have a trusted advisor or coach.[150] Leaders need someone in their life who challenges them to continue growing, a person who recognizes the leader's blind spots and helps them develop a plan to reach their highest level of performance.

Douglas Conant, former president and CEO of the Campbell Soup Company, stressed the importance of a leader's development in his book, *TouchPoints: Creating Powerful Leadership Connections in the Smallest Moments*. Conant notes that the greater your responsibility, the larger the number of variables and the more skills you need. In other words, the higher you go, the greater the number of people who watch you, and the more consistent you must be.

"Furthermore, each time you are promoted, your new peers are likely to have more experience and stronger ideas about how to lead," writes Conant and co-author Mette Norgaard. "To influence them, your voice must be so clear that they can hear you and so credible that they will pay attention to you. To gain such a level of credibility, it is not enough merely to use TouchPoints—you need to master them."[151] The point that Doug and Mette are making is that leaders must master their role in the organization and interactions with team members. The CEO will master these moments by knowing what to say, where to lead, and how to encourage their team members to follow their ideas and vision.

One of the best ways I have discovered of how to grow as a leader is by associating with other wise leaders. I believe there are three levels of learning: 1) by yourself, 2) with a mentor or coach, 3) with a team. Jesus taught a group of people. The church is a team of people. So is a business, and when all learn together, it will amplify the learning impact. I teach that every leader should have a team retreat.[152] Furthermore, all leaders need a team with which to learn, which is why they should join a mastermind group or participate in CEO retreats.

4. Invest in spiritual habits

Leading a business is challenging. Leaders who last will work to develop good daily habits that will sustain them through the seasons of a business. The regular practice of prayer and meditation can go a long way to re-centering the leader during times of chaos or stressful situations.

Early nineteenth-century Christian CEO P.T. Barnum, who built a circus that lasted for nearly 150 years, knew the importance of early morning Bible reading. Barnum used biblical principles to establish his business and care for societal outcasts. In 1959, author Irving Wallace wrote a biography of Barnum titled *The Fabulous Showman*. It is an exciting look at the decisions that Barnum made and the interesting personalities who featured in his shows, as well as the famed showman's attraction to inspirational and biblical writings.

"Barnum readings was partial religious and inspirational works," Irving wrote. "He claimed to read the family Bible regularly, and next to it, he enjoyed a slender anthology of prose and verse by 'wise and holy men of many times' entitled Daily Strength for Daily Needs. He said that he read a page of the latter volume every morning, and on the flyleaf of one of his two copies, he wrote: 'This book I believe teaches the philosophy of life and death. . . . I wish every person would daily read it."[153] Well Done Leaders who wish to improve their leadership will develop daily habits to improve their thinking, stretch their mind, and challenge their ideas."

> **Well Done Leaders who wish to improve their leadership will develop daily habits to improve their thinking, stretch their mind, and challenge their ideas.**

Make Bold, Courageous Spiritual Decisions

To stand for Christ in the marketplace is a bold and risky decision, but it is one God calls every Well Done leader to make. It is essential to take a stand for Christ in business. It might come in the form of boundaries your company not cross because of your faith, or it could be what you will do as you seek to honor God.

> **Experience Question:** What bold and risky decision is God asking you to make pertaining to your business?

Well Done CEO David Novak, former chairman and CEO of YUM Brands, writes about the importance of bold decision-making in *Taking People With You: The Only Way To Make Big Things Happen*. He says that going public with what you want to accomplish is a great way to give yourself some extra motivation to see it through. "Why?" Novak asks. "Because if you don't succeed, everyone will know it. You'll lose credibility and risk seeming ineffectual. To be a good leader, you have to put pressure on yourself, so if it's important to get something done, take a public stand on it. Going public will also give your people purpose. It will show then what you really care about."154

Going public is a good idea not only for big decisions in business but also for the leader's faith. The most natural step for faith-driven leaders is to use the platform of their business to recognize Christ and God before men. There will be times that God might ask a faith-driven leader to do something bold and crazy. The fact that a leader is doing it out of obedience can be a testimony to those that they lead. Every spiritual leader in the Bible had to make a bold and courageous decision.

- Moses made a bold and courageous decision when he stepped into the Red Sea.
- Noah made a bold and courageous decision to build a boat in the middle of a desert.
- Abraham made a bold and courageous decision by taking his son Isaac to the mountain to offer him as a sacrifice.
- Daniel made a bold and courageous decision when he decided to trust the commandments of God rather than the rules of his leader.
- Joshua made a bold and courageous decision when he decided to march and sing around the city of Jericho rather than attack it.
- David made a bold and courageous decision when he chose to fight Goliath with a slingshot rather than a suit of armor.
- Esther made a bold and courageous decision when she went before the king and defended her people even though it might have cost her her life.
- Peter made a bold and courageous decision when he chose to walk on water rather than stay in the boat.
- Paul made a bold and courageous decision by deciding to go on missionary journeys to launch churches across the Mediterranean region.
- Jesus made a bold and courageous decision by going to the cross to die for the sins of mankind.

If every great spiritual and business leader has made a risky and bold decision, then God is still challenging Well Done leaders today to make bold and risky decisions. I challenge you to consider what risky and courageous decision you have made for God in your business. Too many leaders are playing it safe. Playing it safe never built a business, and it never had an impact on the Kingdom of God.

Playing it safe never built a business, and it never had an impact on the Kingdom of God.

> **Experience Question:** What does it mean to you that you can trust God's protection in every trial and issue that you face in your business?

Shine Your Light

In Matthew 5:15-16, Jesus makes a simple statement that makes all the difference: "Neither do people light a lamp and put it under a bowl. Instead, they put it on its stand, and it gives light to everyone in the house. In the same way, let your light shine before others, that they may see your good deeds and glorify your Father in heaven."

> **Experience Question:** How could you shine your light for Christ more in your business?

To shine means to stand out and be different. The light shines brightest in the darkest places. In an ever-darkening world, the faith-driven leader is to be passionate about being different, unique and set apart for a higher calling. Customers, vendors, and employees should see a difference when they are working with a company that seeks to honor Christ in all it does.[155] The Well Done leader should act differently, respond to tough issues peacefully, and embrace a bigger vision than just making another dollar to build a bigger mansion.

Shining your light can be simple. An example is your email signature. Many businesspeople place a catchy statement or quote at the bottom of emails, but faith-driven leaders can use an inspirational Bible verse there. Emails sent to vendors, customers, and employees can testify to the leader's faith. Other ways are offering a better benefits package to employees or giving them time off to take mission trips, supporting a Christian cause, or providing chaplains to their employees who are going through difficult times.[156]

The latter is one of the reasons I promote marketplace chaplains for every kingdom company. Chaplains can become part of a holistic wellness program where they have the opportunity to explore deep personal issues from a spiritual point of view. Chaplaincy can provide business owners with a strategic way to measure spiritual key performance targets for a company. Companies like Marketplace Chaplains (https://mchapusa.com) provide a monthly report of the number of employees using the service, spiritual conversations, and people who make a decision for Christ. A commitment to a chaplain service is a small investment that can have an eternal return of investment. Shining one's light is about intentionally being about God's business rather than your own. Well Done leaders should be strategic in how they share their faith in the marketplace and how they touch others with their business.

Produce Good and Godly Fruit

Godly things grow—sometimes exponentially. Jesus often refers to the importance of good fruit in the Bible, showing how God is about results when it comes to good companies producing good fruit. Faith-driven leaders should have a mindset toward growth and expansion. Leaders who wish to honor God through their business will make sure both their people and the business reach their full capacity.

While striving to do this, we should never operate from the point of exhaustion. Jesus never led while out of breath. He was always where He was supposed to be, and He was there always when He was supposed to be. He reached his peak and established an organization to fulfill its capacity as well.

Business leaders love results. They are always looking for a return on investment. Yet, many faith-driven leaders never inspect results from a kingdom perspective. While passionate about business, they never take time to examine the eternal. One key question I ask every Well Done CEO I interact with: how many salvations has your company produced? This question typically gives faith-driven entrepreneurs pause. Most have never been asked that question, yet it is an essential question to ask to know if a company is making a kingdom impact.

However, don't you think that if God placed a business under your care for years, which touches the lives of thousands, He expects some salvations or spiritual move-

Kingdom companies should become conversion companies.

ment to take place in the company? Kingdom companies should become conversion companies."

While God is all about free will and grace, He also expects results. He wants His leaders to be about His business. He is calling leaders of all size companies to produce good fruit.

I believe strongly in prayer groups, Bible study groups, and learning opportunities for employees to hear the message of Christ in new and different ways.[157] There will be people coming into your business who would never enter a church. The marketplace has always been and will always be a place where God can be elevated.

At CEO Experience, we have developed a Next-Level Leader retreat designed for all employees. The CXP CEO Retreat Guide has pages dedicated to next level leaders and what they should be learning. These leaders receive the entire CEO guide filled with Bible passages and spiritual insights with the idea that faith comes from hearing, and hearing from the Word of God (see Romans 10:17). When they read business insights for themselves, they see spiritual ideas designed for the leader, and it sets them on a path of spiritual growth and development.

See Spiritual Opportunities

In Luke 12:13-21, Jesus tells His disciples an important parable with applications to business and investment: *"Someone in the crowd said to him, 'Teacher, tell my brother to divide the inheritance with me.' Jesus replied, 'Man, who appointed me a judge or an arbiter between you?' Then he said to them, 'Watch out! Be on your guard against all kinds of greed; life does not consist in an abundance of possessions.' And he told them this parable: 'The ground of a certain rich man yielded an abundant harvest. He thought to himself, 'What shall I do? I have no place to store my crops.' Then he said, 'This is what I'll do. I will tear down my barns and build bigger ones, and there I will store my surplus grain. And I'll say to myself, 'You have plenty of grain laid up for many years. Take life easy; eat, drink and be merry.' But God said to him, 'You fool! This very night your life will be demanded from you. Then who will get what you have prepared for yourself?' This is how it will be with whoever stores up things for themselves but is not rich toward God."*

In business, the CEO has the responsibility to see opportunities. "Environmental Scanning" is one business term used to help leaders survey the landscape of competitors, customers, and new innovations for products and services.[158] In the same way, faith-driven CEOs should be looking for opportunities to make a difference in the lives they lead and those their company touches.

The reason Jesus condemns the business owner in this parable isn't that he builds larger barns for himself or his business. That was a wise business decision. He fails, however, to consider the spiritual opportunities before him. God had given this business owner His blessings, yet he never considers other options for the increased revenue. Maybe God wanted him to keep the same size barns and give away the excess, or sell the surplus and give the money to the poor.

> **Win Activity: Kingdom Impact:** Brainstorm ways that you could incorporate Christian values and Christian activities into your company to make a kingdom impact.
>
> 1.
>
> 2.
>
> 3.
>
> 4.

Expand Your Mission Field

Jesus acknowledged His Father in all He did. Christ said His Father was the One who sent Him (John 8:29) Jesus knew He was to do the work the Father sent Him to do (John 6:38). Jesus was clear in His mission: what He did had an eternal impact. Christ challenges all Christians and Well Done leaders to remember to acknowledge Him. As Jesus puts it in Matthew 10:32-33: *"Whoever acknowledges me before others, I will also acknowledge before my Father in heaven. But whoever disowns me before others, I will disown before my Father in heaven."*

Such acknowledgment is part of a winning strategy. Every good business is built on a strategy for success. But for the Well Done, profitability is not enough. Success in God's kingdom looks different. Former Proctor & Gamble executive A.G. Lafley and business professor Roger Martin write about the importance of a winning strategy in their book, *Playing to Win.*

"As you begin articulating your strategic choice cascade, the obvious place to start is at the top," they write. "We've argued that it is essential to define a winning aspiration up front, and it does make sense to begin thinking about strategy by defining the purpose of your enterprise; without having an initial definition of winning, it is difficult to assess the value of any subsequent choice. You need a winning aspiration against which you can weigh different choices."[159]

This aspirational statement of designing the win is essential for Well Done CEOs. Winning in the business that is led by a faith-driven CEO should include the possibility of seeing Jesus in the business they are building. In fact, today unlike any time before in history, businesses have the opportunity to have a global impact, not by traveling to a foreign country, but rather by walking through their organization and talking with their own team members. In my experience, it is not unusual that a small business with 150 employees will at least have team members that represent on average, at least ten different countries around the world. Well Done CEOs have a mission field in their own marketplace and must be strategic and intentional about how to acknowledge Jesus to the people groups under their care.

What does it say about a Christian business that has been in existence for a decade or longer and yet never does anything to acknowledge Christ publicly? Companies have an opportunity to impact thousands touched by the business and may never have another chance to learn about what Christ can do in their lives if they decide to follow Him.

Acknowledge Christ Before People

Let me make one more bold, outrageous statement. I have worked with many Well Done leaders over the years; many have a passion for honoring Christ in their business. I have seen some backdown, however, when it comes to publicly acknowledging Christ, these leaders understand the value of acknowledging Jesus in and throughout the business. To deny Jesus is to weaken their impact by using generic praise for God. Although I applaud any leader's efforts to honor Jesus, I do question their boldness and their ability to hear the words Well Done. These timid leaders are "playing it safe" by trying to placate other faiths that recognize some kind of god. But this is a day for courage and commitment to Christ in the marketplace. Businesses that honor Christ find favor with God; when Well Done leaders get to heaven, they will be acknowledged for their stand for Christ in the marketplace.

Trust God and His Direction

Trust is essential in business. Customers must trust the product. Leaders must trust their people. Teams must trust each other. The wise business owner will trust the Lord.

A principle that has shaped many businesses and leaders is Proverbs 3:5-6: *"Trust in the Lord with all your heart and lean not on your own understanding; in all your ways submit to him, and he will make your paths straight."* Leaders are called on to make many decisions and must set the direction and path for the business to ensure its growth. Therefore, they must know where to find inspiration for their vision and decisions.

Four Areas to Trust God Every Day in Business

1. Business Owners Need to Trust God's Plan

While every Christian business owner knows that God has a plan for his or her life and business, sometimes that plan can be challenging to understand. However, a leader should never doubt that God has a purpose in every situation. When businesswoman LaToya Harris was re-writing her business plan in mid-2017, she saw the need for reliance on God. "If you're writing a business plan, you may have certain ideas about how to go about making your business a success, but remember the Lord knows best. He can steer us in the right direction and help us avoid unnecessary mistakes and trials. By including Him, you can ensure that your vision for your business lines up with His vision and Word."[160]

2. Business Owners Need to Trust God's Principles

God's options are always good, and His principles always prudent. Those who lead with integrity understand and apply God's principles throughout the business. During his life, noted pastor and author A.W. Tozer wrote, "It's not my business to try and make God think like me…but to try, in prayer and penitence, to think like God."[161] Every successful business in applies biblical business principles, even if they don't understand where they found the principle.

> **It's not my business to try and make God think like me…but to try, in prayer and penitence, to think like God.**

3. Business Owners Need to Trust God's Provision

Steward business owners believe that God owns their business. Since they understand everything they have comes from the hand of God, they no longer carry the burden of having to do everything. As stewards, they realize that God knows everything the business needs. Every day they can ask God to provide what the company requires for that day.

4. Business Owners Need to Trust God's Protection

There is much to worry about in running a business. Fear can be the dominant factor driving the leader. Solomon reminds us in Proverbs 3:5-6 that the leader can trust God to direct and guide their steps in even the most difficult situations. Christian business leaders can rest assured that God wants to protect a business that has been built to honor Him.

> **Experience Question:** Do you trust that God can give you everything you need to succeed in the business?

One last second step comment:

It can be difficult for the leader or owner to exhibit such trust. In business, it is always tough to know who and what to trust. I am grateful that amid shifting seasons in life and the world, God offers consistency. It is still wise to "trust in the Lord and lean not on our own understanding." When a leader trusts the right principles and people, possibilities for achievements and accomplishments become limitless. Well Done leaders do things today that impact today and tomorrow.

Best Ideas: Write down two or three best ideas that you heard or learned from this chapter.

WELL DONE

Chapter 12

WORK TO "WELL DONE"

*"Well Done." Those are two of the most powerful words
in the English language.*

*"Therefore go and make disciples of all nations, baptizing them
in the name of the Father and of the Son and of the Holy Spirit,
and teaching them to obey everything I have commanded you.
And surely I am with you always, to the very end of the age."*
Matthew 28:19-20

In one of the most emotional scenes in the Bible, Jesus is completing the
essential work of His life: hanging on the cross in agony to secure forgiveness of sin for all humankind. This final act culminated the work He set out
to do thirty-three years earlier—work He had dreamed about and possessed the
vision to complete before coming to earth. It marked the climax of His three-
year-long earthly ministry; it was the work He had discussed with His disciples as

He trained them to go on without Him. It was His mission, the work the Father designed Him to fulfill.

Here is how the disciple John records this moment in the life of Jesus in his Gospel: *"Later, knowing that everything had now been finished, and so that Scripture would be fulfilled, Jesus said, 'I am thirsty.' A jar of wine vinegar was there, so they soaked a sponge in it, put the sponge on a stalk of the hyssop plant, and lifted it to Jesus' lips. When he had received the drink, Jesus said, 'It is finished.' With that, he bowed his head and gave up his spirit."* (John 19:28-30)

Note the last words that Jesus spoke from the cross. While subtle, they make a profound impact. While completing His most essential work, Christ proclaims: "It is finished." Those are the words that every Well Done leader should be able to state with clarity and convictions."

This phrase, tetelestai (it is finished) is a derivative from the Greek verb teleo. Teleo means "to bring to an end, to complete, to accomplish." According to Vine's Expository Dictionary of New Testament Words: "The word (it is finished) was in His (Jesus) heart before He uttered it."[162] In other words, Jesus had the vision to do good work even before beginning it. He also had the foresight to work to completion before starting."

> **Jesus had the vision to do good work even before beginning it. He also had the foresight to work to completion before starting.**

Jesus set out not only to complete the work, but to do the work well, to the complete satisfaction of His Father. This phrase in the Greek New Testament is an action verb in the perfect tense. A perfect tense action verb in the Greek language means something that had been fulfilled but still has an impact on the present.

This phrase has power for business owners who look to leave a legacy for the future. Every Well Done leader should have the desire to complete works to "it is finished," but still has an impact in the present. I call this principle "working to Well Done." When a leader works to Well Done, they will know they have completed what God called them to do with excellence. They will be able to look back on the work in which they invested their time, energy, and resources to complete, and be able to hear the words: Well Done.

Experience Question: What does your finish line look like? What would you have to do in your business to please God and know that you could say the words, "It is finished?"

Jesus put this principle in practice through how He lived His life and how He worked to complete the tasks that were before Him. In His last statements to His disciples He encourages them to live out this same principle. He states in Matthew 28:19-20: *"Therefore go and make disciples of all nations, baptizing them in the name of the Father and of the Son and of the Holy Spirit, and teaching them to obey everything I have commanded you. And surely I am with you always, to the very end of the age."*

His last commission to His disciples, is the same commission that He himself lived by: Work to Well Done! Jesus is inspiring His team to go and fulfill the mission that He has called them to complete. He desires that they increase their focus, enhance their passion, and fulfill their calling, so at the end of their life, they will be able to hear the words "Well Done."

> **His last commission to His disciples, is the same commission that He himself lived by: Work to Well Done!**

Biblical Business Principle #12: Work To "Well Done"

"Therefore go and make disciples of all nations, baptizing them in the name of the Father and of the Son and of the Holy Spirit, and teaching them to obey everything I have commanded you. And surely I am with you always, to the very end of the age." Matthew 28:19-20

Excellent Work Is Worthy Work. Measure Your Final Product Against Your Mission. Give Away Upgrades and Improvements. Work at Thinking Eternally. Show Your Value Through Products that Are of High Quality. Produce Good Fruit of which You Can Be Proud.

Jesus told another story earlier in his ministry to foreshadow of this principle about working to Well Done. In one of the most dramatic stories Jesus ever tells, He relates the idea of working to Well Done at its best with a story about a man who receives the blessings of abundance and missed the purpose of his real work. This parable is a business story. While Jesus told it to warn about greed, it also has leadership implications. The story is found in Luke 12:13-21. Here is how it reads in the Bible:

"Someone in the crowd said to him, 'Teacher, tell my brother to divide the inheritance with me.' Jesus replied, 'Man, who appointed me a judge or an arbiter between you?' Then he said to them, 'Watch out! Be on your guard against all kinds of greed; life does not consist in an abundance of possessions,' And he told them this parable: 'The ground of a certain rich man yielded an abundant harvest. He thought to himself, 'What shall I do? I have no place to store my crops.' Then he said, 'This is what I'll do. I will tear down my barns and build bigger ones, and there I will store my surplus grain. And I'll say to myself, 'You have plenty of grain laid up for many years. Take life easy; eat, drink and be merry.' But God said to him, 'You fool! This very night your life will be demanded from you. Then who will get what you have prepared for yourself?' This is how it will be with whoever stores up things for themselves but is not rich toward God."

This parable emphasizes accountability with the recognition that in a moment's notice, the business can be taken from the owner of the barns. The parable emphasizes that the owner never owned anything. The business owner thought he owned everything, the fields, the barns, and the crops, but in reality, he didn't own any of it. Indeed, the crops, fields, and barns were all taken from him when he least expected it—that night. The owner of the barns believed that he had worked for it all and deserved to keep it all. He had such a misguided conception. This parable speaks to the importance of working to Well Done every day. At any moment, the Master could return, or you could be taken to the Master and a review of what you did and how you did it will determine a Well Done statement or not. The leader is this parable failed. He had ignored what God wanted of Him, so that he could focus more on building barns and a bigger kingdom for himself. This parable reminds the readers of the importance of being accountable for finishing the work that God has for them. Accountability teaches that every action is important and that every decision matters.

Every Well Done leader must understand a few critical aspects of this parable. First, note the statement that Jesus makes when He begins to teach the parable: "Watch out! Be on your guard against all kinds of greed; life does not consist in an abundance of possessions." In this statement, Jesus reveals that a key to living a Well Done life is maintaining a Well Done perspective. Greed can cause a person to gather more and more for themselves—and only for themselves. A Well Done leader wishes to use everything they have for the benefit of those around them, and ultimately for the Kingdom of God.

Greed always wants more. The leader who thinks like an owner will want more and more. However, leaders with a steward mentality will use the resources under their care to produce exceptional eternal results. Well Done leaders are bigger than their businesses. In this parable, Jesus reminds His listeners how easy it is to fall into the mentality of only becoming like the leader's possessions. Well Done leaders embody the perspective that life is bigger than what they have or what they have acquired.

Next, note verse 17, an easy one to miss. While the business leader in the parable has received an abundant blessing, here is the key phrase to catch: "He thought to himself." In the business world, many leaders like to call themselves "self-made successes." In other words, they consider every blessing they have received to be solely the result of their own hard work and effort. There is no doubt that building a business is grueling work, requiring many hours of effort and conserving resources to keep the business going through the hard times. However, consider also that it is a blessing from God for anyone who receives a blessing from a business. Since God is the owner of all things, therefore He owns every business. He has the ability to bless or curse as well as the ability to build up or to bring low.

Psalm 46:4-6 reads: *"There is a river whose streams make glad the city of God, the holy place where the Most High dwells. God is within her, she will not fall; God will help her at break of day. Nations are in uproar, kingdoms fall; he lifts his voice, the earth melts."* This Psalm speaks to the truth that God can build a nation or destroy one. If that is true, it is also true that God can build a business or destroy one. In this case, it was God who sent the blessing. Yet, this foolish leader only thought about what he should do with all that he had done for himself. Every Well Done leader must examine their heart and test their beliefs to see if they are turning to God for guidance and direction, or whether they are trying to lead their business with only their own wisdom and insight.

The next perspective is revealed in the response of the foolish leader in verse 18: *"This is what I'll do. I will tear down my barns and build bigger ones."* The foolish leader wanted to build something bigger for himself, rather than build something bigger for God. The leader actually made a sound business decision, but he did not make a good life decision. The Well Done leader has a perspective that is bigger than just the moment in which they are living. They think about making a Kingdom impact, knowing that one day they will have to give an account for all they are doing and have done.

In verse 19, the reader gets a full insight into the mind of the foolish leader. The Bible reveals the leader's heart when he reasons: *"I'll say to myself, 'You'll have plenty of grain laid up for many years. Take life easy; eat, drink and be merry.'"* The leader was selfish and had no concern about using his blessings for others' benefit. Well Done leaders make decisions with God in mind. They have the desire to please Him by doing the things that He would have them to do. A Well Done leader is never satisfied to disengage with the gifts and talents God has given them. They want to work diligently throughout their lifetime to always be pleasing the Master until He returns. They never settle for second-best or for a lackluster effort of producing the best results.

At the end of the parable, Jesus makes the statement, *"You fool! This very night your life will be demanded from you. Then who will get what you have prepared for yourself?"* All leaders must consider this condemnation of Jesus a powerful statement indeed. It reveals that the leader was foolish because he had only prepared things for himself on earth and not in heaven. He believed that he had no one to answer to except himself. Well Done leaders always take action today with tomorrow in mind. They continue to strive for success in the world—and in eternity. They prepare by preparing for the return of the true Owner of the business. That is the difference between being foolish and being wise.

> **Experience Question:** What work do you do on a daily basis where it is hard to include God in the process? What could you do to honor God with that work?

Another example of this is referred to in the parable of the talents when the master returns and speaks passionately to two of the servants. Because of their excellent work, he tells them, Well Done. Every CEO who leads and builds a business wants to hear the words Well Done from customers, employees, and vendors. Those words, Well Done can be spoken in terms of employee engagement and productivity, customer retention, vendor relationships, referrals, and longevity. However, for the Well Done CEO who has an audience of One they desire to hear the words, Well Done from God in heaven. His voice is the voice that matters.

Excellent Work Is Worthy Work

Building a business on biblical principles requires a change of perspective. One essential attitude for Christian leaders is practicing excellence at all times and in all situations. The apostle Paul writes these critical words in Colossians 3:23-24: Whatever you do, work at it with all your heart, as working for the Lord, not for human masters, since you know that you will receive an inheritance from the Lord as a reward. It is the Lord Christ; you are serving." Paul was reminding Christian leaders of the higher call that is part of their lives. Christians are not called to do average work, but to do all

> **Whatever you do, work at it with all your heart, as working for the Lord, not for human masters, since you know that you will receive an inheritance from the Lord as a reward. It is the Lord Christ; you are serving.**

their work with excellence, in a way that honors God. When you work towards excellence in everything, you are on your way to hearing, "Well Done" from your customers, employees, vendors, and God.

With that I mind, remember that excellent work is eternal work, which means that:

1. The Well Done Leader Strives for Excellence in ALL of their work.

Note the keyword "whatever" at the beginning of Colossians 3:23. To God, it does not matter what type of work you do. His desire is to be included in your work. In other words, Christian leaders and business owners can honor God in a variety of daily tasks. Indeed, every task matters, a truth Pastor Matthew Barnett addresses in his book, *The Cause within You: Finding the One Great Thing God*

Created You to do in This World. The co-founder of the ground-breaking Dream Center in Los Angeles says that when you were born, God instilled many things within you.

"One of them was a great cause that He wants you to embrace," Barnett writes. "In His unique grandeur, He created a universe in which the cumulative effect of all people faithfully pursuing the cause within them would result in a transformed world—one in which everyone's needs would be met, and every servant's heart would be filled with the joy of blessing others. . . . A transforming cause is never about you—promoting yourself, achieving greater fame or fortune, experiencing more pleasure or comfort, amassing greater power. It is always about using the resources God has given you—skills, relationships, experiences, money, time, intelligence, and all the rest—to make a positive impact in the lives of others."[163]

For the Well Done CEO, it all matters. Everything that is done in and throughout the business is important and will often show up in unexpected or unanticipated places. For example, at In-N-Out Burger, they place a Bible verse on the bottom of their drink cups. SweetFrog Yogurt plays Christian music in their stores and proudly displays their FROG values on the wall behind every register. The F.R.O.G. in SweetFrog stands for Fully Rely On God, and they try to show that by being a good neighbor to every community that they enter. Tyson Foods employs chaplains as part of its wellness program to help employees during difficult times. FoodPRO wrote Bible verses on their floor so that they could stand on the Word of God when they remodeled their corporate offices.

These companies are practicing excellence in their business practices as they seek to fulfill their mission. They are working to hear, Well Done. As Christian leaders, you are called to be excellent in all of your work. Excellence means committing to do your best work before you even begin and knowing that someday you will have to give an account of what you did and why you did it.

2. The Well Done Leader Strives for Excellence in even Small tasks

Excellence shows itself in the small, daily, seemingly inconsequential tasks. Steve Jobs once said, "We don't get a chance to do that many things, and everyone should be really excellent. Because this is our life. Life is brief, and then you die, you know? So this is what we've chosen to do with our life."[164] Jobs excelled at designing and building great products; he did not do as well at doing the excellent things in other areas of his life. Regardless, Jobs was right. Life is short, and Well Done leaders must not miss the opportunity to build excellence in everything.

Every task should be an excellent task. One secret to business success is to do the small things well. Companies that excel pay attention to the details that other companies don't. It could be something like remembering a customer's name, their past order, or recognizing a significant employee milestone in their life of the business.

The apostle Paul reminds his readers to do all things with "all your heart." This perspective includes the small things. In a book I mentioned previously, *The Hospitable Leader*, Terry Smith writes: "Hospitable leadership is differentiated from other kinds of leadership emphases in that hospitable

You can't do things with all your heart and do them badly.

leaders are particularly obsessed with helping followers find their place. We are not only hospitable to people with heads full of dreams; we are also dream refiners. We are insistent that people develop clarity about the life God dreams specifically for them."[165] In other words, Matthew 13:4-8, Jesus taught: you can't do things with all your heart and do them badly.

> **Experience Question:** What small task in your company can you turn into an excellent task?

3. The Well Done Leader Strives for Excellence in all CALLED tasks.

Every person has been called to do good works according to their abilities and experiences. Those areas of life in which we are called are areas of mastery and excellence. To excel in these called areas is how we give glory back to the One who has given us those gifts in the first place. Every person should know his or her strengths and abilities. They should know where they are excellent and then seek to improve their excellence.

One example of a Well Done leader who achieved mastery was Booker T. Washington, one of my father's favorite historical figures. Dad taught me many stories from Washington's life; for that, I am forever grateful. In the book *Christian Business Legends*, the editors write about Washington's journey, recalling the words on the first page of his autobiography, Up From Slavery: "My life had its beginning in the midst of the most miserable, desolate, and discouraging surroundings."

He continues "Not a promising start, but Washington's life of discipline and sheer determination holds many lessons for Christians involved in any business endeavor today . . . by possessing an intense desire to achieve something better for one's self and his fellow man, being aware of one's calling and life purpose, refusing to quit despite setbacks, and trusting in the care and good providence of God. Just what was the desire that consumed young Booker? The desire to learn . . . starting with not much more than Alabama's blessing and his own resolve, by 1915, Washington has built Tuskegee Institute into a school of 107 buildings on. 2,000 acres with over 1,500 students and more than 200 teachers and professors."[166]

To do things with excellence is a difficult task. It was not easy for Booker T. Washington, just as it is not easy for the modern-day faith-driven leader. However, excellence stands out. Excellent products are talked about and used among customers. Exceptional service is appreciated and shared with others. Excellent work is seen and recognized. In short, excellence is hard to keep hidden. Therefore, Christian business owner, you should strive for excellence in all that you do because you are doing the work as if serving Jesus Himself. Moreover, when you practice this attitude, God Himself will reward your life and your business for your excellence.

Measure Your Final Product Against Your Mission

Well Done CEO Cheryl Bachelder excelled at leadership, putting this quality to good use in turning around Popeyes' Louisiana Kitchen. Her drive originated with her desire to serve and lead with purpose. In the book, *Dare to Serve: How to Drive Superior Results by Serving Others*, she writes that during her tenure as CEO of Popeyes, her personal purpose was inspiring purpose-driven leaders to exhibit competence and character in every area of their lives. Such personal purpose was the filter she used for determining how she spent my time in leadership and work.

"Here are just a few of the ways my purpose guided my work life," she says in her book:

- "Mondays and Tuesdays of every week were dedicated to one-on-one coaching sessions with Popeyes leaders, my direct reports. Tuesday mornings were our team meeting to collaborate and make decisions."

- "Every six months, I chose one vice president-level leader to mentor with six ninety-minute sessions on any topics they chose."
- "I toured restaurants each month with the goal of getting to know the restaurant's general manager and finding out how the company could better serve them."
- "When asked to speak at public events, I only spoke on the topic of Dare-to-Serve leadership."

"Purpose helped me decide what to say yes to. Purpose helped me decide what to say no to. I enjoyed my work more than ever because I was doing what I cared most about. I also felt my life had more significance because I was singularly focused on how I wanted to make a difference in the lives of others."[167]

When a leader has an underlying purpose cemented in their thinking, it ignites a passion that keeps burning even when times look bleak and challenging. Jesus found going to the cross depleting and exhausting. The Bible records that the night before He was crucified that He was sweating drops of blood as He prayed to His Father. It was the nobler mission that motivated Him through the dark days to complete the mission so that He knew when it was finished.

Many companies and leaders quit before they are finished. They never get to Well Done because they have no idea what that Well Done looks like. The purpose will give a leader the vision of what working to Well Done looks like at the finish line. Well Done leaders know what the finish line looks like.

In his book, *Leading from Purpose,* Nick Craig writes that purpose is like a sharp sword: "Once you know what your purpose is, you also know immediately when you are leading from it and when you are not. The moment you find your purpose is a moment of waking up; once awake, you see. You instantly stand in the room of purpose. You know what is at stake, and you have a level of motivation and commitment that transcends that of the cold and timid souls sitting on the sidelines."[168]

One way that I help leaders think about finding Well Done is by helping them to see the finish line." I ask them to consider what success at their finish line will look like. Once they have that clear picture in mind, they can be released to build their business

One way that I help leaders think about finding Well Done is by helping them to see the finish line.

and life around that future finish line. Another application of that with teams and employees is to have a team member describe a perfect day in their work in the business. When you work to complete the perfect day, you do better work. Working to the model or standard will help every leader hear the words: Well Done.

Give Away Upgrades

Everyone loves unexpected upgrades and improvements. For the faith-driven CEO, innovation, upgrades, and improvements can be a way to make a kingdom impact and a difference in the lives of those whom they serve.

Many companies build their success through exceptional service. One such company is a luxury hotel chain, The Ritz-Carlton. Business consultant and best-selling author Joseph A. Michelli writes about this mentality in his book, *The New Gold Standard*. In it, he notes that "Wow" moments happen in every workplace. "In some cases, they are the result of a service culture while in others, they are simply the individual acts of a high-performing staff member," Michelli says. "In many businesses, outstanding work is tracked and recognized. Ritz-Carlton takes this one step further. Leadership has designed ways for their 'Wow stories'—remarkable examples of extraordinary service exhibited by their Ladies and Gentlemen—to be used to reinforce existing service excellence and to propel future extraordinary acts."[169]

I believe that God is looking for "Wow" stories from business leaders and companies that have a heart for Him. One of the ways in which companies can create such experiences is by surprising people with unexpected upgrades or improvements — for no reason. These grace-filled moments can remind the Well Done CEOs of the unexpected love their Savior has shown to them by sending His Son, Jesus, to die for the sins of the world. God is a good Father who knows how to give good gifts to His children and companies. Faith-driven leaders should be good at improving their customers' experiences through upgrades and improvements.

Experience Question: How has your business shown the grace of God to others?

After all, savvy business travelers have learned how to ask for free upgrades. When renting a car or checking in at a hotel, they routinely ask, "Are there any upgrades available?" What impact would it have on customers if a company they patronize asks them if they would like a free upgrade—before they ask for it? Theologian Wayne Grudem reminds the business owner of the potential of showing God's grace in business transactions in his book, *Business for the Glory of God*. Grudem writes, "We (workers in the marketplace) can imitate God's attributes each time we buy and sell if we practice honesty, faithfulness to our commitments, fairness, and freedom of choice. Moreover, commercial transactions provide many opportunities for personal interaction, as when I realize that I am buying not just from a store but from a person, to whom I should show kindness and God's grace."[170]

Every Well Done business should have the desire to express the love and grace of God. By setting the course of continual improvement and unexpected upgrades, the company can continue to grow, develop, and impress its consumers and customers.

Work at Thinking Eternally

It is easy for businesses and business leaders to think short-term. The best companies have a long-term focus, which I wrote about in an earlier chapter. Now, I want to challenge you to think even further. Every faith-driven spiritual entrepreneur knows that one day, they will have to give an account for all that have done. Therefore to hear the words, Well Done, leaders have to keep their focus on activities that please their Father, who is in heaven.

A typical business owner can go through an entire day without even considering or thinking anything about God or what would please Him. Yet, there are many opportunities throughout the day-to-day activities of a business to pray with people, show grace, teach biblical values, and act with integrity. Daniel Barenboim, one of the most notable pianists of all time, once said: "Every great work of art has two faces: one toward its own time, and one toward the future, towards eternity."[171]

> **Experience Question:** How would you describe eternal work? What kind of work do you think most pleases God in heaven?

The servant whose master rebuked him in the parable of the talents was thinking only about today, not tomorrow. He never considered what would happen when the leader would return. Good Well Done leaders act today but think eternally.

Eternal work is worthy work.

One way to think eternally is through focusing on work that impacts eternity. Eternal work is worthy work." Things such as praying for a customer, worshipping through the act of your work, or lifting up Christ in some way so that others can see Him, are all acts of eternity. When business leaders focus on eternity, they find more peace in the present.

Show Your Value through Products that are of High Quality

Producing work that is of the highest quality is a way to Well Done. Christian-led companies show their value through the production of their work. Building products to stand the test of time communicates the seriousness that a leader pursues their work.

David and Solomon built a temple that lasted generations. Noah built an ark to survive a flood. Jacob purchased a coat of many colors to give to his son, Joseph. Jesus established a church to stand until the second coming. Faith-driven leaders understand the value of a well-built product and service.

The Well Done leader will seek to build their products to become the best in class compared to their competition. Well Done leaders should never sacrifice quality for price.

They must feel inspired to do their best work and do it as a way of communicating their value in the marketplace. Companies that focus solely on price devalue their products and end up building products that have little lasting value.

> **Experience Question:** Would your customers consider your product "best in class?" Why or why not? What changes would you have to make in order to build a "best in class" product?

Produce Good Fruit of Which You Can be Proud

Good companies produce good and godly results. Jesus was a leader that was concerned about actions and results. In one of the most interesting stories of Jesus with his disciples, he comes upon a tree that is not producing fruit.

In Matthew 21:18-22, the Bible records this story: *"Early in the morning, as Jesus was on his way back to the city, he was hungry. Seeing a fig tree by the road, he went up to it but found nothing on it except leaves. Then he said to it, 'May you never bear fruit again!' Immediately the tree withered. When the disciples saw this, they were amazed. 'How did the fig tree wither so quickly?' they asked. Jesus replied, 'Truly I tell you, if you have faith and do not doubt, not only can you do what was done to the fig tree, but also you can say to this mountain, "Go, throw yourself into the sea," and it will be done. If you believe, you will receive whatever you ask for in prayer.'"*

This story speaks to the power of believing big dreams, but here, a reference is made to the importance of living a Well Done life. Well Done comes from producing excellent results. The tree was created to provide figs. The tree was made with a purpose, and the reality was that the tree was not fulfilling the purpose that it had been given.

Seek to Hear: "Well Done"

"Well Done are two of the most powerful words in the English language." At the end of the parable of the talents, the returning owner expresses his pleasure with the good stewards with those words. Every Christian business owner should long to hear these words at the end of their journey on earth. They should strive for that goal in everything they do, commit to sharing them with excellent employees and other executives and suppliers who excel in their position.

Well Done are two of the most powerful words in the English language.

Companies that only produce earthly results will not receive heavenly praise. God has given businesses to faith-driven leaders for a purpose—to produce faith-driven results. Faith-driven leaders should not shy away from results. Results help to measure if something is working or if time and energy should be placed somewhere else that might be of better benefit for the business. Leaders and teams need to know if they are producing at the right level. They need to measure themselves and their effort against the desired results that they anticipated and expected.

Hans Finzel penned a fascinating book entitled *The Top Ten Mistakes Leaders Make*. In that book, the author wrote about the mistake that many leaders make in not investing in a successor to their leadership. The author writes, "To end well, we must not get too wrapped up in our own indispensability. Humility is the key to finishing well and passing the torch on to our successors. One of the keys to a successful leadership transition is to learn to hold our positions loosely. The tighter the grip, the more pride, and the harder it becomes at any stage to let go. A loose grip is a humble grip, an attitude that knows our finitude and dispensability."[172]

Jesus knew that He needed twelve disciples. What if He got tired and only called eleven? Jesus knew the cities He was to preach in and the miracles that He was to perform. He fulfilled his expectations and achieved the desired results. When a company has no idea about what results they are looking to achieve, they are often led by a leader who has no vision and no passion for hearing the words, Well Done. When a company produces something for the kingdom, God is pleased, and the leader will hear, Well Done.

One last second step comment:

To work to "Well Done" can be the most significant biblical business principle that you embrace as a faith-driven leader. Everything else will fall away at the end of your business career and life if you miss the mark of hearing the words "Well Done."

In the parable of the talents, when the leader returned, the two employees that produced great work heard the words "'Well done, good and faithful servant! You have been faithful with a few things; I will put you in charge of many things. Come and share your master's happiness!'" (Matthew 25:23). These are the words that every faith-driven CEO and business leader longs to hear. This reason is why faith-driven leaders seek to build a business and live a life of significance. This statement is what lies in the balance. There have been many successful businesses and business leaders who built a great kingdom for themselves, but they never heard the words well done. There have been many people who accomplished great feats and were recognized by the throngs of people who never heard the words well done. However, the words well done are available for anyone to hear and those brave souls that are willing to build their business on the biblical principles of Jesus are well on their way to hearing, "Well done, good and faithful servant!"

Win Activity: Well Done: List four people who have done something that impressed you or pleased you and whom you should say the words, Well Done.

1.

2.

3.

4.

Best Ideas: Write down two or three best ideas that you heard or learned from this chapter.

WELL

DONE

SUMMARY OF TERMS

Second Mile Mentality: The perspective to always do a little more than anticipated or expected. Jesus taught this attitude to first-century Christians as a way to be different than others for the purpose of leading people to faith.

Second Mile Satisfaction: The result of a second-mile action. When customers experience the unexpected they are more pleased and joyful over the interaction with the company that has provided exceptional service.

Well Done CEOs: CEOs and business leaders who lead in such a way that at the end of their lives they will hear the words, "Well Done" from the people who have watched them work and from the Savior whom they have worked to please.

Customer Point of View: The step of thinking about what the customer desires and ultimately wants from the business. Faith-driven leaders are passionate about considering other people more important than they consider themselves. They always consider how their decisions and choices impact another person.

HISG: HISG stands for Huge Impossible Spiritual Goal of a HIS G target. Well Done leaders seek to do the impossible, knowing that God is the God that makes the impossible possible. Leaders should consider and imagine Huge Impossible Spiritual Goals they would like to accomplish in and through their business with the help of God.

The Art of the Ask: The art of the ask is the habit of learning what questions to ask and to whom those questions should be asked. Well Done leaders ask more questions than they give answers so others can find the answers to their questions.

CXP Executive Retreat Guide: The retreat guide is a unique resource prepared monthly by CEO Experience to help leaders embrace and practice the 12 Biblical Business Principles that lead to well done. The guide is one part business magazine, one part executive journal, and one part executive coach. Download a free executive guide at www.ceoexperience.com.

Steward Leader: A steward leader is one who recognizes that God is the owner of the business and that a business owner is just a steward of the things under their care. At the end of the line, steward leaders will have to release everything under their care and have to give an account of all the decisions and choices that they made while they lead the business.

Planting Seeds: Every organization has resources at their disposal. How a company chooses to use its resources is how a company plants seed for future growth or a future harvest.

Harvest: The result a company or leader will receive when they made wise choices and decisions. God is the God of the harvest and wants to give good gifts to His children when they acknowledge and recognize Him.

The Art of Sowing: The practice of planting seed or investing for future growth. Every day provides an opportunity for leaders and organizations to sow seeds for future and eternal growth.

Yes and No: The simple practice of reaching a bold and conclusive decision: yes or no.

Profit with Purpose: The perspective that companies and organizations should have a larger mission and purpose for their existence than just to make money.

Kingdom Dreams: The practice of imagining something that would have a significant impact on the kingdom of God. The vision to use business resources to further God's kingdom here on earth.

Seven Year Projects: It took Solomon seven years to build the temple. This blueprint reminds leaders to work on projects that have a future impact. Every organization should be working on projects or tasks that take resources today to make the organization or company better tomorrow. Seven years is a figurative example but can be a good framework to consider a prolonged project.

Second Things: Activities, decisions, and tasks that cloud a leader from knowing and working on the main things of a business. Second things are not necessarily bad things; they are just not first things. "Second Things" are those activities that do not support the betterment of the mission of the organization or your calling as a leader.

First fruits: The art of giving to God before anything else. This was a practice established in the Bible, related to the harvest people reaped in their fields. They would bring the first offering to God as a way of communicating thanksgiving for the blessings they had received.

Next Level Leaders: These are up and coming leaders in your organization who need to be mentored and developed so that your organization can be improved.

Kingdom Companies: Companies led by Well Done leaders who desire to grow profits and have an impact on God's Kingdom.

Kingdom Impact: Actions or behaviors that embody a focus on developing spiritual fruit in a business. Kingdom impact happens through intentionality and focusing on applying biblical business principles that lead customers, employees, and vendors to deep their relationship with God.

Net Promoter Score: A business survey that gauges the level of customer satisfaction with a company after a customer experience. Customers will fall on a scale, ranging from those who promote the business through referring the business to others, to a detractor of the business who tells others to not do business with the organization.

Faith-Driven Leader: A leader who embraces their faith as a part of their leadership. These leaders are guided by their beliefs in their faith teachings and their morals and values.

Masterplan: Five guides that have been developed by CEO Experience for the purpose of strategy and decision-making. CEO Experience offers a vision masterplan, a planning masterplan, a CEO masterplan, and a kingdom masterplan, all designed to enhance the four key areas of leadership success.

CEO Retreat Day: A one-day retreat designed for CEOs to listen to God's voice, hear the best ideas of others, and to develop a monthly strategic plan for decision-making.

Win Walls: A focus on areas of success in life and business. Wins can start small and lead to bigger breakthroughs. When a win is celebrated, it is often repeated. Wins focus on what is working as a company seeks to build momentum.

Financial Finish Line: The amount of money that a steward leader believes is enough for their work. The Well Done CEO will wish to stay in alignment with the peers across the country but not be tempted to work for greed and miss out on the blessings that only God can give.

ENDNOTES

1   Theresia Whitfield, "Second Mile Service," *The Christian Post*, August 11, 2008, https://www.christianpost.com/news/second-mile-service.html.

2   S. Truett Cathy, *Eat Mor' Chikin: Inspire More People: Doing Business the Chick-fil-A Way*, (Decatur, GA: Looking Glass Books, 2002), 26.

3   Tommy Newberry, "How Going the Extra Mile Changes Everything," TN Coaching, September 19, 2016, https://www.tommynewberry.com/the-habit-of-the-extra-mile.

4   Shep Hyken, "There's No Traffic Jam On The Extra Mile," Forbes, February 27, 2016, https://www.forbes.com/sites/shephyken/2016/02/27/theres-no-traffic-jam-on-the-extra-mile/#4f65161679a6.

5   Pat Williams with Jim Denney, *How to Be Like Walt: Capturing the Disney Magic Every Day of Your Life* (Deerfield Beach, FL: Health Communications, 2004), 173.

6   Chris DeRose and Noel Tichy, "Here's How to Actually Empower Customer Service Employees," *Harvard Business Review*, July 1, 2013, https://hbr.org/2013/07/heres-how-to-actually-empower-customer.

7 Jack Trout, "Peter Drucker on Marketing," *Forbes*, July 3, 2006, https://www.forbes.com/2006/06/30/jack-trout-on-marketing-cx_jt_0703drucker.html#67cfaedb555c.

8 Vladimir Botsvadze, PhD, Leading Brands Forward, February 14, 2015, https://vladimerbotsvadze.wordpress.com/2015/02/14/the-purpose-of-business-is-to-create-a-customer-who-creates-more-customers-shiv-singh-quotes-business-success/.

9 Thomas Oppong, "Don't Just Start a Business, Solve A Problem," *Entrepreneur*, August 15, 2014, https://www.entrepreneur.com/article/236522.

10 Chris Denove and James D. Power IV, *Satisfaction: How Every Great Company Listens to the Voice of the Customer* (New York: Penguin Group, 2006), 241.

11 Gregory Ciotti, "These 13 Stories of Remarkable Customer Service Will Put a Smile on Your Face," Help Scout, June 12, 2016, https://www.helpscout.com/blog/remarkable-customer-service/.

12 Tony Hsieh, *Delivering Happiness: A Path to Profits, Passion, and Purpose* (New York: Hachette Book Group, 2010), 160.

13 Gary Vaynerchuk, *The Thank You Economy* (New York: HarperBusiness, 2011), 26.

14 Ken Gosnell, "How My Mother Helped Me Become The Entrepreneur I Am Today," *YSF Magazine*, February 28, 2019, https://yfsmagazine.com/2019/02/28/how-my-mother-helped-me-become-the-entrepreneur-i-am-today/.

15 Kevin and Jackie Freiberg, *NUTS!: Southwest Airlines' Crazy Recipe for Business and Personal Success* (New York: Bard Press, 1996), 216.

16 BrainyQuote', "James Cash Penney Quotes," https://www.brainyquote.com/quotes/james_cash_penney_226548.

17 J.C. Penney, *Fifty Years With The Golden Rule: A Spiritual Autobiography* (New York: Harper and Brothers Publishers, 1950), 64.

18 Ibid., 84.

19 Brenton Hayden, "Why the Golden Rule Must Be Practiced in Business," *Entrepreneur*, September 11, 2016, https://www.entrepreneur.com/article/281387.

20   Steve Sanduski, "Lee Iacocca was right–your success hinges on these 3 things," Belay Advisor, March 23, 2016, https://www.belayadvisor.com/lee-iacocca-your-success/.

21   Patrick Lencioni, *The Advantage: Why Organizational Health Trumps Everything Else in Business* by Patrick Lencioni (San Francisco: Jossey-Bass, 2012), quote from "The Advantage Quotes," GoodReads, https://www.goodreads.com/work/quotes/18134034-the-advantage.

22   Jeff Bezos, "2016 Letter to Shareholders," April 17, 2017, https://blog.aboutamazon.com/company-news/2016-letter-to-shareholders.

23   Matthew Dollinger, "Starbucks, 'The Third Place', and Creating the Ultimate Customer Experience," *Fast Company*, June 6, 2008, https://www.fastcompany.com/887990/starbucks-third-place-and-creating-ultimate-customer-experience.

24   Gavin Doyle, "Disney History and Why Theme Parks Ever Happened," Disney Dose, September 22, 2014, http://disneydose.com/disneyland-history/#axzz5jIQQjwBe.

25   Lee Cockerell, *The Customer Rules, The 39 Essential Rules for Delivering Sensational Service* (New York: Crown Business, 2013), 61,65

26   Dick Parker, "Humble Beginnings, " The Chicken Wire, November 11, 2016, https://thechickenwire.chick-fil-a.com/inside-chick-fil-a/Humble-Beginnings-How-Truett-Cathys-Love-for-Customers-Grew-From-a-Coke-and-Smile.

27   Rani Molla, "American consumers spent more on Airbnb than on Hilton last year," Recode, March 25, 2019, https://www.recode.net/2019/3/25/18276296/airbnb-hotels-hilton-marriott-us-spending

28   Leigh Gallagher, *The Airbnb Story: How Three Ordinary Guys Disrupted an Industry, Made Billions . . . and Created Plenty of Controversy* (Boston: Houghton Mifflin Harcourt, 2017), 7.

29   Nikki Gilliland, "Seven innovators of the in-store customer experience," Econsultancy, March 12, 2019, https://econsultancy.com/in-store-customer-experience/.

30   "Why the Customer Experience Matters," McKinsey & Company podcast, May 2016 podcast, https://www.mckinsey.com/business-functions/marketing-and-sales/our-insights/why-the-customer-experience-matters.

31   Dan Dowling, "I'm Buying Your Customer Experience, Not Your Prod-
      uct," *Entrepreneur*, August 2, 2017, https://www.entrepreneur.com/arti-
      cle/297498.

32   Shep Hyken, "Six Ways Listening Improves The Customer Expe-
      rience," *Forbes*, April 29, 2017, https://www.forbes.com/sites/
      shephyken/2017/04/29/six-ways-listening-improves-the-customer-experi-
      ence/#116e61e372da.

33   Eve Tahmincioglu, "Friends Don't Always Make Good Partners," *The New
      York Times*, September 7, 2006, https://www.nytimes.com/2006/09/07/
      business/07sbiz.html.

34   *The Thank You Economy*, 26.

35   Megan Ritter, "Why Efficient Customer Service is Better than Friendly,"
      business.com, February 22, 2017, https://www.business.com/articles/why-
      efficient-customer-service-is-better-than-friendly/.

36   *Fifty Years With The Golden Rule*, 197.

37   "Why the Golden Rule Must Be Practiced in Business."

38   Blake Mycoskie, *Start Something That Matters* (New York: Spiegel & Grau,
      2011), 159.

39   "Blake Mycoskie: A Conversation," Fresh Life Church, January 6, 2019,
      https://subsplash.com/freshlifechurch/messages/mi/+dh8nv6q.

40   *Start Something That Matters*, 32.

41   W. Edwards Deming, *Out of the Crisis* (Cambridge, MA: The MIT Press,
      1982), 139

42   Henry Ford, *The Great To-Day and Greater Future* (New York: Cosimo
      Classics), 35.

43   Brendon Burchard, "The Charged Life: Start Something That Matters,"
      May 20, 2015, http://brendonburchard.tumblr.com/post/119430801458/
      start-something-that-matters.

44   Sebastian Buck, "How Motivating Is Your Company's Purpose?" *Fast
      Company*, October 17, 2016, https://www.fastcompany.com/3064570/
      how-motivating-is-your-companys-purpose.

45   Chris MeLeod, "The inspirational reason why the CEO of a $250M
      company limited his salary to $140,000," *The Business Journals*, November

24, 2015, https://www.bizjournals.com/bizjournals/how-to/growth-strate-gies/2015/11/alan-barnhart-limits-salary-to-help-missions.html.

46 "How and Why I Gave my Business to God," Ray Hilbert, Bottom Line Faith podcast, May 23, 2017, https://truthatwork.org/alan-barnhart-bot-tom-line-faith-episode-17/.

47 Susan Stamberg, "How Andrew Carnegie Turned His Fortune Into A Library Legacy," NPR, August 1, 2013, https://www.npr.org/2013/08/01/207272849/how-andrew-carnegie-turned-his-fortune-in-to-a-library-legacy.

48 "History of the Pledge," The Giving Pledge, https://givingpledge.org/About.aspx.

49 Bill Peel, "Why RG LeTourneau Gave 90 Percent," Center for Faith and Work, https://centerforfaithandwork.com/article/why-rg-letourneau-gave-90-percent.

50 R.G. LeTourneau, *Mover of Men and Mountains* (Chicago: Moody Press, 1967), 279.

51 Jodi Glickman, "Be Generous at Work," *Harvard Business Review*, June 8, 2011, https://hbr.org/2011/06/be-generous-at-work.html.

52 Anthony S. Boyce, Levi R. G. Nieminen, Michael A. Gillespie, Ann Marie Ryan, and Daniel R. Denison, "Which comes first, organizational culture or performance? A longitudinal study of causal priority with automobile dealerships," *Journal of Organizational Behavior*, January 15, 2015, https://onlinelibrary.wiley.com/doi/abs/10.1002/job.1985.

53 Sharon Lipinski, "The Business Case: How Generosity Can Transform Your Corporate Culture," Conscious Company Media, May 14, 2018, https://consciouscompanymedia.com/workplace-culture/the-busi-ness-case-how-generosity-can-transform-your-corporate-culture/.

54 Frank Sonnenberg, *Follow Your Conscience: Make a Difference in Your Life & in the Lives of Others* (New York: CreateSpace, 2014), excerpt at https://www.franksonnenbergonline.com/blog/honor-your-word-is-your-bond/.

55 *Eat Mor' Chikin*, 89.

56 Ibid., 90.

57 Elena L. Botelho and Kim R. Powell, *The CEO Next Door, The Behaviors that Transform Ordinary People Into World-Class Leaders* (New York: Crown Publishing, 2018), 29.

58 Joel Trammell, *The CEO Tightrope: How to Master the Balancing Act of a Successful CEO* (Austin, TX: Greenleaf Book Group Press, 2014), 10.

59 *Winners Dream*, 141.

60 BrainyQuote®, "Tony Blair Quotes," https://www.brainyquote.com/quotes/tony_blair_384839.

61 Anne Fisher, "Don't Blow Your New Job: Managers are switching companies like never before, but a startling number don't last 18 months. Here's why," *Forbes*, June 22, 1998, http://archive.fortune.com/magazines/fortune/fortune_archive/1998/06/22/244154/index.htm.

62 GoodReads, "Andrew Carnegie Quotes," https://www.goodreads.com/quotes/251192-teamwork-is-the-ability-to-work-together-toward-a-common.

63 John Maxwell, *The 21 Irrefutable Laws of Leadership* (Nashville, TN: Thomas Nelson Publishers, 2007), 7.

64 Todd Stocker, *Becoming the Fulfilled Leader: 10 Personal Leadership Principles Learned Through An Unlikely Friendship* (New York: CreateSpace, 2014), 72.

65 Kevan Lee, "How Successful People Start Their Day: The Best Morning Routines for Feeling Great and Getting Work Done," Buffer, July 21, 2014, https://open.buffer.com/morning-routines-of-successful-people/.

66 AZQuotes, "Peter Drucker Quotes," https://www.azquotes.com/quote/459993.

67 Ken Gosnell, "Leaders, Don't Wait To Make Your Next Business Decision," Forbes, https://www.forbes.com/sites/forbescoachescouncil/2019/08/27/leaders-dont-wait-to-make-your-next-business-decision/#378905c14802.

68 "Local Businessman, Humanitarian Turns 100 Years Old," Your Hometown Stations, September 19, 2015, https://www.hometownstations.com/news/local-businessman-humanitarian-turns-years-old/article_2c0bc07b-1e8c-5ddd-8db5-6c0b93966313.html

69 *God Owns My Business*, 62.

70   Ken Gosnell, "6 Shifts for a Christian CEO," Biblical Leadership, November 11, 2018, https://www.biblicalleadership.com/blogs/6-shifts-for-a-christian-ceo/.

71   Linda Sasser, "4 Things Every Leader Must Steward," Impacting Leaders blog, December 18, 2013, http://www.impactingleaders.com/2013/12/18/4-things-every-leader-must-steward/

72   Randy Alcorn, *The Treasure Principle* (Colorado Springs, CO: Multnomah Books, 2005), 11.

73   Hugh Whelchel, *How Then Should We Work?* (Bloomington, IN: Westbow Press, 2012), 48.

74   Will Yakowicz, "Why You Need to Get Employees to Challenge Your Decisions," *Inc.*, May 7, 2015, https://www.inc.com/will-yakowicz/the-reason-why-companies-like-kodak-fail.html.

75   John Maxwell, *Leadershift: The 11 Essential Changes Every Leader Must Embrace* (New York: HarperCollins Leadership, 2019), 19

76   Max De Pree, *Leadership is an Art* (New York: Currency, 1989), 50.

77   David Green, *More Than a Hobby* (Nashville, TN: Nelson Business, 2005), 164.

78   Wayne Grudem, *Business for the Glory of God*, (Wheaton, IL: Crossway, 2003).

79   "Hobby Lobby: Our Story," https://www.hobbylobby.com/about-us/our-story.

80   David Green, *More Than a Hobby: How a $600 Startup Became America's Home and Craft Superstore* (Nashville, TN: Nelson Business, 2005), 110.

81   Daniel J. Martin, *Rich Soil: Transforming Your Organization's Landscape for Maximum Effectiveness* (Kansas City: Beacon Press, 2014), 27.

82   Bob Adams, "How to Build a Solid Foundation for Your Business," Business.com, August 18, 2017, https://www.business.com/articles/how-to-build-a-solid-foundation-for-your-business/

83   BrainyQuote®, "Robert Louis Stevenson Quotes," https://www.brainyquote.com/quotes/robert_louis_stevenson_101230

84   Dave Ramsey, *EntreLeadership: 20 Years of Practical Business Wisdom from the Trenches*, (New York: Howard Books, 2011) 118.

85 *Rich Soil*, 25.

86 Ken Gosnell, "The disciplines of disruption," Biblical Leadership, April 5, 2018, https://www.biblicalleadership.com/blogs/the-disciplines-of-disruption-in-servant-leadership/.

87 Rabbi Daniel Lapin, *Business Secrets from the Bible: Spiritual Success Strategies for Financial Abundance* (Hoboken, NJ; Wiley, 2014), 161.

88 John C. Abell, "Jan. 19, 1983: Apple Gets Graphic with Lisa," *Wired*, January 19, 2010, https://www.wired.com/2010/01/0119apple-unveils-lisa/

89 "The Wright Brothers - First Flight, 1903," EyeWitness to History.com, http://www.eyewitnesstohistory.com/wright.htm.

90 Simon Sinek, *Leaders Eat Last: Why Some Teams Pull Together and Others Don't* (New York: Penguin Random House, 2014), 121.

91 Ken Walker, "Holy Spirit at the Helm: Steering the ship at Florida's gospel-driven Regal Marine Industries," *Ministry Today*, May/June 2017, 51.

92 Andy Stanley, *Visioneering: God's Blueprint for Developing and Maintaining Personal Vision* (Colorado Springs, CO: Multnomah Books, 1999), 14.

93 David Novak, *Taking People with You: The Only Way to Make BIG Things Happen* (New York: Penguin Group, 2012), 84.

94 Bill McDermott with Joanne Gordon, *Winners Dream: A Journey from Corner Store to Corner Office* (New York: Simon and Schuster, 2014), 180.

95 Quotes.net, "Pamela Vaull Starr," https://www.quotes.net/quote/42664.

96 BrainyQuote®, "Walt Disney Quotes," https://www.brainyquote.com/quotes/walt_disney_130027

97 Jim Collins, "BHAG – Big Hairy Audacious Goal," https://www.jimcollins.com/article_topics/articles/BHAG.html

98 Ken Gosnell, "The disciplines of disruption," Biblical Leadership, April 5, 2018, https://www.biblicalleadership.com/blogs/the-disciplines-of-disruption-in-servant-leadership/.

99 John Maxwell, *Good Leaders Ask Great Questions: Your Foundation for Successful Leadership* (New York: Center Street, 2014), 14.

100 Brandon Showalter, "Chick-fil-A to become 3rd largest fast-food chain in US sales amid growing popularity," *ChristianPost,* May 9, 2019, https://www.christianpost.com/news/chick-fil-a-to-become-3rd-largest-fast-food-

chain-in-us-sales-amid-growing-popularity.html.

101 Stanley Tam, *God Owns My Business: They Said It Couldn't Be Done, But Formally and Legally . . .* (Camp Hill, PA: Wing Spread Publishers, 1969), 62.

102 Regi Campbell, *About My Father's Business: Taking Your Faith to Work* (Colorado Springs, CO: Multnomah Books, 2009), 77.

103 Rick Williams and Jared Crooks, *Christian Business Legends: Lessons from History, Volume 1* (Linville, VA: Business Reform, 2004), 34.

104 Religion News Service, "Faith and Facials: The Religion of Mary Kay," *The Orlando Sentinel*, January 4, 1997, https://www.orlandosentinel.com/news/os-xpm-1997-01-04-9701021026-story.html.

105 Bible Study Tools Staff, "Bible Verse About Rocks," Bible Study Tools, May 1, 2018, https://www.biblestudytools.com/topical-verses/bible-verse-about-rocks/

106 Bill George with Peter Sims, *True North: Discover Your Authentic Leadership* (San Francisco: Jossey-Bass, 2007), quoted on Pinterest, https://www.pinterest.com/pin/518195500850223416/

107 Brainy Quote®, "Dwight D. Eisenhower Quotes," https://www.brainy-quote.com/quotes/dwight_d_eisenhower_164720.

108 "Frequently Asked Questions," U.S. Small Business Administration, Office of Advocacy, June 2016, https://www.sba.gov/sites/default/files/advocacy/SB-FAQ-2016_WEB.pdf.

109 John Sporleder, "Leadership in the Workplace: The Importance of Integrity," PayScale, May 8, 2009, https://www.payscale.com/compensation-to-day/2009/05/leadership-in-the-workplace.

110 Dr. Maynard Brusman, "Leading with Values: Walking the Talk," Working Resources, http://www.workingresources.com/professionaleffectivenessarticles/leading-with-values-walking-the-talk.html.

111 "20 Years of Surveys Show Key Differences in the Faith of America's Men and Women," Barna Group, August 1, 2011, https://www.barna.com/research/20-years-of-surveys-show-key-differences-in-the-faith-of-americas-men-and-women/.

112 "What Faith Looks Like In The Workplace," Barna Group, October 30, 2018, https://www.barna.com/research/faith-workplace/.

113 Ramit Sethi, "Why Successful People Take 10 Years to 'Succeed Over-night,'" *Inc.*, May 11, 2016, https://www.inc.com/empact/why-successful-people-take-10-years-to-succeed-overnight.html

114 Adam Grant, *Originals: How Non-Conformists Move The World* (New York: Penguin Books, 2016), 35.

115 Caitlin Jordan, "A showcase of 100 design quotes to ignite your inspira-tion," Canva, https://www.canva.com/learn/design-quotes/.

116 Quotefancy, "Wayne Muller," https://quotefancy.com/quote/1708473/Wayne-Muller-In-the-soil-of-the- quick-fix-is-the-seed-of-a-new-problem-because-our-quiet.

117 Ken Gosnell, "How To Hire Your Next A-Player," *YSF Magazine*, May 27, 2019, https://yfsmagazine.com/2019/05/27/how-to-hire-your-next-a-player/.

118 Steve Robinson, *Covert Cows and Chick-Fil-A: How Faith, Cows, and Chicken Built an Iconic Brand*, (Nashville, TN: Nelson Books, 2019), 70.

119 Harry Levinson, "Conflicts That Plague Family Businesses," *Har-vard Business Review*, March 1971, https://hbr.org/1971/03/con-flicts-that-plague-family-businesses.

120 Ken Gosnell, "How Leaders Can Balance Marriage With Running A Business," *Forbes*, April 19, 2018, https://www.forbes.com/sites/forbes-coachescouncil/2018/04/19/how-leaders-can-balance-marriage-with-run-ning-a-business/#57512e267d70.

121 Harvey Mackay, "6 Keys to Building a Service Culture," *Inc.*, April 17, 2012, https://www.inc.com/harvey-mackay/6-keys-build-service-culture.html.

122 John Burley, "Building A Business That Is Bigger Than You: The viewpoint of an experienced buyer and the advice of an expert on increasing your company's value," *Inc.*, June 21, 2017, https://www.inc.com/john-burley/every-founder-should-learn-get-customers-to-identify-with-the-business-and-not-t.html.

123 Steven Covey, *7 Habits of Highly Successful People: Powerful Lessons in Per-sonal Change* (New York: Simon and Schuster, 1989), 148.

124 Peter Drucker, *The Effective Executive: The Definitive Guide to Getting the Right Things Done* (New York: HarperCollins Publishing, 2006), 103.

125 Stephanie Vozza, "Personal Mission Statements Of 5 Famous CEOs (And Why You Should Write One Too)," *Fast Company*, February 25, 2014, https://www.fastcompany.com/3026791/personal-mission-statements-of-5-famous-ceos-and-why-you-should-write-one-too.

126 Ashley Stahl, "Three Reasons You Need To Say 'No' More Often," *Forbes*, October 2, 2015, https://www.forbes.com/sites/ashleystahl/2015/10/02/three-reasons-you-need-to-say-no-more-often/#2e3443bb3ff3.

127 James Clear, "A Scientific Guide to Saying "No": How to Avoid Temptation and Distraction," Buffer, March 28, 2013, https://buffer.com/resources/a-scientific-guide-to-saying-no-how-to-avoid-temptation-and-distraction.

128 AZ Quotes, "Peter Drucker Quotes," https://www.azquotes.com/quote/863677.

129 Visier, "2015 Human Capital Institute Survey," http://www.hci.org/files/field_content_file/Visier-Executive-Survey-Results-Changing-Expectations-for-HR-Leadership.pdf

130 Robert Kaplan and David Norton, *The Strategy-Focused Organization: How Balanced Scorecard Companies Thrive in the New Business Environment* (Cambridge, MA: Harvard Business Review Press, 2000), 234.

131 Ben Lamorte, "Goal Summit 2015: John Doerr & Kris Duggan on OKRs," April 21, 2015, https://www.okrs.com/2015/04/goal-summit-2015-john-doerr-kris-duggan-on-okrs/.

132 Quotes.net, "William Edwards Deming Quotes," https://www.quotes.net/quote/8537.

133 Nick Nicholaou, "Tithing Considerations for Business Owners," 2006, https://www.mbsinc.com/tithing-considerations-for-business-owners/.

134 Randy Alcorn, *The Law of Rewards: Giving what you can't keep to gain what you can't lose* (Carol Stream, IL: Tyndale House Publishing, 2003), 39-40.

135 Christopher Klein, "Ford and Edison's Excellent Camping Adventures," History Channel, July 30, 2013, https://www.history.com/news/ford-and-edisons-excellent-camping-adventures.

136 Randy Ross, *Relationomics, Business Powered By Relationships* (Grand Rapids, MI: Baker Books, 2019), 264.

137 Terry A. Smith, *The Hospitable Leader: Create Environments Where People and Dreams Flourish* (Minneapolis: Bethany House, 2018), 33.

138 Christine Comaford, *Smart Tribes: How Teams Become Brilliant Together* (New York: Penguin Group, 2013), 184.

139 Lee Colon, "4 Powerful Leadership Lessons From Jesus," *Inc.*, January 20, 2016, https://www.inc.com/lee-colan/4-powerful-leadership-lessons-from-jesus.html.

140 Ken Gosnell, "What every leader can learn from Jesus," Biblical Leadership, July 1, 2018, https://www.biblicalleadership.com/blogs/what-every-leader-can-learn-from-jesus-2/.

141 Oliver Rui, "Challenges Ahead for China's Family Businesses," *Forbes*, June 5, 2014, https://www.forbes.com/sites/ceibs/2014/06/05/challenges-ahead-for-chinas-family-businesses/#6319472e14cd.

142 Peter F. Drucker, *Post-Capitalist Society* (Oxford, England: Butterworth-Heinemann, 1993), 41.

143 "ForbesQuotes: Thoughts on the Business of Life," https://www.forbes.com/quotes/8958/.

144 Richard Sheridan, *Joy, Inc.: How We Build a Workplace People Love* (New York: Penguin Group, 2013), 145.

145 LeadershipNow, Leading Blog, "The Wisdom of Booker T. Washington," leadershipnow.com, February 14, 2011, https://www.leadershipnow.com/leadingblog/2011/02/the_wisdom_of_booker_t_washing.html.

146 Sydney Finkelstein, *Superbosses: How Exceptional Leaders Master the Flow of Talent* (New York: Penguin Random House, 2016), 140-141

147 Jon Gordon, *The Energy Bus, 10 Rules to Fuel Your Life, Work, and Team with Positive Energy* (Hoboken, New Jersey, 2007), 124.

148 BrainyQuote˚, "John Wooden Quotes," https://www.brainyquote.com/quotes/john_wooden_106379.

149 Regi Campbell, *Mentor Like Jesus: His Radical Approach To Building the Church* (Atlanta: RM Press, 2016), 7-8.

150 Ken Gosnell, "Why Every Entrepreneur Needs A Business Coach," *YSF Magazine*, December 10, 2018, https://yfsmagazine.com/2018/12/10/why-every-entrepreneur-needs-a-business-coach/.

151 Douglas Conant and Mette Norgaard, *TouchPoints: Creating Powerful Leadership Connections in the Smallest Moments* (San Francisco: Jossey-Bass, 2011), 25-26.

152 Ken Gosnell, "Four Reasons Why Company Retreats Are Good For Business," *YSF Magazine*, October 30, 2018, https://yfsmagazine.com/2018/10/30/company-retreats-are-good-for-business/.

153 Irving Wallace, *The Fabulous Showman: The Life and Times of P.T. Barnum* (New York: Alfred Knopf, 1959), 160.

154 *Taking People With You*, 175.

155 Mark Oppenheimer, "At Christian Companies, Religious Principles Complement Business Practices," *New York Times*, August 2, 2013, https://www.nytimes.com/2013/08/03/us/at-christian-companies-religious-principles-complement-business-practices.html.

156 Emma Green, "Finding Jesus at Work," *The Atlantic*, February 17, 2016, https://www.theatlantic.com/business/archive/2016/02/work-secularization-chaplaincies/462987/.

157 David Gibbs, "The Legal Implications of Witnessing at Work," CBN, 2005, https://www1.cbn.com/legal-implications-witnessing-work-1.

158 Drumm McNaughton, "Strategic Planning and Environmental Scanning," The Change Leader, Inc. blog, Mar. 3, 2018, https://thechangeleader.com/strategic-planning-and-environmental-scanning/.

159 A.G. Lafley and Roger Martin, *Playing to Win: How Strategy Really Works* (Brighton, MA: Harvard Business Review Press, 2013), 159.

160 LaToya Harris, "Why You Should Include God in Your Business Plan," The Praying Woman, June 28, 2017, https://theprayingwoman.com/why-you-should-include-god-in-your-business-plan/.

161 AZ Quotes, "Aiden Wilson Tozer Quotes," https://www.azquotes.com/quote/662694.

162 W.E. Vine, *A Comprehensive Dictionary of the Original Greek Words with their Precise Meaning for English Readers* (Peabody, MA: Hendrickson Publishers, 1996), 441.

163 Matthew Barnett, *The Cause within You: Finding the One Great Thing God Created You to Do In This World* (Wheaton, IL: Tyndale House Publishers, 2011), 33-34.

164 BrainyQuote@, "Steve Jobs Quotes," https://www.brainyquote.com/quotes/steve_jobs_416878.

165 *The Hospitable Leader*, 105-106.

166 *Christian Business Legends*, 37-40.

167 Cheryl Bachelder, *Dare to Serve: How to Drive Superior Results by Serving Others* (Oakland, CA: Berrett-Koehler Publishers, Expanded/Updated Edition, 2018), 149-150.

168 Nick Craig, *Leading from Purpose: Clarity and the Confidence to Act When it Matters Most* (New York: Hachette Books, 2018), 248.

169 Joseph A. Michelli, *The New Gold Standard: 5 Leadership Principles for Creating a Legendary Customer Experience Courtesy of The Ritz-Carlton Hotel Company* (New York: McGraw Hill, 2008), 187.

170 Wayne Grudem, *Business for the Glory of God: The Bible's Teaching on the Moral Goodness of Business* (Wheaton, IL: Crossway, 2003), 37.

171 Quotespictures, "Motivational Work Quote by Daniel Barenboim," http://quotespictures.com/motivational-work-quote-by-daniel-barenboim-every-great-work-of-art-has-two-faces-one-toward-its-own-time-and-one-toward-the-future-toward-eternity/.

172 Hans Finzel, *The Top Ten Mistakes Leaders Make* (Colorado Springs, Colorado: Victor Cook Communications, 2000), 171.

THE WAY TO WELL DONE

Well Done leaders always take the second step, just as Jesus did.

Well Done leaders have a Kingdom impact, just as Jesus did.

Well Done leaders find second step solutions, just as Jesus did.

Well Done leaders consider the other person's point of view, just as Jesus did.

Well Done leaders work the Golden Rule, because they know the Golden Rule works, just as Jesus did.

Well Done leaders have an ultimate purpose that they are striving to complete, just as Jesus did.

Well Done leaders listen to the concerns of others, just as Jesus did.

Well Done leaders find innovation through focusing on consideration for their customers.

Well Done leaders are inspirational and encouraging.

Well Done leaders appreciate their customers.

Well Done leaders know how to set healthy boundaries for themselves, just as Jesus did.

Well Done leaders are generous and give to others freely, just as Jesus did.

Well Done leaders practice excellence, just as Jesus did.

Well Done leaders lead according to purpose, plotting their paths intentionally since they know that clearness in their courses will be reflected throughout their organizations, just as Jesus did.

Well Done leaders focus on utilizing their resources to produce the best results for their company or organization, just as Jesus did.

Well Done leaders make the switch from being driven by profits to driving profits in order to accomplish a higher purpose, just as Jesus did.

Well Done leaders can impact both their company and communities when they strive to make a profit with a purpose, just as Jesus did.

Well Done leaders embrace the idea of profitability while executing a strategic plan to grow profits with a purpose, just as Jesus did.

Well Done leaders embrace the importance of good decision-making, just as Jesus did.

Well Done leaders are credible leaders because they know what they can do, what they shouldn't be doing, and what they won't do, just as Jesus did.

Well Done leaders find their yes, just as Jesus did.

Well Done leaders walk away from waits, just as Jesus did.

Well Done leaders make the move from ownership to overseer, just as Jesus did.

Well Done leaders consistently ask themselves the question, "If I had to give an account to God today for my decisions and actions in the business that I steward, would He say to me, Well Done," just as Jesus did.

Well Done leaders focus their time on how to develop a better seed and plant it in better soil, just as Jesus did.

Well Done leaders know that the harvest they are reaping today comes from the seeds that they planted yesterday, just as Jesus did.

Well Done leaders know that it is essential that they plant seeds for God's Kingdom, just as Jesus did.

Well Done leaders sow seeds into their lives and into the life of the business, knowing that the tomorrows of the company depend on the work of today, just as Jesus did.

Well Done leaders understand the leader they were yesterday will not be able to lead effectively tomorrow unless they improve today, just as Jesus did.

Well Done leaders will use their imagination to see the world in new and different ways, just as Jesus did.

Well Done leaders always consider what brighter future they are trying to create, just as Jesus did.

Well Done leaders challenge their people to find solutions instead of making excuses, just as Jesus did.

Well Done leaders create huge impossible spiritual goals, just as Jesus did.

Well Done leaders create win walls, just as Jesus did.

Well Done leaders never forget to give praise to the One who does the hard work in the business, just as Jesus did.

Well Done leaders do not forget where their wins come from, and they pause long enough to thank the One that can give new wins in the future, just as Jesus did.

Well Done leaders are not short-sighted leaders, but they build something that can bless future generations, just as Jesus did.

Well Done leaders follow sound principles, just as Jesus did.

Well Done leaders continue leading with persistence, just as Jesus did.

Well Done leaders lead by developing and preparing firm plans, just as Jesus did.

Well Done leaders know that the right foundation is vital to success in this world and is of significance in the world to come, just as Jesus did.

Well Done leaders become clear about their vision so that they can drive clarity in those they lead, just as Jesus did.

Well Done leaders always review their Kingdom impact, just as Jesus did.

Well Done leaders have a vision of creating an organization that lasts at least one hundred years, just as Jesus did.

Well Done leaders know their order of things, just as Jesus did.

Well Done leaders build organizations that can continue even when the leader is not able to continue, just as Jesus did.

Well Done leaders examine their choices and behaviors to ensure that they are not involved in second things, just as Jesus did.

Well Done leaders don't just automatically commit to something without a more significant cause that is motivating them, just Jesus did.

Well Done leaders understand the essential truth of team performance and team effort, just as Jesus did.

Well Done leaders improve their team to improve their organization, just as Jesus did.

Well Done leaders recognize that the best use of time is to be around others who can help them, just as Jesus did.

Well Done leaders learn how to step back so that they can move forward, just as Jesus did.

Well Done leaders focus on finding and retaining the best talent, just as Jesus did.

Well Done leaders will develop daily habits to improve their thinking, stretch their minds, and challenge their ideas, just as Jesus did.

Well Done leaders have a mission field in their own towns and villages, just as Jesus did.

Well Done leaders acknowledge God to the people groups under their care, just as Jesus did.

Well Done leaders do things today that impact today and tomorrow, just as Jesus did.

Well Done leader wish to use everything they have for the benefit of those around them, and ultimately for the Kingdom of God, just as Jesus did.

Well Done leaders always take action today with tomorrow in mind, just as Jesus did.

Well Done leaders have an audience of One, just as Jesus did.

Well Done leaders take bold and risky faith decisions, just as Jesus did.

Well Done leaders do not miss the opportunity to build excellence in everything they do, just as Jesus did.

Well Done leaders know what the finish line looks like, just as Jesus did.

Well Done leaders have the desire to express the love and grace of God, just as Jesus did.

Well Done leaders produce good fruit, just as Jesus did.

Well Done leaders recognize excellence in others, just as Jesus did.,~

Well Done leaders seek to build their products to become the best in class, just as Jesus did.

Well Done leaders will hear the words "well done, good and faithful servant," just as Jesus did.

ACKNOWLEDGMENTS

A principle that I reviewed in this book is to "improve your team to improve your organization." I have experienced this principle personally. I have been improved by so many people who have poured into me throughout the years and who have worked tremendously hard to bring this book to completion.

I first want to acknowledge my father and mother. I believe that the seeds they planted in me at a young age are what enabled me to understand and experience the biblical business principles as not only good for business but life. I remember watching my parents work in hard and laborious jobs that many would not want to engage in, and yet they worked diligently as stewards of all that was under their care. They showed me how faith could come to life and bring transformation to decisions and attitudes. I have often said that both my father and mother taught me everything that I needed to know about how to lead a company and live a life.

I also want to thank my wife, Shonda, who is a true partner in my life and business. I want to thank her for the encouragement to write and to share my best ideas with the world. It was only after hours, days, and years of discussing the principles of this book with her that I felt courageous enough to put my thoughts on paper and define the biblical business principles. I appreciate her words of encouragement and support for the hours of working on this book during vacations, evenings, and mornings when I could have been doing so many other things. Her love for God and her love for me brings a smile to my face and joy to my heart.

I have to acknowledge CEO Experience CEOs whom I have had the privilege to work alongside over the past decade. These Well Done leaders are the men and women who embody Christian values in their daily business interactions. I have no doubt they will one day hear the words: "Well Done." Some of these first adopters include Joe Connolly, Ebere Okoye, Vaughn Thurman, Tom Boyer, Stu Welsh, Doug Hillmuth, Harry Plack, Pat Wheeler, Dennis Carter, and Tim Manley. These leaders and other current CXP CEOs inspire me daily and are my mentors, as well as my friends.

I want to acknowledge Ken Walker, who helped to edit and shape the ideas in this book and who helps me with the monthly executive retreat guides. Ken has become a trusted advisor and friend who poured his heart over each word and each chapter to ensure that together we conveyed the right ideas and right principles that could impact CEOs and leaders around the world. Ken's insights have proven to be wise and beneficial. He is a true master of his trade.

I am appreciative of Matt Christ and Orsolya Herbein of Brand3, who helped to shape the identity of CEO Experience and who has a servant's heart in everything they do. I want to acknowledge Nelson Anderson and his team, which help to produce and print the CXP *CEO Executive Guides*. I want to thank Krystal Trimble, who works diligently to design the guide and ensure that the guides are always beautiful and engaging.

Thanks also goes to the Chief Experience Officers who lead CXP retreats with Well Done CEOs. Tracy Graves Stevens, Dwight Delgado, Tom Crea, and Jason Milbrandt have helped to shoulder the load over the last year as I have dedicated time and energy to write and produce tools, executive guides, and resources that have gone into the pages of this book. These Chief Experience Officers are outstanding market leaders, and I am honored that they have chosen to partner with me to help build CEO Experience.

Randy Ross, the author of *Remarkable!* and *Relationomics*, is a man that I greatly admired. I appreciate his words at the beginning of this book and his friendship. He is truly a remarkable leader.

I want to acknowledge the men and women who have a passion for working with Christian CEOs. Men and women like Steve Simpson, Bryan Hyzdu, Mike Sipe, and Rick Ferris and Diana Furr. These Christian coaches, advisors, and leaders pour themselves into leaders as their life's work. They are excellent leaders and inspire me by their servant's heart and their obedience to sacrifice the recognition on earth so that they can be recognized for eternity.

Don Barefoot and Buck Jacobs are two men who shaped by concepts of the impact of Christian CEOs. These men have dedicated their lives to produce results that would please God at the Bema seat of Christ.

I want to thank Morgan James Publishing for their excellent work to bring this work to life through their publishing efforts. The publishing team has been excellent to work with through this process, and I highly recommend their team to others.

Finally, I want to acknowledge the CEOs and Well Done leaders mentioned in this book as those kinds of faith-driven leaders who lead their business for kingdom impact. Leaders like JC Penny, Truett Cathy, B.T. Barnum, Stanley Tam, Mary Kay Ash, and R.G. LeTourneau These leaders do not always get acknowledged publicly, but they make a difference in their communities and the Kingdom. Yet God knows their work, and one day, every leader who practices biblical business principles will hear the words, Well Done.

ABOUT THE AUTHOR

Ken Gosnell is the CEO and Servant Leader of CEO Experience (CXP). His company serves Christian CEOs and leaders by helping them to hear the words Well Done. He is a keynote speaker, executive coach, and strategic partner with CEOs and successful business leaders. His business concepts and ideas have been sought out by leaders around the world, and he writes articles with a focus on business, leadership, team, management, and CEOs for several business magazines and publications, including Forbes, Business.com,

YFS Magazine, The Startup, and Executive Vine. He is the publisher of the CXP CEO Executive Retreat Guide that is designed to help leaders learn the biblical business principles that will help them to grow their business with Kingdom impact. He trains and equips Chief Experience Officers to lead CXP Retreats in their communities.

Ken leads a team of Chief Experience Officers at CEO Experience, a full consulting organization that specializes in providing strategic retreat experiences to help CEOS hear the words Well Done. The CXP CEO retreats have help CEOs work to improve their business as a platform for kingdom impact as well as improve the overall performance of their leadership teams, strategic vision, operational excellence, and sales performance.

Ken has a passion for education and self-improvement. He received a double master's degree from Regent University with a focus on business and divinity. He started in his consulting career with the Dale Carnegie organization, where he became a master trainer for the organization and consulted with Fortune 500 companies. He has read thousands of books and has spent many hours in the study of business and peak performance, but he has learned that the secrets to success in life and business are in just one book, The Bible.

He lives in the Washington DC area with his amazing wife, Shonda. They have four children, Carli, Caleb, Kaiden, and Kyston. You can connect with Ken at @ken_gosnell on Twitter, https://www.linkedin.com/in/kengosnell/ on Linkedin, or by email at kengosnell@ceoexperience.com

Printed in the USA
CPSIA information can be obtained
at www.ICGtesting.com
LVHW091532080824
787695LV00002B/287